How to Start and Run an eBay® Consignment Business

Skip McGrath

McGraw-Hill

New York   Chicago   San Francisco   Lisbon
London   Madrid   Mexico City   Milan   New Delhi
San Juan   Seoul   Singapore   Sydney   Toronto

The McGraw·Hill Companies

McGraw-Hill books are available at special quantity discounts to use as premiums and sales promotions, or for use in corporate training programs. For more information, please write to the Director of Special Sales, Professional Publishing, McGraw-Hill, Two Penn Plaza, New York, NY 10121-2298. Or contact your local bookstore.

How to Start and Run an eBay® Consignment Business

1234567890 FGR FGR 019876

ISBN 0-07-226277-X

The sponsoring editor for this book was Margie McAneny and the project editor was Carolyn Welch. The copy editor was Bob Campbell, the proofreader was Susie Elkind, and the indexer was Claire Splan. Composition and illustration by International Typesetting & Composition. Cover design by Jeff Weeks

This book was composed with Adobe® InDesign®.

Information contained in this work has been obtained by The McGraw-Hill Companies, Inc. from sources believed to be reliable. However, because of the possibility of human or mechanical error by our sources, McGraw-Hill, or others, McGraw-Hill does not guarantee the accuracy, adequacy, or completeness of any information and is not responsible for any errors or omissions or the results obtained from the use of such information.

Library of Congress Cataloging-in-Publication Data

McGrath, Skip.
  How to start and run an eBay consignment business : make
real money as an eBay trading assistant / by Skip McGrath.-- 1st ed.
       p. cm.

  ISBN 0-07-226277-X
  1. eBay (Firm) 2. Internet auctions. 3. Consignment sales I. Title.
  HF5478.M387 2006
  658.8'7--dc22

                              2005035665

Dedication

This book is dedicated to my many readers who keep me honest
by pointing out my mistakes, and who are a constant source of questions,
ideas, and suggestions that give my writing direction.

Contents

Acknowledgments

I would like to thank my agent Marilyn Allen for her ideas and inspiration; my wife, Karen, who gives me the time to write by putting up with my long hours and doing all the hard work running our day-to-day eBay business; and my editors, Margie McAneny and Agatha Kim, who help keep the writing clean and tight by catching my mistakes and oversights before they make it into print.

Introduction

Selling other people's goods on eBay on consignment is the fastest-growing segment of the online auction industry. Finding products to sell is one of the most difficult challenges the everyday eBay seller faces. This book solves that problem. If you master the techniques of marketing and running this business, you will have an endless supply of merchandise to sell with no risk and very little investment on your part.

I sold my first item on consignment in 2002. A neighbor approached me who had a large collection of cookie jars. I knew that collecting cookie jars was hot, but I didn't really know anything about them. I started by listing two of the cookie jars at $1.00 no-reserve. One of them, a Planter's Peanut cookie jar, sold for over $200 and the other one (I can't remember the style) sold for over $90. Within four weeks I sold the rest of the cookie jars at prices ranging from $60 to over $170 each. My commission was 20 percent. (I now charge 30 percent.)

I was instantly hooked on eBay consignment selling. It was amazing. All I had to do was put out the word to my friends and neighbors that I would sell their stuff for them on eBay, and I had a virtually unlimited supply of goods to sell.

Now, not everything sells on eBay. I know; I have a garage full of stuff I purchased that I later learned couldn't sell. But this deal was perfect—if something didn't sell, I simply returned it to the person who gave it to me, or if they didn't want it back, I donated it to the local thrift shop and took a tax deduction for my trouble.

I have now been selling on consignment for three years, during which time I have sold over 2,000 items for other people. I would like to tell you it's easy, but it's not. Like anything you do that can earn large amounts of money, there is some work involved and techniques you have to learn, but it's not THAT hard. *How to Start and Run an eBay Consignment Business* contains all of the tips, tricks, and techniques I have used to start, run, and grow a successful eBay consignment business. I hope you will enjoy the book, and I hope to see you selling on eBay within a few weeks.

One of the things I hate about reading books about web sites and online auctions is that they are full of URL links to other web sites containing resources, tools, and additional information. So, I have created a special page on my web site just for readers of this book that contains all of the links and resources mentioned in the book, plus links to my newsletter archives, free articles, and tons of additional free resources. Just go to www.skipmcgrath.com/consignment to access the page.

Part I

Setting Up Your Consignment Business

Chapter 1

Why Start a Consignment Business on eBay?

When I told my friends I was going to write this book, everyone said, "Why would someone pay you to sell their goods on eBay, if they could do it themselves?" Good question. Well, it turns out there are a lot of reasons.

For every successful eBay seller, there are a lot of people who can't figure out how to sell effectively or profitably on eBay. And, believe it or not, there are still a lot of people who either do not believe eBay really works, are afraid to try it, and/or are computer illiterate.

There are also plenty of people in this world who just don't have the time.

If you think there isn't a market for selling other people's goods on eBay, consider this: In 2002 eBay launched the Trading Assistants Program. A Trading Assistant is an eBay seller who volunteers to sell products for eBay members who don't know how or don't want to sell themselves. If you go to the eBay home page and click the Services tab, you will see a link to Trading Assistants.

By 2005 there were 80,000 Trading Assistants helping others sell on eBay. Here is what eBay says about the program:

"To become a Trading Assistant, you need to have sold at least one item in the last 30 days, have a feedback rating of 50 or higher, and have greater than 97 percent of your feedback as positive. You also must be in good standing with eBay.

"Including yourself in our Trading Assistants Program directory is a lot like running a classified ad for your services. Trading Assistants are not employees or independent contractors of eBay. Nor do we endorse or approve them. Each Trading Assistant runs his or her own independent business free from any involvement by eBay."

What Are the Benefits of Becoming a Trading Assistant?

When you join the Trading Assistants directory (see Figure 1-1), you tell the world that you are willing to sell for others. Trading Assistants charge fees or commissions for their services. Selling as a Trading Assistant allows you to leverage your selling expertise without having to find products yourself; clients provide the items, and you are compensated for your efforts on terms that you decide. Many sellers already do this as a way of making money on eBay, and profit margins can be significant for higher-priced items.

Basically, eBay has already given any eBay seller who qualifies an opportunity to start a consignment business. When an eBay member is looking for a Trading Assistant, they are directed to a directory page where they can type in their location (ZIP code) and search for an assistant in their own hometown.

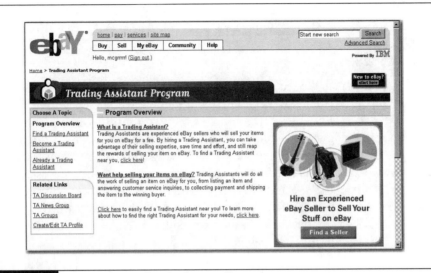

FIGURE 1-1   The eBay Trading Assistants directory

eBay also provides promotional material. There is a Marketing Collateral link on the Trading Assistant page where you can download posters and flyers in Microsoft Word format that you can print out and use in your marketing efforts. (See the example in Appendix B.)

Signing up to be an eBay Trading Assistant should be your first step to start a consignment business.

Are There Successful Consignment Businesses Operating Now?

There are thousands of eBay sellers running consignment businesses. These range from regular sellers who sell consignments as a side business to full-time large commercial businesses operating out of retail storefronts. A recent story in AuctionBytes (www .auctionbytes.com, a weekly newsletter for the online auction industry) reported that there are now over 4,000 eBay drop-off stores open in the U.S.

A woman in my hometown used to own a consignment store right in the heart of the retail district. She sold good-quality antiques and collectibles on consignment and had a very nice business for several years. Three years ago she tried putting some of the goods in her shop on eBay. After some trial and error, she began doing very well. Earlier this year, she closed the shop and now sells on eBay

Pro Tip   Use eBay to Help Others

There are more than monetary awards to running a consignment business.

Lori, an eBay Trading Assistant in South Florida, wrote me the following e-mail:

Skip: I'm doing more and more consignments, especially for the elderly retirees in my area. It makes me sick when I see what estate sale companies do to these people. I can make real good money handling someone's estate on a consignment basis. But, I get an immense sense of gratification from knowing that I'm helping them keep a LOT more of their hard-earned money, too! Likewise, I help local churches with consignment sales to help them raise money . . . it sure beats what they get at a rummage sale!

—Lori Enzo—eBay Powerseller

full time. She finds people with goods to sell by placing ads in the local paper, from her previous customers who know her, by putting notices on free community bulletin boards, and by word of mouth.

Consignment selling on eBay is not a new idea. eBay professionals have been doing it for several years. Recently a venture capital-funded startup in San Francisco has created more interest and excitement in this business model.

Recently I was in San Jose, California, on business. I was driving north on the 101 freeway when I saw a billboard that said:

Drop Off Your Item and We'll
Sell It On eBay
Call 1-866-DROP-IT-OFF

When I got home, I called the number to ask about the service. The company, called AuctionDrop, is a professional consignment service (see Figure 1-2). The owners have been so successful they raised $500,000 in startup venture capital to build the business and recently raised another $2.5 million to expand the business to Los Angeles and New York. AuctionDrop plans to go public in 2006. You can visit their web site at www.auctiondrop.com. In 2005 AuctionDrop partnered with UPS to set up UPS Stores as drop-off locations for merchandise they will sell on eBay.

FIGURE 1-2   The AuctionDrop home page

This business will certainly invite competition. As you will see in this book, eBay consignment selling is a business you can start with very little capital and very low barriers to entry. Auctiondrop's strategy is obviously to grow fast and to dominate the market with prime locations, advertising, and a well-known brand name.

Does this mean you shouldn't enter the market? Not at all. Starbucks dominates the coffee market in the United States, but they still represent only 16 percent of all the premium coffee outlets in the country and less than 2 percent worldwide. There are plenty of other people making good money selling coffee for $1.75 a cup. AuctionDrop will have plenty of competitors too.

Another example is a large eBay seller in Los Angeles: He contracts with the various movie studios to sell the props and costumes on eBay once the movie is finished filming. He regularly sells over $1 million a year.

How Big Can an eBay Consignment Business Grow?

That really depends on how big you want to grow your business, what your resources are, and how much you can invest. AuctionDrop is a private company and does not release its sales figures. But, by watching its auctions on eBay, I estimate the company is closing about $50,000 worth of auctions a week.

Its basic commission schedule is 40 percent, so that works out to a gross margin of $20,000 per week. Now, you aren't going to do this without a large investment, several employees, advertising, and so on, but I firmly believe that anyone who is well skilled selling on eBay can develop a small business that can realize a gross margin of $1,000 to $5,000 a week. This would require you to launch an average of 30–60 auctions per week. Many power sellers today routinely launch over 100 auctions a week, so this is not an unrealistic number. Later we will talk about automating some of the common tasks that will allow you to do this.

To answer the question posed in the preceding heading, the amount of money you can make is only limited by your imagination and your ability to conceive, start, run, and grow the business. According to *Business Week* magazine, the consignment or secondhand business is already a $2 billon plus business in the U.S. Many of these stores already sell on eBay. I predict that within five years there will be over 10,000 eBay consignment storefronts in the U.S. Cities such as New York and Los Angeles will have hundreds of stores in their respective metro areas. Some of these stores will be little Mom & Pop operations, others will be specialty shops selling antiques or collectibles, while others will be owned by large franchise operations.

I-Sold-it.com, a company in Pasadena, California, has been selling eBay consignment business franchises for over two years and now has over 100 eBay drop-off franchise stores operating nationwide. Another leading company is QuikDrop in Costa Mesa, California. Their franchise sells for $25,000. QuickDrop has over 76 locations open and has sold another 50 franchises that will open in 2005–2006.

You don't need an expensive franchise to start a Trading Assistant business, although that is one way to go. If you would like to explore franchise sellers in a competitive environment, you should attend eBay's annual convention, eBay Live, which is held every year in June. Almost all of the franchise sellers exhibit at the show, as do several companies that sell software, hardware, and services to consignment sellers.

You can also link to several franchise company web sites on the special web page for readers who purchase this book. This page is located at www.skipmcgrath.com/consignment.

Even with 80,000 registered Trading Assistants and over 4,000 eBay consignment drop-off stores operating, there is still plenty of room for growth. If one eBay consignment location can service a community of 20,000 people, with a population of 360 million in the U.S., that works out to a market potential of over 18,000 drop-off stores.

Chapter 2

Get Started

Okay, where do I start? First of all, you will need experience selling on eBay. If you bought this book and you have either never sold on eBay or only sold very little, I suggest you visit the Auction Seller's web site at: www.skipmcgrath.com.

We offer several basic and advanced instruction manuals for eBay sellers. Before purchasing one of our books from the web site, send us an e-mail and let us know you bought this book and you would like to upgrade to the others. We will offer you a substantial discount and send you an e-mail with payment instructions. You can also e-mail us at auctions@isomedia.com for advice on this subject.

That said, let us assume that you have the required experience selling on eBay. What is enough experience? I would say you should have listed and converted (sold) at least 50 auctions, have a positive feedback score of at least 100, and a feedback rating of at least 98 percent. I am not saying you cannot be successful with less experience than this; however, your chances of success will increase, and more important, you will have the credibility to point to when you go out and find customers to consign goods to sell on eBay.

Another requirement is a retail personality. You have to like people and enjoy being around them. There are thousands of successful eBay sellers who could not be successful in a consignment business because they don't have the people skills to succeed.

Setting Up Your Business

You will need to look and act like a business if you want prospective consignors to take you seriously. As you will see later in this book, you will not only be dealing with little old ladies that want to sell their collection of ceramic roosters, but you will potentially also be dealing with retail store owners, estate agents, estate and bankruptcy attorneys, and other business people.

The first step is to name your business, and to get a business address, a phone number, letterhead, business cards, and a business license.

Naming Your Business

Be careful naming your business. If you are in one line of business only, then a specific name is good because it gives you credibility as a specialist. Some examples might be: Steve's Collectibles, Westwood Jewelry Sales, and Nautical Antiques & Collectibles.

If you will be selling various types of products, you may wish to use a more general business name. Some examples might be Vision-One Marketing, Sell-It-Now, On-Line Consignments, and Northwest Marketing.

Be careful using the words Inc., Incorporated, Partners, and Limited (Ltd), as these all have specific legal meaning. It is illegal to call yourself a corporation if you are not incorporated.

If you specifically want to promote your consignment business, you should pick a name such as Consignments On-Line or Auction Consignment Service. (Note that you cannot use the word "eBay" in your business name, but you can say that you sell on eBay on your letterhead or business card with a subhead under the business name.) Here is an example: "Consignments Online, the eBay consignment specialists." You can also use the word eBay on your business cards and flyers. If you are a registered eBay Trading Assistant, then you can use the eBay logo in your material as well. (The word *eBay* in the flyer shown here could be in the eBay primary colors.)

On-line Auction Specialists, Inc.

Earn Top Dollar Selling
Your Valuable Goods on eBay

703-555-1111

eBay Trading Assistant

Business Types

The most common way to start a business is as a *sole proprietorship*. Even if you are married and jointly own the business, it can still be a "sole proprietorship," if you live in a community property state. If not, consult a local CPA if you want to own a business jointly with your spouse and ask how to register it. If you wish to own a business solely without your spouse, then you can be a sole proprietor in any state.

Another approach is to actually *incorporate*, which can be done very inexpensively in most states. There are several web sites where you can incorporate for as little as $100. One of the most popular is www.mycorporation.com. Once incorporated, you can register an unlimited number of DBAs (Doing Business As). These are company names controlled by the master corporation.

Once your income goes over $50,000 per year gross, you may wish to incorporate for tax reasons. I will not deal with that here, but there are excellent tax breaks available to corporations. You should consult a CPA for advice on tax issues. A few hundred dollars spent on a CPA can save you thousands of dollars in taxes.

The third type of business ownership is a *partnership*. I personally would avoid this, as it leads to more lawsuits than any other type of business. If you wish to become partners with someone, you should incorporate and decide who gets the controlling (51 percent) share of stock. Equal partnerships are usually a disaster waiting to happen when it comes to small business.

Business Licenses

There are two types of business licenses:

- A local business license

- A sales tax license, sometime called a sales tax ID number

A local business license is *needed only if you are going to open a physical storefront.* You do not need a local (city or county) business license to sell on eBay out of your home unless your home is also zoned as commercial property.

If you plan to purchase goods from wholesalers, or sell on consignment to people in the state you live in, then you *will* need a sales tax number for your state, or a state business license number (if your state does not have sales tax).

Almost every state has a web site that gives information about how to obtain a sales tax number, and most states will let you apply over the web or download the forms to apply. For example, go to http://www.wa.gov, the web site for Washington State. Substitute the two-letter abbreviation for your state in this URL to get the government site for your home state. All states charge a fee (usually less than $50). Some states require a deposit based on your annual estimated sales. The minimum deposit is usually $200–400.

If you live in a state that charges sales tax, you must charge (or pay) sales tax on all transactions shipped to buyers *in your state.* Not doing so can result in fines and eventually loss of your sales tax license.

One thing you may need to determine is if your state charges sales tax on any fees you charge the buyer. Commissions are tax-free in most states, but if you are charging a listing fee, then you may have to collect tax on that fee.

When you get a sales tax number, ask your state authority for a pamphlet or instructions that specify exactly what products and services are taxable. Many states exempt food, vitamins, commissions, user fees, periodicals, books, etc., from sales tax. If you are selling one of these items, you need to know if they are taxable or not.

Another benefit of getting a sales tax number is that you can open a business account at Costco or Sam's Club. Now you can purchase items there for resale without paying sales tax. A friend of mine on our town's police force shops at

Costco weekly for bargains and sells them on eBay. His latest purchase was ten sets of Hoffritz BBQ tools he bought for $18 each and sold on eBay for $29.95. You can also buy shipping supplies such as boxes, tape, bubble pack, labels, and ink cartridges for your printer without paying sales tax; since you are charging for shipping, this is part of your product cost.

If you plan to open a retail location where customers can drop off their merchandise, you may also need a local business license from your city or township. If you live in a small town, just go to city hall for information about getting a business license. If you live in a large city, you can usually find information online or check with the local chamber of commerce for advice.

Some cities require a special license to sell secondhand goods. This is to allow the police to track stolen merchandise. In some cases, you have to file a list of the items you sell with the police and wait a number of days until you can sell an item. If this is the case where you live, it will cause a complication if you have a store. You may want to locate your business in a nearby suburb that does not require a special license to sell secondhand goods.

If you incorporate or plan to hire an employee, you will also need an IRS Employer Identification Number (EIN). You can download a form to apply for this from the IRS web site at www.irs.gov. It is faster, however, to apply by phone. Taxpayers can obtain an EIN immediately by calling the Business & Specialty Tax Line (800-829-4933). The hours of operation are 7:00 a.m. to 10:00 p.m. local time, Monday through Friday. An assistant takes the information, assigns the EIN, and provides the number to an authorized individual over the telephone. There is no charge to get an EIN.

Business Telephone

You should have a business telephone number that is separate from your home phone if you are doing business at home. Train your children not to answer it and get voice mail (not an answering machine) from the phone company.

An inexpensive alternative to a second phone line is the "distinctive ring" line. Most phone companies will give you an additional phone number at a small charge of only $5–10 per month. There is no installation charge because it is just a phone number that rings on your regular line with a distinctive sounding ring. When you hear this ring, you know it is a business call. Even if you are sitting in the kitchen in your bathrobe, you pick up the phone and say: "Good morning, Annie's Consignments, may I help you?"

Of course, today a lot of people just use a cell phone as their business phone.

Eventually, as your business grows you will want to install a separate phone line for your business. In the meantime, the distinctive-ring phone line can provide the credibility you need to tell the world you are running a business. Many people nowadays just use their cell phone, although the quality can still be a problem in some areas.

Letterhead and Business Cards

If you are at all handy with the computer, you can create letterhead and business cards from your word processing program. There are also several inexpensive software programs that will create beautiful letterheads and business cards complete with logos. Office Max and Staples sell several of these for under $15.

A professional-looking letterhead and business card are essential to be taken seriously by many businesses. Remember, you will be dealing with business owners, lawyers, and bankers.

Computer and Software Resources

You can run an auction or web business from almost any kind of computer. It does help to have a fast computer and a fast modem, DSL or cable, as you will be spending a fair amount of time surfing the Web, sending e-mails, and entering auction descriptions.

Photography will also become very important to your success. You will need a good digital camera and photo lighting set up to take good photos. A dedicated place for photography is a real plus.

You will also need a dedicated shipping station. If your business is successful, you will be doing a lot of shipping. This means you will want to invest in tape guns, paper rolls, and a postage scale. You will also want to open an account with UPS. Endicia (www.endicia.com) is a great site for time-saving shipping solutions if you use the post office for shipping.

The best e-mail program for running a business is Eudora Pro. The full version sells for about $49.95. You can download a free version of Eudora at www.eudora .com. The free version works just like the full version, but it has an advertising logo in a lower corner. The other professional e-mail program is Outlook, which comes with Microsoft Office. Internet programs such as Yahoo and Hotmail should be your secondary mail system for traffic so you don't clog up your primary mail.

Microsoft Word is also an excellent program for word processing for web-based businesses because it has preformatted e-mail templates and web page templates.

QuickBooks is an excellent program for keeping your books. Whether you use a program such as QuickBooks or keep your books manually, it is important to keep good records. Good bookkeeping is vital to the success of a consignment business. Really, this issue can make or break your business, so don't scrimp here. I strongly recommend you use a bookkeeping system such as QuickBooks to make sure this part of your business is professionally run.

Don't rush out and buy a new computer and a ton of software right away (unless someone just gave you a hundred thousand dollars in venture capital), but you should have a plan to buy what you need to run a professional business. Set some money aside each month to purchase what you need, and buy it when you can afford it. Do not take on loans or debt to get your business started.

Insurance

You will be responsible for the goods you take in from consignors. Therefore, you need to carry adequate fire, theft, and damage insurance. Make sure your car insurance covers contents that could be stolen or damaged in an accident. In many states, insurance can be very difficult to find for businesses in the home. First, check with your homeowners insurance company, because many of them offer low-cost riders for such businesses.

Find an independent broker to buy your insurance from. Brokers represent several insurance companies, and they can shop around to find you the best deal. Tell your insurance agent that you are running a business and you need *commercial coverage.* This is a little more expensive than your standard home and auto insurance. But if you have a loss and the insurance company finds out you are using your home or car for business (and didn't tell them), they can deny the claim if you do not have a business policy.

One problem you will have is that the value of the goods you have in your possession will vary from time to time. Unless you have a bonded warehouse with security, you probably cannot buy a policy with variable limits. You will just have to estimate the value of goods you have at any one time and buy that much insurance. You can obviously start out small and raise the limit later. I would suggest $10,000 coverage to start with, as this is probably the minimum you can purchase. A policy such as this should cost less than $500 a year. Remember too, the very fact you have an insurance policy you can show to consignors will help you get more business.

There is a new service available for eBay sellers called buySAFE, which bonds all your auctions against fraud and is underwritten by the Liberty Mutual Insurance Company. Print out your buySAFE page and carry it with you to show that you are a bonded seller. This can help your credibility with consignors. You can apply at www.buysafe.com. buySAFE is also working with Liberty Mutual to develop an insurance policy for eBay Trading Assistants. Check our web site at www .skipmcgrath.com for the latest information on this service.

Later we will talk about your presentation, or "pitch" book. You will want to carry a copy of your business insurance policy and/or your bond with you and show it to people as part of your presentation.

Another important reason for having insurance is that you will occasionally run into consignors who are reluctant to let you hold the merchandise you are going to sell. Showing them your insurance policy and/or bonding certificate will often solve this problem for you.

Should you decide to open a retail store, you will also want liability insurance to cover someone who gets injured on your property.

Reference Material

You will be doing a lot of writing, creating auction ads, sending e-mails, etc., so you should have a good dictionary, thesaurus, and style manual handy.

If you will be selling antiques and collectibles, you will want some reference books and price guides.

My most valuable reference tool is a series of three-ring notebooks I keep next to my computer. It is frustrating and time-consuming to be working on a document or an e-mail and have to flip back and forth to a web page or other file for information. I find it much easier to open a notebook next to my computer where I have printed out copies of web pages, pages from catalogs, the eBay help files, and information that I tend to refer to often.

The Official eBay Bible by Jim Griffin (Gotham, 2003, available from our online bookstore) is a good general eBay reference and how-to guide. Once you master the basics of selling on eBay, my advanced eBay training manual, *The Complete eBay Marketing System*, is available at the www.skipmcgrath.com web site.

Record Keeping

Keep good files. Keep a hard copy of each transaction and back up your computer records on disk or with an online backup service. Also, keep good financial records for tax purposes. We will talk about this in greater detail in later sections of this book.

Taxes

As a small business owner, you will have to pay taxes on your income. There are thousands of people selling on eBay on a cash basis that never claim the income. I don't recommend this unless you are placing only a few auctions a month.

If you are ever audited, the IRS will have a look at your bank and credit card records. If they see a lot of charges by eBay and/or a lot of miscellaneous deposits, you will have some explaining to do.

I am not licensed to give tax advice, but I would like to point out that as a small business owner you have dozens of tax breaks and deductions available to you. These became even better under the 2003 Tax Reform Act, which improved tax breaks for small businesses.

You can safely write off an office in the home, automobile expenses, costs for computers, software, Internet service, telephone, utilities, transportation, meals, entertainment, and so on.

Instead of paying your kids an "allowance," you can hire them as "casual laborers" and deduct what you now pay them as an allowance. (We use our children to clean up our office, wrap packages, deliver mail to the post office, stuff envelopes, etc.)

Legal Issues

There are some very important legal issues to be aware of when doing consignment selling. Some states and cities have regulations that require you to hold any consignment goods valued at over $100 for a period of up to ten days to give the police time to determine if they are stolen merchandise. In these locations, you have to fax the police a description of the merchandise and any serial numbers of computers, stereos, cameras, and so on. If you don't hear back from them within seven to ten days, you can then go ahead and sell the item.

Pro Tip   **Protect Yourself from Illegal Activity**

What is the best way to protect yourself from illegal activity? It is actually very easy. Create a sales policy that lays out this information:

Anyone wanting you to sell goods has to provide a driver's license, which you should photocopy. You explain to your consignors that you pay all consignment proceeds by check only and you will only mail the check to the address on the driver's license.

Now any thief would be crazy to provide you his real name and address. If he is stupid enough to do this and the goods turn out to be stolen, you simply give the information to the police and you are legally off the hook. If anyone approaches you to sell goods and wants to be paid in cash, simply show them a copy of your (written) policy and explain that you are sorry, but this is the only way you will do business.

Even if your location does not have any such regulations, you want to be very careful about selling stolen goods. I guarantee as soon as you advertise that you are an eBay consignment seller or open a consignment storefront, you will be approached by someone (or several people) attempting to sell stolen goods. If you do not take due diligence, and the police determine that you have sold stolen goods, you could be in deep trouble.

Getting Help

Most community colleges offer courses in starting and running a small business and some have free business resource centers that can help with all sorts of things you may run into.

A great resource is SCORE. This stands for the Service Core of Retired Executives (www.score.org). SCORE is a government-sponsored volunteer organization of retired small business owners who provide consulting and advice to new startup business owners. These folks are often very well connected in the community and can introduce you to lots of valuable contacts. They can also be a source of potential investors.

Taking the time to set up and organize your business correctly will pay dividends almost immediately and save you time and energy as you build and grow your business.

Chapter 3

How Much Should I Charge?

How much money you charge and how you charge for your services are very important decisions. Unfortunately, there isn't one answer. What to charge and how much to charge depend on the type of merchandise you are specializing in (if you are specializing), competition in your area, and how successful you are at running auctions. If you are very selective in the merchandise you accept and very good at running auctions with a high conversion rate, then you can often charge less than your competition and still make a lot of money.

Consignment Math

Ultimately, you will have to decide how much to charge on the basis of the issues just raised. But before you start, it helps to understand what it takes to make money in this business.

If you visit the AuctionDrop web site at www.auctiondrop.com, you will see their fees start at 40 percent and go down as the selling price of the item increases. However, this company has a lot of overhead that you will not have at first.

A lot depends on how much you sell and your average selling price. To start, I would not accept any item that you believe will not sell for more than $50, unless the consignor is giving you dozens of items to sell.

Think about this a moment: If you were closing 25 successful auctions a week and charging 25 percent of the selling price as a commission, what would you gross at different price points? Some examples are shown in Table 3-1.

Obviously, even at the $50 minimum, you don't want to do all of this work for $312.50 a week. Remember, though, we are talking about minimums. In reality, if you set your minimum at $50, you will have a lot of sales above this.

Minimum Sales Price	25% Commission	Gross @ 25 Auctions/Week
$10	$2.50	$62.50
$20	$5.00	$125
$30	$7.50	$187.50
$40	$10.00	$250
$50	$12.50	$312.50
$75	$18.75	$468.75

TABLE 3-1   Commission Table

POWER TIP *Don't make the mistake of charging too little. It is much easier to lower your prices than to raise them. Another important consideration is consistency. You should charge everyone the same rates unless someone can bring you a large volume of merchandise consistently. If you charge different people different prices, word will get around and everyone will try to negotiate fees with you.*

Later we will talk about selling large-ticket items that sell for thousands of dollars. On these goods, you might take only a 5 percent or 10 percent commission, but you could earn thousands of dollars on one sale.

The short answer to the question "How much should I charge?" simply depends on the volume and type of merchandise you can access. If you specialize in higher-end merchandise, you can charge a lower commission and still make more money. If you sell low-cost items, you will have to charge a higher commission and/or do a huge amount of volume.

Suggested Commission Schedule

Whatever you do, don't start out with a low commission schedule, because it will be hard to raise it later. Also, don't think 25 percent to 30 percent is too high—this is what most consignment stores charge.

Here is a schedule I use; you can adjust this as necessary to fit your business model:

Sale Value	Commission
Under $300	30%
$301–500	+25% of the amount over $300
$501–20,000	+10% of the amount over $500
Over $20,000	Negotiated amount

To the basic commission, I add a listing fee and, optionally, a couple of further fees:

- **Listing fee** $3 for the first item and $1.00 for each additional item

- **Reserve fee** $5 (optional if the client insists on a reserve)

- **Optional promotion fee** $25 (This gets a category feature and a bold listing. I recommend this only for items that should sell for over $250.)

So what does this mean? If you sold an item for $795.00, what would your commission be?

$300 @ 30% =	$90.00
$200 @ 25% =	$50.00
$295 @ 10% =	$29.50
Total: $795	**$169.50**

(21.3 percent of the selling cost + your fees)

Add your listing fee of $3; your gross is $172.50.

How much would you net from this fee schedule? First, subtract your eBay listing fees, any special feature fees, and the eBay final value fee. If you accepted payment via PayPal or credit card, you would also incur that fee (approx 2.75 percent, or $21.86).

If we assume all of these fees totaled about 5 percent ($39.75), then you would make $172.50 – $39.75 = $132.75.

If you did ten sales a week at this level, you would net $1,327.50 per week.

Flat Fees

Another approach is to charge a flat fee of $5 or $10 per item, whether the item sells or not. Even at $10 per auction, you would have to launch 50 auctions just to make $500. There is one occasion on which you may want to use this method. That is when you use a Dutch auction or list something at a fixed price in your eBay store. If someone gave you 500 each of an identical item to sell, you could either sell it as a wholesale lot or sell the items individually. Selling them individually may net the consignor more profit. If the items are small and easy to ship (for example, jewelry, a CD, or a small book), then you could break your $50 rule and sell them individually at a fixed price. This also works well if you sell the items at a Dutch auction.

Your Unique Selling Proposition

Now you might ask, "Why would someone pay these fees, when they could take their merchandise to a local auctioneer who only charges a 5 or 10 percent selling fee?" This is the heart of your proposition. If you are selling a highly collectible art object and you live in London, Paris, New York, or Los Angeles, then yes, you could take your artwork, antique, or collectible to a big-name auction house and get top dollar for it. The seller would only pay a 5 percent commission.

But let's face it. If you are selling a nice piece of art glass and you take it to a small-town auction house—or even an auction house in a medium-sized city such as Pittsburgh, Seattle, or St. Louis—you will not get nearly the national exposure you get on eBay. There are professional dealers who attend auctions in small and medium-sized cities. They buy only the finest objects in each auction, take them to New York, and sell them at Christie's and Sotheby's for a nice profit. Some of these professionals are now selling on eBay instead of with Christie's or Sotheby's.

eBay gives you national and even international exposure. Your auctions are exposed to literally millions of potential buyers. (eBay currently has over 140 million registered users worldwide and is growing by 50,000 per week.)

Here are some simple examples:

A local woman tried to sell a hand-tooled decorative western saddle at a garage sale for $300. There were no takers, so she gave it to me to list on eBay. I sold the saddle for over $800.

I recently bought an early Coca-Cola tray at a Seattle auction house for $190. I put it on eBay, where it sold for over $400 to a collector in Germany.

When I was in the antique business in upstate New York, I once bought a small Marquetry desk for $600 from a picker who came down from Canada about twice a year. I sold it to an antique dealer from White Plains, New York, for $1,100. He put it up for auction at Sotheby's, where it sold for $2,100 to a New York City antique dealer. The NYC dealer sold it out of his shop for $3,900.

That was five years ago. This desk was very unusual, and I could recognize it instantly. In January of 2002, it sold on eBay for over $7,000.

I recently sold an old camera for a neighbor that he was going to sell at a garage sale for $50. He knew I sold on eBay and checked with me first. It went for over $200 on eBay. (He didn't mind paying the 30 percent commission.)

A woman recently approached me to sell some quality ladies' clothing. The mixed lot consisted of expensive name-brand silk blouses, good wool suits, blazers, and slacks. They were all size 10, which is a very popular size. I sold the suits and blazers separately and the rest as a lot. The total came to over $900 on eBay. She was about to donate them to the local Rotary Thrift shop before a friend recommended me to her.

There is a leading auction house where I live in Seattle that routinely auctions off high-end art, antiques, and collectibles—mostly from local estates and dot-com millionaires who have fallen on hard times. Every three or four months, I attend with a friend of mine who is an expert in old woodworking tools, nautical antiques, and early instruments. Very few of the things he buys ever come up at auction. But when they do, he buys them and sells them on eBay for a 200 percent to 300 percent profit. The last time we went, he bought an old mercury thermometer

Pro Tip   Can I Sell Successfully in a Small Town?

I am often asked if you can make a living as an eBay consignment seller in a small town. I live in a town of 10,000 with another 5,000 in the nearby county area. There are four consignment sellers in my area, and three of us are doing very well. The forth one works in a very narrow specialty (movie memorabilia) and has trouble finding merchandise locally to sell, but he does very well when he can.

and barometer from the late 1800s. The bidding was very fierce, and he eventually won the item for just over $900. He sold it on eBay a week later for over $2,000.

In Seattle, the antique barometer was exposed to perhaps a dozen or so knowledgeable dealers or collectors. On eBay, it was exposed to thousands.

From my experience, I can honestly say that almost any top-quality artwork, antique, or collectible you buy at a small town or regional auction can be sold on eBay for profits upward of 100 percent.

Suppose you were the executor of an estate, and I approached you with these facts and said, "Look, you can give your goods to a local auctioneer who will charge you 10 percent and net $50,000 for the estate you are trying to sell. Or you can give it to me. I will net you closer to $150,000 and charge you an average commission of 18 percent." Do the math. Which would you pick?

Let's go back to the commission schedule. There is another way to look at this. In the example, we were calculating the commission if someone gave you one object to sell. If someone is willing to bring you a large amount of merchandise to sell (such as an estate), then you could make a deal based on the total value of the estate or the amount that sold each week. Calculate the total goods sold in one week's auctions and calculate the commission. If someone gave you merchandise to sell that went for a total of $50,000, then the commission could be much lower than 21 percent and you would still make a nice profit.

You may also run into the opportunity to sell real estate, aircraft, boats, cars, trucks, industrial equipment, or large wholesale lots when the selling price of one item is in the thousands of dollars. In general, I would not work for less than 10 percent, although this is really up to you and your cost structure. If I had a chance to sell a jet aircraft for $2.2 million, then yes, I would probably negotiate a lower fee.

Please remember that the commission structures I have used here are just examples. I would use them as your starting point to develop a commission schedule that is appropriate for your area, your competitive situation, and the goods you sell. Competition is also a factor. If a local competitor is charging a generous commission schedule, you may wish to set your rates slightly below his or hers. If, however, another local consignment seller is charging a very low schedule, do not try to compete on rates—just be patient and he or she will most likely go out of business unless that seller has incredibly high volume. Instead, compete on service. One thing I like to do is have a very high commission schedule but give people generous discounts for volume or repeat business.

Chapter 4

Find Consignment Customers

L et's get some legal terminology out of the way before discussing this topic. A person who brings you something to sell is called the *consignor.* You, as the seller, are called the *consignee.* This section is about finding consignors.

If you already know how to sell on eBay, this chapter is probably the most important. If you can find people who are willing to give you something to sell without your paying for it unless it sells, then you have created an unstoppable money machine. With this business you get the inventory in your hand before you sell it, but your inventory is free.

Think about this a moment: What is the biggest problem eBay sellers face? It's finding goods to sell on eBay that they can buy at a low enough cost to make a profit.

A lot of eBayers try drop shipping. This is where you list an item on eBay and if it sells, you send your money to a wholesaler who agrees to ship the item directly to your customer. The problem with this is that the drop ship company must charge for this service, meaning you end up paying more for the item than if you bought a box of them outright. The margins end up being pretty small. You have to sell an awful lot of stuff using the drop ship technique to make a good living on eBay. An additional hazard is that the drop shipper isn't responsible to the buyer. If they ship late, or ship the wrong item, then it's your feedback that suffers.

The other alternative is the one taken by the eBay seller who buys a large quantity of items at wholesale. He or she gets a great price but has the risk of selling them. If the items they purchased don't sell, then they're stuck with the merchandise.

What could be better than the consignment business? There is no investment in merchandise. If an item sells, you make a profit with little or no investment—or risk. If it doesn't sell, you simply call the consignor up and ask them to come and pick up their goods.

So, simply put, if you can find enough good merchandise to sell, this is a win-win business. The consignor ends up getting more for their merchandise than they could get from a garage sale or by selling it in a local auction, and you make a commission with little or no risk to you beyond the eBay listing fees.

Assuming you know how to sell on eBay, and you can handle the administrative and bookkeeping side of this business, you really can't lose as long as you find a steady supply of people with merchandise to sell. Let's explore the ways to do this.

Marketing Your Business

Marketing your business or, put another way, selling your service is the key to success in the eBay consignment opportunity. This includes all forms of advertising, networking, and public relations. Marketing is a continuous process. If you stop marketing, you will stop growing. How you plan to market your services is the most important part of your business plan. The money you spend on marketing will most likely be the largest single category of expense you have after rent and labor.

You should spend your marketing dollars very carefully. Make sure you test every advertisement for effectiveness before running it again. Always start small. Most advertising venues such as newspapers, magazines, and radio will give you large discounts for signing up for a program instead of doing just one or two ads. This is highly negotiable, however. My standard answer to an advertising salesperson is "I will buy three spots (or ads) and test them. If they work, I will sign up for a larger program. If I go ahead with the larger program, I want you to credit my first three ads with the program discount." Because advertising is very competitive, the sales rep will agree to this most of the time. If he doesn't, then talk to his competitor first before making a decision.

Advertising

Advertising is probably the easiest way to build a clientele. Advertising takes many forms and has a wide variety of costs, depending on the reach and frequency of the advertising you do. The great thing about advertising is that you can start small, reinvest your earnings, and grow with very little financial risk. Avoid the temptation to jump in and commit to a large program. Test your ads first in small papers and journals, before spending large sums to advertise in larger publications.

Print Advertising

Starting out, local advertising is probably your best source of merchandise. I stress the word "local." This is a relevant term. If you live in a small town (under 100,000 population), you can take out a classified ad for very little money (usually under $15). If you live in New York City or Los Angeles, a classified ad in the major newspapers can cost over $50. If I lived in New York City and were starting out on a small budget, I would forgo the *New York Times* and place an ad in one of the neighborhood journals, such as the *West Side Journal*. On the other hand, in a small town I could afford to advertise in the largest newspaper.

There are also plenty of small publications such as the *Ad Server, Little Nickel*, and so on. These are very inexpensive to advertise in.

If you take your business to a higher level with employees and/or a storefront, then you will be able to afford advertising in the major newspapers.

Here is an example of a classified ad that I have used with success:

> **Make money selling your valuable goods on eBay.** ConsignOnLine does all the work for you. We photograph the items, list and launch the auctions, collect the money, and ship the goods. We sell art, antiques, collectibles, computers, small electronics, and good quality clothing, jewelry, and accessories.
>
> Call 206-555-7777.

Here are some shorter ads that also work:

> I will sell your items on eBay.
> Low fees. Call Skip at 306-555-5555.
>
> Professional eBay seller will get top dollar for your valuable goods.
> Low fees, quick payment. 703-555-5555.
>
> eBay seller works for you. Get top dollar for your antiques and collectibles.
> 212-444-4444.

Yellow Pages

Yellow Page advertising works very well but is also very expensive. A small ad in a small town yellow page book can run $25 to $50 per month. The same ad in a major city would cost over $200 per month. This is something that should wait until you grow your business or until you open a storefront.

Radio Advertising

Local radio stations can also be very inexpensive and effective. Small local radio stations sell 30-second spots very cheaply. For example, I once purchased 25 spots for $300. One half of the spots ran in prime time. I received over 70 calls from the spots. About 20 of those resulted in acquiring merchandise to sell on eBay. Those sales netted over $6,000. What is more important, a few of the people I dealt with are still in touch with me and bring me merchandise on a regular basis.

Bulletin Boards and Posters

Another source of advertising is local bulletin boards in supermarkets, book stores, laundromats, senior centers, neighborhood kiosks, and so on. Yes, people actually read these.

Post as many as you can and check them on a regular basis. You can also put those little tabs with phone numbers on the bottom that people can tear off.

Here is the card our local consignment shop uses (I have changed the phone number at her request):

CONSIGN IT
eBay Auction Service
We get "Roadshow" prices for quality antiques & collectibles.
Glassware, Pottery, Paintings, Prints, Sterling Silver, Art Glass, Antiques,
Collectibles, Old Books, Old Lamps, Vintage Jewelry, & other unique items
Sliding Scale Commission Rates
Call Angelina at 360-555-1111

She has been using this same card for over three years, and it continues to bring her a steady stream of customers. More important, she has developed a good reputation and today most of her business comes via word of mouth.

Here is a sign I saw in downtown Seattle. It was an 8" × 10" poster similar to the concert posters that are pasted on lampposts all over town. I called the seller and interviewed her. She claims the signs bring her anywhere from 10 to 15 calls a week. She is very selective in the merchandise she accepts, so she may take merchandise from only four or five of the people who call, but many of them have more than one thing to sell.

STOP SELLING YOUR TREASURES AT GARAGE SALE PRICES

I CAN GET YOU TOP DOLLAR ON EBAY

I ALSO PAY IMMEDIATE CASH FOR THE RIGHT MERCHANDISE

Electronics, Small Appliances, Antiques,
Collectibles, Jewelry, & Watches

Consign Today: 206-555-5555

Most of her business is consignment, but she also pays cash for merchandise that she knows will sell.

This woman also advertises in small neighborhood papers. An investment of $20 per week usually brings in several pieces of good merchandise. One seller gave her over 100 vintage movie posters to sell. She sold all of them individually over a six-week period. She charged the consignor 20 percent and grossed over $30,000.

Cold Calling

Lots of people sell things at garage sales that they could sell for much more money on eBay. There are hundreds of eBay power sellers who cruise garage sales, tag sales, and estate sales buying up good used items they can sell on eBay for three or four times the cost. If you want to sell on consignment, however, getting to the sale when it opens is too late.

Instead, try this: On Wednesday or Thursday, get a list of sales from your local paper. Go to the house and knock on the door and explain what you do and offer to look at what they are selling to see if you could get more money for them on eBay. If you are too shy to do this, you could also just prepare a short note or a flyer explaining what you do and either drop it off on their door or send it in the mail timed to arrive a couple of days before the sale.

Another source of cold-calling is dropping into small antiques and collectible stores. Today a lot of dealers are already selling on eBay themselves, but I know a few dealers who want to sell more on eBay but just don't have the time. There are other, old-fashioned dealers who have never tried eBay and probably never will. These people are very approachable. eBay and the soft economy of the past few years have been cutting into their sales, and many small antique dealers are struggling. Your efforts can really help some of these small-town dealers stay in business.

You can do this with any business, but the advantage of antiques and collectibles is that they are usually higher priced than most used goods.

Charities

Local charities are always looking to raise money. You should approach them and offer to sell goods on eBay that are donated by their members.

You can also approach the local nonprofit thrift shops and explain that eBay sellers come into thrift shops every day and buy stuff cheaply that they turn around and sell on eBay for a nice profit. You could offer to sell their better merchandise for them directly on eBay instead.

Estate Sales and Garage Sales

Another technique I use is to visit estate sales and garage sales at the end of the day just before they close. Sometimes people have things that wouldn't sell, because either there is no local market or they priced them too high for a garage sale. Often you can sell these items at a higher price on eBay.

Pro Tip   **Offer Your TA Services**

TA services are invaluable to people going through significant life changes, so network with senior centers, moving companies, storage facilities, retirement homes, and the like. Many people are excited to find out there's a smarter way to liquidate their treasures when they need to because they are downsizing their lifestyle due to retirement, illness, etc.

Take one day a month to visit these facilities to provide free buying classes, informal sessions on eBay values for their items (a mini-*Antiques Road Show* with realistic eBay prices), or just volunteer your time and get to know the facility's management staff. You'll gain their trust and help a few people out in the process.

—eBay Powerseller and TA, myjeweldogsupplies

Networking

You should volunteer to speak before community groups such as the Lions Club, Rotary, the senior center, chamber meetings, and so on. Give a talk about "How to sell on eBay." This will help get your name out in the community. Your talk should not be a sales pitch for your services, but you can mention what you do at the end of your talk and most groups will let you hand out business cards or flyers.

Join your local Chamber of Commerce, where you can meet bankers, attorneys, and local business owners. The best way to meet and develop a relationship with these folks is to volunteer for some of the committees, such as the speaker committee or dinner committee, or else for events the chamber sponsors. This will bring you in close contact with other members and people will look upon you as someone who really cares rather than someone who joined the chamber just for the business contacts.

As a chamber member, you will also be allowed to advertise in the chamber newsletter or magazine and will have a directory of all the members that you can use for direct mail.

Presenting Yourself

As you will see later, you will be dealing with various types of business people— attorneys, storeowners, and other business owners. You will need to look presentable.

This doesn't mean you have to wear a suit. The corporate casual look is very acceptable. Nice slacks, a blouse or shirt, and perhaps a blazer if you are speaking to a group, or meeting a business owner, will work fine.

Creating a Presentation Book

Prepare and carry a presentation book (or a "pitch book" as it's called by salespeople). Buy a three-ring notebook and plastic sleeves that hold an 8" × 10" sheet of paper. Prepare inserts as follows:

- Facts about eBay (see Appendix E)

- Facts about you (feedback status, power seller status, years of eBay experience, and so on)

- A screen shot of your feedback page with comments

- Examples of common items selling on eBay

- Some screen shots of successful auctions you have completed

- Your fee schedule

- A list of local references

You should also carry extra copies of your fee schedule, your flyer or card, and a consignment contract to leave at the end of the meeting. (We will cover contracts later in this manual.)

Practice giving your presentation until you can give a concise "pitch" in about ten minutes. You will be reading upside down (people seldom sit side by side in a business meeting), so you will need to memorize what you want to say about each page.

Your presentation should be concise, informative, and to the point. When you get to the end of your presentation, don't forget to ask for the business. Do not say something lame, such as "Well, what do you think?" Instead, say something along the lines of, "Mr. Jones, do you have any merchandise that you would like me to try selling for you?" Or you might say, "Mrs. Brown, would you like to give me a couple of items to test-market for you before making a final decision?"

If you take one thing away from this chapter, it should be that consignors will not beat a path to your door. It is not enough to announce to the world that you are in business. You have to proactively go out and look for consignors. I would try all of the techniques listed here. Over time, you will learn which ones work best for you and your particular market.

If you do any type of paid advertising, be sure to keep records of how many calls you received, and how much merchandise you ended up selling from each advertisement you run. This way you will learn very quickly where to spend your advertising dollars most effectively.

Public Relations

Public relations is another name for press relations. When you open your business, you will want to send out a press release to the local media. At first a lot of media will not cover the opening of your store, but media members file press releases under subjects. If a news story about eBay comes up, they will pull the press release out and call you for commentary and information.

There are also several free press release distribution services on the Web. One of the best known is www.ecomwire.com. (You can find several others by Googling "free press release.") A lot of local newspapers monitor these press release services for local content.

The eBay Co-Op Advertising Program

eBay runs a program for Trading Assistants where they will pay 25 percent of the cost of print advertising in any publication with a circulation greater than 10,000. You can apply for the program via the Trading Assistant portal. You must be at least a Bronze-level power seller to apply for the program.

There are five steps to participate in the program:

1. Fill out the Co-op Advertising Registration Form and agree to the Terms and Conditions of the program.

2. eBay will send you an e-mail confirming your eligibility. Once you receive this e-mail, you're ready to get started.

3. Build your ad with eBay's Ad Creation Wizard.

4. Once your ad is complete, submit it for preapproval from the My Ads page.

5. All ads must be preapproved prior to placement to be eligible for reimbursement.

Once your ad starts running, visit the Submit Reimbursement page to fill out the Reimbursement Request Form. Submit your reimbursement request.

The reimbursement request must include all of the following information to be eligible for reimbursement:

- A completed Co-op Reimbursement Form

- An original tear sheet of the ad as it appeared in publication (Please make sure to include the entire page your ad appeared on, not just your ad.)

- A copy of the invoice for the advertisement

- A published rate card including circulation numbers (10,000 minimum)

You will need a PayPal account, as this is the only way eBay will reimburse you.

Chapter 5

What Sells on eBay?

This is a very important chapter. One of the keys to your success is knowing what sells—and what doesn't sell—on eBay. My wife, Karen, and I spent years in the antiques business. People would walk into our store all the time with all sorts of old items that they were sure were valuable. When we first started out, we used to buy almost anything. Boy, did we get stuck with a lot of stuff. Over time we learned to discriminate.

In the consignment business your challenge will be even greater because you will be offered all types of merchandise. You will see many things that you just don't know anything about. You will have to be very careful what you accept, or you will be relisting auctions and filling up your garage with useless junk.

What Sells on eBay

What sells on eBay? Well, almost anything. The key word in that sentence is "almost." If you are going to be successful with an eBay consignment business, you will have to spend a lot of time on eBay learning what sells and learning how to search for an item to see if any have actually sold—and at what price.

It does very little good to search ongoing auctions. Until the auction ends, you just won't know if the item sold, if it hit its reserve, and what the final price was.

At the top of eBay's main pages there is a navigation link box that says Search. If you click this box, it will take you to eBay's main search page. Once on that page, look at the navigation bars next to the search box and you will see a tab that says Advanced Search (see Figure 5-1).

There is a list of boxes to check. One of them says: "Completed Items Only." If you check this box, your search will only turn up auctions that have ended within the last 30 days. When you get to this list, you can see if any of the items sold and what they sold for. Remember, you are looking at items that sold for over $50.

Another great research tool is available from the Andale auction service at www.andale.com. Click on the Research tab at the top of the page. This will bring up a box where you enter the product name. Andale's search engine will then bring up the last five to ten items matching your search that actually sold. The info will

FIGURE 5-1   The eBay Advanced Search page

also tell you the best day to end an auction for what you are selling, and the best category to list it in.

If a consignor brings you an item to sell that you are not familiar with, it is always a good idea to check both of these sources to determine if a) there is a market for the item on eBay and b) what the likely or approximate selling price will be. Taking the time to do this research will save you lots of time, eBay fees, and unhappy consignors.

So back to the question: what sells on eBay? Obviously, there is a ready market for most popular antiques and virtually every type of collectible. But there is also a market for a wide variety of used goods.

A power seller I met at eBay Live sells nothing but used hi-fi and stereo equipment. He describes it as "vintage stereo." He gets almost all of his supply at garage sales, thrift stores, and pawnshops. He sells over $5,000 a month.

Plenty of people sell new and used clothing on eBay. Specialized items such as plus-sized clothing, western clothing, and vintage clothing are really big sellers. One buyer specializes in selling "lots" of clothing of the same size. For example, instead of selling individual dresses and jackets, she will assemble a lot of size 8 dresses, jackets, and blouses and sell them all in one auction. This way she has to launch fewer auctions, and she has less work to ship, less bookkeeping, and a higher average sale. Many of these lots are purchased for less than $20 but can sell for over $100 and more. Used clothing if it is in good condition and manufactured by name-brand companies provides some great consignment items.

Another excellent category is used sporting goods. Plenty of people buy used skis, helmets, hockey sticks, golf clubs, baseball gloves, tents, fishing gear, and so on. Again, you don't want to get into selling small individual items. But keep your eyes open for more expensive items that would bring far more on eBay than at a local tag sale. Sets of golf clubs are ideal.

All types of computers, accessories, consumer electronics, small appliances, and general consumer goods do very well on eBay. You can sell both new and used. You would be amazed at the number of people with an espresso machine or a pasta machine that has been used only once and is still in the original box with instructions. Right after Christmas is a great time to find these types of goods. If you sell anything electronic, be sure to plug it in first to test it before putting it on eBay.

About 65 percent of eBay buyers find items on eBay by searching. Knowing the search terms they use can be very helpful in finding out what sells. The following list shows some popular search words from just one day on eBay. The number to the right of the term is the number of times that term was searched in one 24-hour period.

1. Rod Reel 37612
2. Collections 37024
3. Avon 36547
4. Animals 36494
5. Tattoo Gun 36224
6. Royal Lace 36183
7. Weather 36167
8. Jazz 35939
9. Hockey 35796
10. USB 35761
11. Beaded Lamp 35469
12. Pliers 35420
13. Ornaments 35332
14. Wolverine 35222
15. Southern Comfort 35194
16. Sleeping Bag 35073
17. Canon 34999
18. Marquise 34964
19. Star Wars 34924
20. Linen 34547
21. Ticket Stub 34517
22. Plumbing 34308
23. Superboy 34273
24. Gretsch 34211
25. Spoons 34133
26. Mary Kay 34088
27. Canon 34064
28. Oral Care 34015
29. Rugby 33979
30. LCD 33933
31. Patterns 33911
32. Buttons 33817
33. Rifle 33765
34. Wholesale Lot 33697
35. Lexmark 33652
36. Emergency 33551
37. Scorecards 33462
38. 450 MHz 33190
39. Motorcycle 32736
40. Grateful Dead 32689
41. Fushigi Yuugi 32644
42. Tripod 32585
43. Concert Memorabilia 32226
44. Authentic 32134
45. Photos 31981
46. Orrefors 31961
47. Stands 31840
48. Rugs 31743
49. Cables 31408
50. Novelties 31363
51. Science Fiction 31318
52. Scissors 31277
53. Sociology 31242
54. Farm 31030
55. Batting 30967
56. Science 30903
57. Camel 30890
58. Birds 30712
59. Shears 30478
60. Political 30354
61. Cisco 30198
62. Vintage 30137
63. Graded 29897
64. Role Playing 29776
65. Tole Painting 29593
66. Platinum 29383
67. Family 29240
68. Mouse 28899
69. Skates 28854
70. RDRAM 28845
71. Family 28813
72. Golf Balls 28693
73. Topaz 28331
74. Indicator 28281
75. Tee Time 28042
76. Cymbals 27994
77. Baskets 27949
78. Vials 27937
79. Jackets 27921
80. Big Game Fishing 27877
81. Jacket 27815
82. Royal Ruby 27650
83. Components 27643
84. Jersey 27327
85. Westclox 27260
86. Florida 27117
87. Shirt 27076
88. Harley Davidson 26970
89. Cap Hat 26965
90. Emerald 26794
91. Diamond Necklace 26755
92. Coffee Grinder 26754
93. Zircon 26684
94. Washington Wizards 26527
95. Bowling 26450
96. Editing 26375
97. Sacramento Kings 26161
98. San Diego Padres 26111
99. Jesco 26067
100. Play Station 2 26037
101. New York Rangers 26024
102. Texas Rangers 25948
103. Racquet 25796
104. Amplifier 25220
105. AMD 24964
106. USB Cable 24712
107. Hat 23663
108. Mixer 23326
109. Flatware 23213

110. Men's Size 23110
111. Vacuum Bags 23058
112. Water Purifier 22952
113. Desk Lamp 22898
114. Circuit Breaker 22802
115. Bed Skirt 22771
116. Juicer 22729
117. Photoplay 22703
118. Blank Tapes 22600
119. Cutlery 22558
120. Lumber 22347
121. Stove 22309
122. Alabama 22261
123. Antique 22194
124. Router 22160
125. Japan 22074
126. Flag 22027
127. Gag Gift 22002
128. Flowers 21842
129. Montana 21803
130. Gas Powered 21676
131. Diapers 21627
132. Bachmann 21593
133. New Jersey 21582
134. Air Pump 21446
135. Xbox Systems 21341
136. Candelabra 21262
137. Taylor Made 21255
138. Map 21192
139. Wedge 21131
140. Press Kit 20779
141. Attic 20706
142. Irons Set 20651
143. Fujitsu 20620
144. Callaway 20510
145. 12 Inch 20340
146. Sebring 20071
147. Pacific Rim 19308
148. Generator 19265
149. Ancient 19030
150. Conan 18921

This list is amazing. Just look at the variety. Would you have thought that over 21,000 people search for the term "air pump" in one day? Or that there were over 19,265 searches for a generator? This list was compiled during the summertime. That is why there are so many searches for sporting goods. If you did a similar report in the wintertime, the most searched keywords would change dramatically. You can subscribe to a service that sends you these reports at: http://auctionkeywords.com. eBay also now has the hot keywords in all categories updated monthly in the Seller Central section of eBay.

Brand names are also popular search terms: Sony, Hitachi, All Clad, Gucci, Rolex, Compaq, IBM, Lexmark, and so on.

Should I Specialize?

In general, the answer to this is yes if you live in an area where there is a good supply of whatever it is you specialize in. If you want to specialize in glass collectibles and you live in a small Midwest town, you may not find enough people to supply you with consignment goods. If you specialize in the broader area of antiques and collectibles, you can find something to sell almost anywhere in the country—or the world, for that matter.

If you are a regular eBay seller buying and also selling for your own account, then I strongly recommend you specialize in one area you can become knowledgeable in. However, this may not be true of the consignment business. There are, however, some broad areas you can specialize in such as automotive, business and industrial equipment, restaurant equipment, medical equipment, and many others.

In a sense, just by being a consignment dealer, you are engaged in a specialized occupation. Most people buying this book are just learning the basics of consignment selling. I would suggest at first that you agree to sell anything you think will sell, and make the decision to specialize after you have some experience. The first priority is to generate a steady cash flow and build a client base.

Business and Industrial Category

The Business and Industrial category on eBay is the fastest-growing category in terms of gross merchandise sales. This is because the merchandise and goods that sell in this category tend to be of much higher value or average selling price. The main categories within Business and Industrial include:

- Agriculture and Forestry
- Construction
- Food Service and Retail
- Health care, Lab, and Life Science
- Industrial, Electrical, and Test
- Industrial Supply, MRO
- Manufacturing and Metalworking
- Office, Printing, and Shipping
- Other Industrial Supplies

This category offers one of the largest money-making opportunities for the eBay consignment seller. There are thousands of auctions in the B2B categories where goods sell for over $25,000 each and some auctions can go over $100,000.

Go for Quality

At first, you will be excited to find people who want you to sell things and you may just jump at anything. Resist this temptation. Only sell quality goods. Don't sell a piece of junk even if it could command over $50. Remember it is your feedback—not the consignor's—that is on the line. This is especially true of the category of antiques and collectibles. Someone may not mind buying a contemporary used fishing reel with a few dings in it, but someone buying an older, highly collectible fly-fishing reel will be looking for a near-perfect example for their collection.

Other Considerations

Be careful about large items, or items that are difficult to ship. If you grow this into a large business with employees to help you, then you can jump into larger items. I would concentrate on items that weigh less than 50 pounds and can fit into a standard-sized shipping box.

As you gain experience, you may wish to sell larger industrial items and other large products that require specialized shipping. We will deal with this subject in a later chapter.

Part II

Marketing Your Business

Chapter 6

Sell Retail Store Closeouts

Have you ever noticed how often retail stores have sales? In fact, even when they are not having a storewide sale, there is often a sale table or a sale rack.

Cash flow and inventory turnover are the dual mantras of every retail storeowner. Their fixed costs are so high (rent, utilities, insurance, employees, etc.) that they must move slow-moving inventory, even if doing so means selling at cost or a small loss. Space is also a major issue for retailers, especially small individual stores, as opposed to the chain stores that tend to have warehouses.

After a retail store has a sale, anything left is usually offered to a closeout dealer or liquidator. Closeout dealers will usually give a retail store 10 percent to 15 percent on the dollar for most merchandise. They turn around and sell the goods to you for 25 percent on the dollar, and you put them on eBay, where they sell for about 50 percent of the original retail price.

You can approach a retailer and offer to sell their slow-moving merchandise on eBay. They will get more money than they would from a closeout dealer, and you will earn a commission.

What Types of Retailers Should I Approach?

These are typical retail stores that have sales and are sources of merchandise:

- Gift stores

- Clothing stores

- Sporting goods

- Electronics stores (Radio Shacks often have excess goods)

- Camera stores

- Kitchen stores

- Gourmet food stores

- Hardware and tool stores

- Arts and crafts supply stores

These are the normal stores to contact for retail goods, but really, all types of stores such as plumbing and electrical supply stores, marine supply stores, beauty supply stores, and others are also great candidates. Even highly specialized stores

Pro Tip

Enhance Your Auction Prices by Using Your Local Library

A no-cost way to add value to your auctions is to use the research materials available at the library. When we needed to write up auctions for someone selling a large collection of Hummel's, when we needed to know if it was legal to sell the zebra pelt (we used a children's reference book to determine it was a zebra not on the endangered species list), and when we needed to know how old the Madame Alexander doll was (which was not anywhere as old as the client told us), we found our answers using the local library. This maximizes the prices you get for the auction items (the bidders are comfortable that you know what you are talking about) and the clients are impressed that you made the effort. Word of mouth from satisfied clients is still your best source of new customers.

—Kathleen Connors and Eileen Martin,
eBay username: ezmoneyauctions in Topsham, Maine

can supply great goods. I once sold several sets of beer and winemaking kits that a brewery supply store was closing out. They sold on eBay for 25 percent more than they were selling on his sale table for.

Virtually any retail store is a candidate, but remember, you don't want to get into launching hundreds of small auctions for low-dollar items. If you visit a clothing store, explain to the owner that you can move their higher-cost items. Alternatively, if a storeowner has hundreds of low-cost items, such as socks, you could make up a "large wholesale lot" or break them into sublots of 10 or 20 items and sell them in eBay's Wholesale, Large & Small Lots section of the clothing category.

This is where breadth versus depth comes into play. If you have 200 identical items and launch them all on eBay at the same time, you will have created the illusion of oversupply and drive down the prices. In a sense, you will be competing with yourself. On the other hand, if you have 200 different items, yet all in the same category, you now have breadth of supply. If a retailer gives you 600 pair of nearly identical athletic shoes, they will probably be spread over certain sizes, but you still have a lot of identical items of each size to sell. But if you have 600 dress and casual shoes, in different styles and sizes, you now have much more breadth of product and can run plenty of auctions without competing with yourself.

Clothing stores are prime candidates for your business because their business is very seasonal. Look for stores that sell brand names. Shoe stores and children's clothing stores are also good candidates, but stick with the more expensive name brands.

I like working with retailers more than with manufacturers or distributors. Manufacturers and distributors will often have one item that they are having trouble selling. They will offer you 1,000 pieces of one particular piece of merchandise. A retailer, on the other hand, carries a large variety of inventory and can give you dozens of different items to sell at the same time.

I have also had success approaching the stores in factory outlet malls. Some of them already have outlets for their overstock, but I have found many of them willing to supply goods to sell. The really high-volume factory outlet stores have to move a lot of merchandise very quickly and are often open to the opportunity.

There is an outlet mall near my home with a Van Husen Clothing Store. Once they were closing out a line of very nice dress shirts. These normally retailed for $29.95. They were selling them for $14.95, and you got one free shirt for every two you bought. As a lark, I bought four shirts (which got me six), all in the same size but different colors. My total cost was $59.80. I sold three of them as a lot for $57. I sold the other three individually for $19, $21.33, and $22.05. I went back the following Monday to buy more. When I got to the store, the manager told me the sale was over. I asked him what happened to the shirts. He said they had about 40 shirts left and they just donated them to a local clothing bank. I told him about my selling the shirts on eBay and he said he wasn't authorized to do consignment business, but he would have sold me the shirts for $5 each if I had been willing to take the whole lot when the sale was finished. We traded business cards and I stayed in touch. The manager has contacted me with several opportunities over the past year that have worked out well for both of us.

It can be okay to violate your $50 rule if you have a substantial volume and the retailer is someone you can work with over and over. If you have enough merchandise to move, it might pay to hire someone to help you place the auctions and pack and ship the goods.

This brings up another issue. Sometimes you will run into opportunities to purchase goods at a great price even though the person is not willing to sell on consignment. Is it okay to do this? The answer is yes if two conditions are met. Can you afford it? Don't get into a situation where you would have to borrow money to buy the items. Second, are you absolutely positive you can sell the goods on eBay at a profit? This is where the research tools we discussed in Chapter 5 come in. Never buy a large quantity of goods without researching their sale price and potential on eBay first.

You will also occasionally be presented with an ethical issue. When I was selling antiques on eBay, someone brought me a large Flow Blue platter. The lady asked me if I would give her $50 for it. It was a very large piece in perfect condition and from a very rare pattern. I knew it was worth at least $250 and probably more. I had a choice. I could pay her $50 and then have trouble sleeping for the next few nights, or I could pay her a fair value of $200, which would allow me to make a small profit. My third choice was to offer to sell it on consignment for a 30 percent commission. She declined the offer because she really wanted money now. So I paid her $200, which made her very happy, and I knew I was being fair. Well, I had really underestimated the value of the platter. It sold on eBay for $490.

When your business is small, you cannot tolerate a lot of risk. The whole point of a consignment business is to make money with a minimal investment on your part. When you are selling on consignment, you are essentially using other people's money. They own the goods until you sell them.

What Fees Should I Charge Retailers?

We have already covered commissions, but you may need to adjust your schedule to deal with retailers. A large portion of your time and money will be spent searching out people to give you goods to sell on consignment. If you connect with a retailer who can give you a steady supply of merchandise, then your cost structure is reduced. You can reduce your commissions and make up the difference in volume. Just don't reduce them too much. If you charge a retailer 20 percent to sell 100 items at $25 each, you will gross $500. Now subtract your eBay and PayPal fees (5 percent = $25) and shipping supplies to ship 100 items (at $1/item = $100) and you are left with $375 ($500 – 25 – 100 = $375). Launching and shipping 100 items is a lot of work for $375.

This is why you should stick to more expensive items, or sell the retail closeout items in lots. In the preceding example, if you sold 10 lots at $250 each, you would make about the same amount of money, but with much less work.

The best way to find retailers is simply to walk into the store in person and ask to speak with the owner. If the clerk asks you what it is about, just say that you are an inventory disposal specialist. That will usually get the owner's attention.

Once you meet the owner, you should make a presentation using your pitch book. This is where professionalism and appearance will come in. Remember, a lot of people who are not familiar with eBay have no idea how large and important a market it is. Putting this information out in the first part of your presentation will usually get their attention.

The other way to connect with retailers is through networking, such as by joining the chamber of commerce. You can also create a direct mail campaign. Simply write a standard letter introducing yourself as a "retail inventory disposal specialist." Mention that you sell on eBay, the world's largest online shopping site, and that you can dispose of surplus inventory at much higher prices than they would get from a liquidation dealer—who is going to mark up the goods and sell them on eBay anyway.

POWER TIP   *Use eBay's subsidized advertising program described in Chapter 4 to promote your business to retailers. Look for specialized business journals and other publications that retailers and other business people read to advertise in, as this will better target your advertising for greater effectiveness.*

Be sure to follow up each mailing with a phone call or a visit to the store. Also, be sure to mail more than once. Direct mail is just like advertising: the more someone sees it, the greater the chance they will take action. If you have 100 retail stores in your area, you could mail all of them the same letter every three months. Every time you mail, you will get more respondents.

Merchandise to Avoid

Almost everything sells on eBay. But, the key word in that sentence is *almost*. There are some things that just won't sell. I was once approached by a foot doctor who had invented a foot powder that really cured chronic smelly feet. I have never had that particular problem, so I had to take his word for it. But, he did have some incredible testimonials from customers. He wanted me to try selling the foot powder on consignment on eBay. I tried every trick I knew. After dozens of auctions and only one sale, I finally gave up. I guess people who use eBay just don't have smelly feet.

The point is that there are goods that just won't sell on eBay. This brings up the importance of doing your homework. Before agreeing to sell anything on eBay that I have no experience with, I now do the research first. I use eBay's search engine to learn what, if any, identical or similar goods sold for on eBay. I have also lately started using a new, very powerful search engine from a company called Terapeak at www.terapeak.com. It searches all the eBay categories in great depth and will give you results for the past 90 days, whereas the eBay search engine goes back only 30 days. We are going to cover research and research tools in Chapter 23.

Chapter 7

Raise Money for Nonprofit Organizations

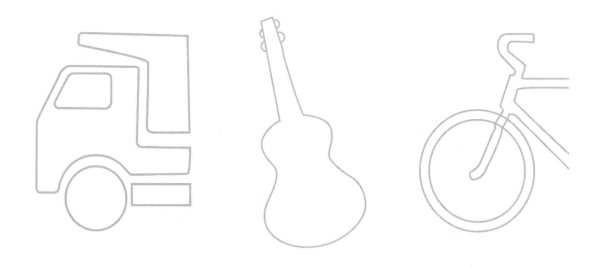

Working with nonprofit organizations can be a very lucrative area for a consignment seller. It has the added advantage that you get to help local churches, charities, and nonprofit organizations raise money to fund their good works. You help the community *and* make a profit at the same time.

Local Charities

You will want to work with small local charities to begin with. Just look in your phone book, and you will be surprised at how many local charities there are. Some of the charities listed in the county I live in include:

- Over seventy churches

- Five senior centers

- Three not-for-profit hospitals

- Three little theater groups

- A battered-women's center

- Two teen centers

- The local offices of the Red Cross and the Salvation Army

- Four food banks

- Three homeless shelters

I live in a very small county, less than 100,000 in population. And this list does not include service groups and thrift shops operated by Rotary, Lions, the Jaycees, and others.

How many times have you seen a local church or senior center holding a weekend flea market, auction, or tag sale to raise money? Typically, the members of the organization donate goods that are sold at one of the events, and the organization keeps the profits.

Most of the merchandise at these events is junk that would never sell on eBay, but often there is some really good stuff that could bring the charity good money if it were exposed to eBay's national audience. For example, at a recent auction held to benefit a local private school for disabled children, a very nice original signed Calder drawing went for the ridiculous sum of $90. This drawing would have brought over $500 on eBay. I also saw a very old Zenith radio in good working condition go for $12. These old radios are highly collectible and would have brought anywhere from $75 to $100 on eBay.

How do you get into this business? Start by contacting the local churches, charities, and nonprofit organizations in your area by mail (we have included a sample letter in Appendix A), followed up with a phone call.

Explain the concept in a simple, straightforward way, much as you would to an estate attorney or small business owner. Explain that instead of holding a flea market or local auction, you would sell the donated merchandise for them on eBay and take out your fees. Because they are a nonprofit, you may want to give them a small discount from your normal fee. You could also waive your normal listing fees (if you charge them), as this would make it more attractive to them if they don't have to invest any money up front.

Now here is the trick to making this really successful. You need to explain that a lot of people could donate stuff that may not sell on eBay. After all, you are the expert and you don't want to be stuck, or the organization to be stuck, with a lot of junk you have to return or dispose of. Therefore, you will draft a letter (or a flyer) that the organization sends out to their members describing the kind of goods you are looking for.

There are two advantages to this approach. First, you will get mostly salable merchandise, and this will result in a much more successful sale. Second, your letter will give people ideas that they may not have thought of.

For example: Your letter says you are looking for good quality books on sports, art, antiques, photography, etc. Someone seeing this may say, "Oh, my—I have that nice set of Ansell Adams photography books I haven't opened in years."

You should do your own research, but here is a list of items that regularly sell well on eBay:

- Collectibles such as china, glassware, celebrity (Elvis, Madonna, Beatles, etc.) memorabilia, and licensed sports items such as NASCAR, NBA, and NFL merchandise

- Nonfiction books in good condition on history, local geography, art, antiques, photography, sports, cars, motorcycles, trains, etc.

- Small appliances such as pasta machines, espresso machines, mixers, or dehydrators, in good working condition

- Art by recognized artists (preferably signed and/or numbered)

- Power tools in good condition

- Designer brand-name clothes and accessories

- Hi-fi and stereo equipment (amplifiers, tape decks, eight-track tapes and decks, etc.)

- CDs in good condition by well-known artists

- Movie DVDs

- Sporting equipment such as golf clubs, water skis, and snow skis

- Horse tack

- Coins and stamps

- Collections of sports cards (not individual cards unless they are very rare such as a Joe Montana rookie card)

- Old cameras

- Fountain pens

- Pre-1970 eyeglasses and sunglasses

- Older fishing rods, reels, and lures

- Pre-1970 kitchen pottery, dish sets, and older kitchen tools

- Old pocket knives

This is just a sample list to start from, but you get the idea.

An ideal situation is if the charity invites you to a meeting where you can explain what you are looking for (I would still hand out the list) and answer questions. At that time, you can also mention that you are happy to sell goods on consignment privately if anyone has any valuable goods they want to get rid of that they don't wish to donate. You should do this in a subtle way so that it doesn't look like you are taking advantage of the charity to contact their members.

As I've mentioned, I would start with small local charities. If you run a successful auction, be sure to ask for a letter of reference. Once you have some experience and some letters of reference, then it is time to contact the large charities in your nearest large city.

Working with Large Charities and Nonprofits

Larger nonprofits such as museums, hospitals, ballets, and operas usually have very wealthy donors. These are the kind of people who can donate that Christian Dior dress they wore once and can't be seen in again, or the Picasso painting the ex-husband bought that reminds her of him every time she sees it. Typically, there are also corporate donors that donate airline tickets or gift certificates to theaters

Pro Tip   **Nonprofits: An Insider's View**

One of our best clients is a local nonprofit. They have a treasure trove of items that had been donated over the years, things that had nothing to do with the mission of the organization today. They were glad to have a way to turn their clutter into cash discretely. It also enabled them to accept noncash donations from Board Members for their annual gifts, which made the Board happy.

—Kathleen Connors and Eileen Martin,
TA and Powerseller, ezmoneyauctions

and restaurants. I attended a charity auction for Children's Hospital here in Seattle a few years ago where over $90,000 worth of goods were auctioned off in an evening. These goods would have brought much, much more on eBay today.

This is a field where you can use your imagination to come up with all sorts of ideas. The nonprofit community is a very small community, and these people change jobs often and network closely with each other. Once you get a reputation in the nonprofit community as someone who can deliver profits to the organization, your business should explode.

Almost every nonprofit organization has a minimum level of donor participation. For example, the ballet here in Seattle sells memberships for the minimum level of $50 to be an annual sponsor. Once you join, you will be invited to various events and get a chance to meet the development officers. *Development officer* is the term large nonprofits use for the people charged with fund-raising.

Once you have worked with a few small charities and obtained a few letters of reference, you should start by approaching the development officers. These people tend to be very cultured and well educated—and they usually dress well. So this is the time to spiff up your appearance and make sure your presentation book is very professional. You might even want to create a PowerPoint presentation. Make sure your presentation book contains your letters of reference from other nonprofits and testimonials from satisfied customers.

Getting your first deal may prove a little difficult, but you should persist. Large nonprofits need to raise millions of dollars a year, and they are always on the lookout for new sources of revenue. Part of your presentation should point out that they are always asking their wealthy donors for cash. This is an opportunity for their traditional donors to donate something they may not want any more and get a full-value tax deduction for it, while giving the ballet, opera, or hospital the funds they earn from the auction.

The other advantage of working with these larger nonprofits is that you will come in contact with a lot of wealthy people who will often also have expensive goods to sell.

The eBay Giving Works Program

eBay Giving Works is an eBay-sponsored program that enables you to list your items on eBay and donate part of or the entire final sale price to nonprofit organizations. When you list an item through the Giving Works portal on eBay, eBay will promote your listings and place a special icon in the listing.

eBay Giving Works listings tend to sell at higher final prices, because buyers are more willing to purchase and often pay more for items that benefit a nonprofit. You can enhance buyer trust and loyalty by aligning with a cause, and you will receive a receipt for your tax-deductible donations. Your listings receive additional visibility through specialized search functionality reserved exclusively for eBay Giving Works listings.

Having said all that, Giving Works does not work for eBay consignment sales. To participate in Giving Works, you must first open an account with Mission Fish (an organization eBay contracts with to process donations) and put up a credit card to guarantee payment. The problem is that if you do a listing and agree to donate 70 percent to a nonprofit, and the buyer doesn't pay you, then you are stuck with the donation. If you file a final value fee refund request through eBay, you can then apply for a refund from Mission Fish, but they will still keep their processing costs.

This lack of functionality for Trading Assistants has been a complaint for quite a while. eBay has promised to address this issue, but as of this writing it has not come up with a workable system.

Chapter 8

Conduct Estate Auctions

Disposing of estates can be an enormously profitable area for an eBay consignment seller. I attended a recent estate auction in a small town near Seattle where the total value of the goods sold was over $40,000. Some of the goods were not appropriate for eBay, but most of them would have sold on eBay for much, much more than they brought. In fact, I purchased two items, a set of silver-plated candlesticks and a box of old stoneware jars. I easily doubled my money on the candlesticks and sold several of the individual jars for more than double what I had paid for the whole box.

There are two types of estate sales: I call them "unofficial" and "official." Whenever someone dies, there are usually goods to be gotten rid of. Sometimes a husband or wife dies, leaving a surviving spouse. In this case, the surviving spouse is not forced to sell her husband's possessions, because in most states the possessions are community property. In this event, the surviving spouse will often hold an "unofficial" estate sale.

When someone dies intestate (without a will), or with no way to pass items to survivors, the goods must often be sold in an official estate auction supervised by a court-appointed attorney.

Unofficial Estate Sales

When a spouse dies, after Mom or Dad's stuff is given away to the kids, there are usually a lot of things left over that no one in the family wants or needs. In some cases, the surviving spouse may need money or may be moving into a smaller house or apartment and will need to get rid of things.

Rather than force these people to have a tag sale or an estate sale in their house, you can offer to sell the goods on eBay for them. This protects their privacy and dignity at a very difficult time and can raise far more cash than they would realize in a private garage sale or estate sale.

You will see all types of items at these sales. These could include clothing and other personal goods, luggage, jewelry, coin and stamp collections and books, musical instruments, old records, tools, and all sorts of hobby equipment and supplies. They could even include furniture and appliances if someone is downsizing to a smaller house. Not everything will be a candidate to sell on eBay, but unless you agree to handle all of it, you may have a difficult time convincing the person to use your services.

Therefore, you must be prepared to first sell the goods on eBay that will sell, and then to somehow dispose of the other things that won't. You have several ways to do this. Almost every town has a secondhand dealer, who will often make a cash offer for the remaining goods. Or a secondhand furniture dealer may take the furnishings off your hands. Finally, you could hold a garage sale for the remaining merchandise. After you have tried all of these approaches, you may be able to donate the remainder to a thrift shop, which will give the consignor a tax deduction.

POWER TIP   *The major point to remember here is to offer a full service beyond just selling on eBay. This is a business that will grow by word of mouth, so you want all of your customers to be thankful and appreciative of your services. Remember also that these people are dealing with grief and memories. They may need to sell the goods, but that doesn't make it any less painful. Besides offering them your services, take a little time to chat and have a cup of tea or coffee with them. They are going through a lonely and difficult time and could use a sympathetic ear. This is not just good business; it's the caring thing to do.*

How Do I Contact These People?

One way to reach potential consignors is to introduce yourself to all of the funeral directors and lawyers in your neighborhood or town. They are in a position to know who could use your service. This can also be a word-of-mouth process. As you grow your business, you will be meeting with and speaking to a lot of people. Let them know you can handle this type of situation. You can add the words "estate sales" to your business cards. Some sellers actually prepare a small flyer specifically aimed at the estate market. If you do this, you can mail the flyer to all the local estate attorneys along with the cover letter shown in Appendix A. You can also distribute the flyer at places where seniors hang out, such as coffee shops, the senior center, and so on. If you like to work in the community, volunteering at your local senior center or nursing home can give you a rewarding experience as well as be a good source of contacts.

Estate sales do not always involve a death. Once you start networking in this community, you will also encounter elderly people who are moving or downsizing due to illness, someone being placed in a nursing home, or just folks who are moving out of that two-story home into a single-story one because it's easier to get around. Be sure to stay in contact with real estate agents, moving companies, nursing homes, and so on. Believe me, not only can you make a lot of money, but these people are really grateful for someone honest who can help them realize more money for their goods than can a lot of the local so-called "estate dealers" who prey on this market.

Official Estate Sales

When someone dies in a situation that an estate has to be distributed among the heirs or sold to satisfy creditors, someone is appointed as the executor of the estate. This person is usually, but not always, an attorney. If the executor is not an attorney, they will usually hire one to assist them.

Attorneys are accustomed to dealing with local auction houses. In fact, professional auctioneers market their services to estate and probate attorneys. These attorneys are appointed by the court and directed to hold an auction on behalf of the estate. It is their legal and ethical obligation to get the highest dollar value for the estate within reason.

How Do I Contact Estate Attorneys?

Estate attorneys are listed in the yellow pages. A more important question is, "What do I say to them when I contact them?"

First of all, I would recommend writing a short business letter setting out your proposition. The letter should cover your experience and qualifications and give them examples of the difference between prices realized on eBay and those obtained through an estate sale or by taking the goods to a local auctioneer. You can also talk about timing. You can start selling goods on eBay immediately, whereas a lot of local auctions are held only once a month or so.

Visit a local auction house and keep notes of popular items that sell and how much they sold for. Next, research these items on eBay and see what they sold for. (Use the Completed Items Search feature.) Create a list of at least twenty items. List these on a single sheet of paper that you include with the letter. (We have constructed a sample list like this in Appendix A.)

All types of property are sold at auction, so don't just list antiques and collectibles. Be sure to show prices for a variety of items, such as tools, industrial goods, clothing items, books, artworks, coins, jewelry, electronics, and musical instruments.

You letter should always end with a call to action. You can state at the end of your letter to the attorney that you will call him or her the following week. In the meantime, if he or she has any questions, you should invite the attorney to call you. You could even offer him or her a free "eBay fact sheet" if they call you. This could be a four- or five-page document containing information about eBay: how many auctions are held each day, how many members they have, a list of the categories, examples of items that routinely sell on eBay, and the prices they bring.

I have spoken with a number of attorneys who didn't have a clue about eBay. They thought eBay was a hobby site where people traded Beanie Babies and baseball cards. Most lawyers are amazed when I tell them that you can buy computers, office equipment, industrial machinery, cars, boats, planes, and real estate on eBay. Remember, although eBay has about 50 million registered users in the United States, that represents only 17 percent of the population. There are still plenty of people who have no idea what eBay is all about.

Marketing to Attorneys

I am reluctantly forgoing several attorney jokes at this point so that we can focus on the topic at hand. Attorneys prefer to deal with other professionals. When you speak to them on the phone, be polite and businesslike. Don't address them by their first name unless they invite you to do so. If you get an appointment, dress in business attire and be prepared to give a professional presentation with lots of facts and data.

If you are just starting out in the consignment business, you might want to wait until you have some experience to cite, a high feedback rating, and perhaps even a professional office or retail storefront. If you live in a small town, you may find it easier dealing with local attorneys than the big-city attorneys. This would be a logical place to start. If you live in a large city, you might want to start marketing your services in the nearby suburbs and smaller towns first until you gain some experience, references, and contacts.

Be sure to use your presentation book or a PowerPoint presentation when dealing with an attorney. It will help establish your credibility and keep you focused on the discussion and what you are there for.

Estate and probate attorneys are used to dealing with established auction houses and estate sale agents. If they are hesitant to turn an entire estate over to you, you might suggest they give you a few items to sell to see how you do, and emphasize that you are professional and reliable.

Pro Tip **How Can I Get an Attorney to Refer Me?**

A well-composed letter to estate attorneys and estate appraisers can lead to a great referral source. Simply check your local yellow pages for a list of names and addresses. Follow each letter up with a phone call and offer to meet with them in person. At the meeting be prepared to answer their question about why they should refer you.

—Mrs. List-it, TA and eBay Power Seller

You will need to provide a complete and detailed accounting at the end of the sale. Keep detailed records on each sale, fees and costs, your commissions, and so on. When the sale is finished, prepare a complete report. I like to use an Excel spreadsheet with everything listed individually and with the results beside each item. Furthermore, some attorneys may require payment by certified check so that they can access any monies immediately.

Other Considerations

Occasionally you will come across very valuable art, antiques, or collectibles. You want to be careful that you know the real value of something so that you do not inadvertently sell it for a pittance. This is where doing your research comes in.

If you are not sure about the value of something, or if you come across an item you are just not familiar with, take the time to research it with Kovels or one of the other research engines (see Chapter 23).

If you can't find a source of value information, there is always the National Association of Master Appraisers at www.masterappraisers.org. Not only can you find a local appraiser, having an appraisal will often raise the final value of the item when it sells on eBay. I was trying to sell a diamond ring for a lady and couldn't reach her reserve of $1,900 after several tries. I then spent $30 to have the ring appraised. It appraised for $2,800, and I included a copy of the appraisal in my auction. The next time I launched it, the ring was snapped up with buy-it-now feature for $2,499. The appraisal cost me $30, but I realized an extra $600 in the final value.

Chapter 9

Conduct Bankruptcy and Repossession Sales

Whenever a person or a business with substantial assets goes bankrupt, the bankruptcy court appoints an agent to conduct a sale of the assets. The agent is almost always an attorney, but there are some nonattorney professional bankruptcy agents. The goods owned by the bankrupt person or company are almost always sold at auction.

Bankruptcy Auction Overview

A bankruptcy auction is conducted much like an estate auction as discussed in the preceding chapter. You will be dealing with bankruptcy lawyers and court personnel. The local auction houses are your competition.

Those who are responsible for selling bankruptcy assets are first required to seek bankruptcy court approval before selling bankruptcy assets to third parties. As a part of this process, most courts require only that notice be given to all creditors and interested parties who are involved with the bankrupt person or company who owns the assets.

A notice is prepared by the professional and is sent by the court to all parties involved with the bankruptcy case. There used to be a requirement to notify the general public of the bankruptcy sale, but this is no longer true. Advertising a bankruptcy sale is expensive, especially if the advertisement is in the national media. In most cases bankruptcy estates do not have any funds to pay for advertising until the asset is sold; therefore, advertising is simply not possible.

As a consignment seller you don't have to worry about this except to ask the question, "Have you already sent out the appropriate notices?" to the attorney or agent giving you the goods. You just want to make sure that all the proper notifications have been made and that the court has approved the sale of the assets.

Most bankruptcy asset sales are *as is where is with no warranties implied or stated.* This means that after the sale is complete, the buyer cannot obtain a refund if the asset they bought does not meet their expectations. If a buyer is unhappy with the sale, they first contact the professional who is responsible for the sale (you). If you cannot solve the buyer's complaint, the buyer could seek relief by going to the bankruptcy court for that particular bankruptcy case. (Some buyers may seek relief by filing an action at their local court; however, the matter will most likely be moved to the bankruptcy court responsible for the case in which the asset is held.) Most bankruptcy courts rule for the professional, since it is commonly understood that bankruptcy sales are *as is where is with no warranties implied or stated*. Just make sure those words appear prominently in your auction description.

Bankruptcy sales are also sometimes *subject to any existing liens and encumbrances*. This means that there may be some existing liens against the property sold and the buyer should expect to satisfy the lien prior to taking possession of the property. Since bankruptcy sales are *as is where is with no warranties implied or stated*, an ultimate buyer will be presumed to have exercised their own "due diligence" regarding the property prior to bidding on that asset.

Some bankruptcy sales are sold *free and clear of all liens and encumbrances*. In these sales, a buyer receives the property with a guarantee that the asset purchased is free and clear of any existing liens. In these situations, the funds received from the buyer are held by the professional, who will later pay off any existing liens after approval from the bankruptcy court. Often, a buyer will receive a court order approving the sale if it is sold *free and clear of liens and encumbrances*.

Most bankruptcy sales of real property such as raw land and timeshares are done without title insurance or with the assistance of a title agency. These real estate assets are also sold *as is where is with no warranties implied or stated subject to any existing liens and encumbrances*. Buyers must exercise their own due diligence prior to bidding and will usually only receive a "bankruptcy trustee's deed" after the sale is complete. Buyers should expect to incur the costs to record and transfer the property to their name without the assistance of the bankruptcy professional. If a buyer wants to utilize a title agency, the buyer should expect to incur the cost of the agency, as the bankruptcy professional will not share or pay for the cost of this service.

Personal property is also sold by bankruptcy professionals. Personal property is usually sold *as is where is*. Buyers are responsible for the removal and transfer of the items purchased. If there are any costs in the transfer of ownership, those costs are born by the buyer. Usually a buyer will check with you regarding the terms and conditions of the sale, but you should have them clearly stated in your item description in any event. That buyers are responsible for everything doesn't mean you can't assist them. You might need to communicate with buyers to explain the terms, help them arrange shipping or storage, find a title company, and so on. Offering this additional service costs you nothing but will tend to give your buyers confidence.

Be careful if a nonattorney approaches you. You want to make sure they are not trying to sell goods from a bankruptcy in progress, where there may be claims on the goods. This usually happens when someone files for bankruptcy but the court hasn't heard the case or there is a pending appeal from a creditor. You should also be aware that sellers of stolen goods may contact you claiming to represent a bankruptcy attorney. Always check with the attorney someone purports to represent if you do not know them.

Marketing Your Bankruptcy Auction Business

Bankruptcy auctions can be a tougher business to break into. For one thing, this area is fraught with corruption. The big auction houses court the court personnel, so to speak. It is not uncommon for cash or favors to change hands. In smaller towns and counties, the situation can sometimes be as simple as that the local auctioneer went to high school with the clerk of the bankruptcy court—or there can be other ties. Nevertheless, you should still try to work this angle. (After all, not every place is corrupt or overly politicized. If, however, you have any political connections, this might be a good place to use them.)

Contact all the bankruptcy attorneys in your county, visit the clerk of the bankruptcy court at your county courthouse, and learn the procedures to apply for a sale. One problem you may occasionally run into is laws that require you to be a licensed auctioneer to dispose of goods related to a court proceeding. In some states this is very easy, but in others you must attend a school and take an exam. In most states, this is fairly inexpensive: typically, a two- or three-day auctioneers' school should cost less than $500.

If you would like to find bankruptcy attorneys in your area, visit the web site shown in Figure 9-1, the American Bankruptcy Institute. There is a link on the web site where you can locate bankruptcy attorneys in your area by ZIP code.

Some attorneys may insist that you take everything for sale, even if you know some of it will not sell on eBay. About the only thing you can hope to do here is partner with a local auction company or a secondhand dealer to sell those things. A local auction company is unlikely to do this, but an out-of-town auctioneer may come in to do the sale, or the goods could be trucked to their facility.

In addition to handling actual bankruptcies, attorneys often know which local companies are in danger of going bankrupt. The commercial loan officer at your local bank will often also have this information. These people and companies need to raise immediate cash and will want to sell assets quickly and quietly to avoid bankruptcy. Because eBay is a national marketplace, you can offer them the confidentiality they would not get by dealing with a local auctioneer and local

FIGURE 9-1   American Bankruptcy Institute web site

buyers. This can be a great source of revenue for the consignment seller if you can develop a reputation for performance and discretion.

Police and Sheriffs' Auctions

Police and Sheriffs' auctions are probably harder to do, but once you are well set up in business, it would pay to contact local police headquarters and the county sheriff's offices to see if they would agree to let you sell their seized goods on eBay. Many large counties are already selling on eBay, and several large metropolitan areas have signed up with one of eBay's competitors, Bid4Assets. Your opportunity here lies in the smaller rural counties and small cities and towns.

The PoliceAuctions.com web site, www.policeauctions.com (see Figure 9-2), provides a service that can help you locate local police and sheriffs' auctions in your community.

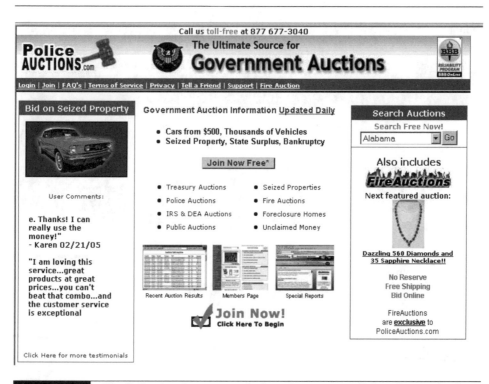

FIGURE 9-2   The PoliceAuctions.com web site, where you can link to thousands of police auctions around the country.

Distressed Companies and Corporate Downsizing

Another source of consignment goods is distressed companies. Although not bankrupt, a lot of companies fall on hard times. If you read about a local company laying off staff or closing facilities, approach that company about selling off the office equipment and furniture. Companies usually sell these types of goods to a local used furniture dealer who seldom pays more than ten cents on the dollar.

I have seen complete offices selling on eBay, including the cubicles, telephones, computers, file cabinets, and so on. Some of these sales can net thousands of dollars. It can be a lot of work to get it shipped. You will have to use a professional moving company, but the buyer pays this anyway. All you have to do is make the arrangements.

Finally, there is the area of repossessions. Although this does not technically mean a bankruptcy (these people may soon be bankrupt), a bank or finance company wants to get rid of the goods and turn the assets into cash as soon as possible. All medium- and large-sized cities have a weekly wholesale auto auction. These consist of cars coming off lease and bank and finance company repossessions. The problem for the bank is that it is a *wholesale* auto auction. Used car dealers go there to buy cars that they can in turn mark up 20 percent to 40 percent and sell on their lot. If you can convince your local bank to let you sell their repo cars on eBay, you can get them more money than at a wholesale auto auction.

POWER TIP   *Most states require you to have an automobile dealer's license if you sell more than three or four cars a year. You can avoid this requirement by collaborating with a small local auto dealer to handle the actual title transfers for you. This also gives you a space to store the vehicle while it is listed on eBay.*

This is an area where it would help to prepare a special flyer describing your services that is aimed specifically at this market. People are more likely to give you business if they perceive that you specialize in a specific market.

Chapter 10

Corporate Consignment Sales

Another great method to find consignment goods is to call on local businesses, contractors, and medical/dental professionals. Businesses often upgrade their computers, copy machines, and telephone systems. These products sell very well on eBay.

The Business & Industrial category on eBay is one of the hottest and fastest growing categories. Just examine the various subcategories listed in Table 10-1 to get an idea of the kind of goods you can sell. Notice that many of these items are very high-value goods that sell for thousands of dollars. This is an incredible area of opportunity for eBay consignment selling.

Farm	Healthcare	Electronic Components
Farm & Livestock Supplies	Equipment	Assemblies, EM Devices
Gear, Apparel	Furniture	Books and Manuals
Implements	Instruments	Interconnects, Wire, Cable
Manuals & Books	Supplies & Disposables	Semiconductors, Actives
Motors, Engines	Teaching, Education Supplies	Passive Components
Tractors & Tractor Parts	Other	Tubes, Acoustics
Vintage Tractors & Equipment	**Restaurant**	Wholesale Lots
Other	Buffet & Catering	Other
Wholesale Lots	Cookware, Cutlery, Utensils	**Websites & Businesses for Sale**
Metalworking	Equipment	Advertising Inventory
Cutting Tools, Consumables	Furniture	Home-Based Businesses
Inspection, Measuring	Hotel, Motel, Casino	Internet Businesses, Websites
Machine Tool Accessories	Lights, Signs & Menu Boards	Manufacturing
Machine Tools, Fab Machines	Point-of-Sale, Paging Systems	Marketing
Raw Materials & Scrap	Supplies	Patents, Trademarks
Shop Essentials	Tabletop	Retail, General Stores
Welding Equipment, Supplies	Vending Machines	Service Businesses
Wholesale Lots	Wholesale Lots, Bulk Foods	Vending, Coin-Op
Other Metalworking Equipment	Other	Wholesale Trade & Distribution
		Other

TABLE 10-1　Business and Industrial Categories on eBay

Farm	Healthcare	Electronic Components
Industrial Supply, MRO	**Test Equipment**	**Other Industries**
Cleaning Equipment & Supplies	Broadcast Measurement	Apparel Manufacturing
Commercial Radios	Calibrators, Standards	Chemical, Petrochemical
Compressors	Data Acquisition, Recorders	Food & Beverage Production
Electrical Equipment	Datacom/Telecom Measurement	Government & Public Safety
Generators	Electrical Power Measurement	Mining, Forestry
HVAC	Frequency Power Meters	Oil & Gas
Industrial Automation, Control	Gas Testers	Plastics & Rubber
Manuals, Books	Impedance, LCR (QZ) Meters	Power & Utilities
Forklifts & Material Handling	Logic Analyzers	Process Equipment
Motors, Transmissions	Manuals, Books	Rail & Marine
Pneumatics	Meters	Semiconductor Manufacturing
Professional Tools & Hardware	Network Analyzers	Specialty Manufacturing
Pumps	Oscilloscopes	Woodworking
Safety & Security	Parts, Accessories, Plug-Ins	Wholesale Lots
Wholesale Lots	Power Supplies	Other
Other	Probes	**Retail Equipment & Supplies**
Printing & Graphic Arts	Signal Sources, Generators	Credit Card Equipment, POS
Commercial Copiers	Sound, Audio Measurement	Cash Registers & Peripherals
Commercial Printing Presses	Spectrum Analyzers	Labels, Tagging, Price Guns
Direct Mail Equipment	Thermometers	Mannequins, Shelving & Racks
Finishing Equipment	Other	Retail Security Systems
Paper, Ink, Plates & Film	**Construction**	Shipping & Packing Supplies
Plotters, Wide Format Printing	Building Materials, Supplies	Signage
Pre-Press Equipment	Construction Apparel	**Laboratory Equipment**
Printing & Graphic Essentials	Contractor Tools	Analytical Instruments
Screen Printing	Equipment	General Lab Equipment
Sign Making Supplies	Manuals, Books	Glassware
Specialty Printing Equipment	Surveying Equipment	Microscopes & Accessories
Wholesale Lots	Other	Supplies
Other	Wholesale Lots	Other

TABLE 10-1   Business and Industrial Categories on eBay (*Continued*)

How to Find Big-Ticket Merchandise to Sell on eBay

There are several categories of big-ticket items, as you can see from Table 10-1. Let's take a look at some of them.

Construction Equipment

Contractors and construction firms replace their tools and equipment every few years. Sometimes they will buy equipment for a certain project and then sell it at the end of the contract because they do not want to endure the carrying costs until they get their next contract. Contractors sell everything from small power tools to wheelbarrows to bulldozers. Here is a sample of the equipment I have seen on eBay for sale lately:

- Rock crushers
- Cable laying machines
- Small cranes
- Trenching machines
- Gravel washers
- Paving machines
- Track loaders
- Welding machines

All of these machines were used—many well used. Nevertheless, they were selling for thousands of dollars.

POWER TIP *The Business & Industrial category offers hundreds of possible niche markets that a person could specialize in. If you do this and become well known for offering a large variety of merchandise or equipment within a sector, you've gained the opportunity to reach beyond your immediate geographic area and to find consignors from all over the United States.*

Agricultural Equipment

Farmers and landscape companies are another great source of expensive equipment. Take a look at the high-priced farm and garden equipment that sells on eBay. You can get a farmer far more money for a used tractor on eBay than he can get trading it in on a new tractor at the dealership. There are both common types of farm equipment such as tractors and tillers and specialized machines such as blueberry picking machines. There is a market for both on eBay. This is an excellent category to specialize in if you live in a rural farming area.

Here are some of the farm machines I have seen selling regularly on eBay:

- Small tractors

- Large tractors

- Aerators

- Large irrigation setups

- Knockdown greenhouses

- Air seeders

- Articulating loaders

- Augur trucks

- Bale wrappers

- Milking machines

- Egg gatherers and transporter

- Grinders/mixers

- Pruning towers

- Orchard sprayers

The list goes on. On just one day, I saw over 10,000 auctions ending for various types of farm and agricultural equipment.

Farmers are very easy to contact if you live in a rural or semirural area. If you live in the big city, you may be too far removed to serve this market. Most farmers gather at feed and fertilizer stores. These types of stores often have bulletin boards where you can advertise. Also, almost every state or even large rural area has a weekly newspaper that services the agricultural community.

Medical Equipment

Doctors, dentists, opticians, hospitals, and laboratories often upgrade their equipment. Getting rid of the old equipment is always a chore, but this stuff sells very well on eBay. Some of it sells to new doctors just setting up their offices, and some of it goes overseas to countries where this old equipment is considered "new" in their country. (India is a huge market for used medical and dental equipment.)

Here is just a short list of some of the types of medical equipment selling on eBay on any given day:

- Complete dental chair system

- Large lot of surgical instruments

- Dentist lighting system

- Dynamic stress rheometer

- Sterilizing oven

- Olympus laboratory microscope

- Pulse oxymeter

- Gastroscope/endoscope

- Hospital beds

- X-ray machines

On the day I compiled this list, there was also a listing for the entire assets of a hospital, not including the real estate that was listed by an eBay trading assistant. The starting bid was $2.7 million. Let's see, 10 percent commission × $2.7 million: Hmmmmm? That works out to a $270,000 commission. Not a bad week's work for a Trading Assistant.

Corporate Equipment Sales

Companies are always upsizing, downsizing, merging, and just replacing equipment. This can be true of office equipment such as cubicles, copy and fax machines, office furniture, computers, and telephone systems. Manufacturing companies also have various types of manufacturing and test equipment available. This equipment spans a lot of categories, so I will not show a typical list here. The best way to stay on top of this market is to read the local business journals to stay abreast of what is happening to companies in your location. When you see an opportunity, simply contact the company and ask who handles asset disposition. If they don't have a specific person for that, then ask for the purchasing department. Asset disposition will usually be handled by someone in purchasing.

Other Considerations

One thought to keep in mind when you sell used equipment: A lot of used equipment really looks "used." It can really pay to take the time to clean or even paint the equipment, before taking the photos. If the equipment looks good, it will sell at a higher price. When you are selling goods worth thousands of dollars, it pays to spend a few dollars up front if it will raise the final bid by a few percent. Spending $10 to rent a pressure washer to clean up a piece of dirty construction equipment can often add several hundred dollars to the final value.

Using the lists above for the category that interests you, look in your yellow pages for companies that would use that specific kind of equipment. You can call, write, or visit them in person. I would suggest a targeted letter campaign using one of the sales letters in Appendix A modified to mention the specific products you are looking for. Then I would follow the letter up with a phone call a week later. When you get an appointment, be sure and bring your pitch book so that you can give a professional presentation.

Part III

Running Your Business for Maximum Profits

Chapter 11

Set Up for Mass Production

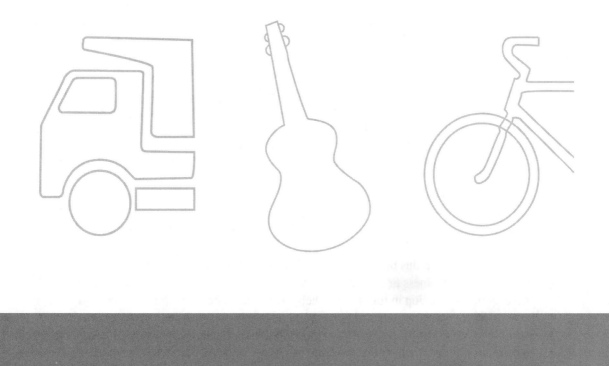

Take some time to think about and study the economics of this business. If you launched 50 auctions a week and 75 percent of them sold with an average final value of $85, what sort of income would this produce?

50 × 75% = 38 auctions × $85 = $3,230 Gross Merchandise Sales (GMS)

Use an average commission of 25 percent. This equals $807.50 income/week, less average eBay and PayPal fees of 6 percent ($48.45) = $759.05. We will assume you broke even on shipping.

Therefore, you have a gross income of $759 per week, or about $3,188 per month (there are 4.2 weeks in the average month). Not counting the time you spent finding consignors, talking to them, and picking up the merchandise, you could probably take and upload the photos, launch the auctions, and ship the goods at an average of about 30 minutes per auction if you are automated. (We will cover this process later.) Let us add in 2 hours for administration. This works out to 27 hours total.

You work 27 hours for a weekly income of $759. That works out to $28.11 per hour. That is not a fortune but is considered a respectable income by many people. If you worked 40 hours a week at this wage, you would earn $59,072 per year. That puts you in the top 20 percent of all income earners in the United States. Of course, this is before overhead costs such as gas, computer payments, ISP fees, and so on.

Anyone can handle running 50 auctions a week. Thousands of eBay sellers do this routinely. What if you doubled or tripled this effort? Well, you would be working a lot more hours a week, but many small business owners and professionals do this already. In fact, there are a lot of "Moms" on eBay who launch more than 50 auctions a week and still find time to raise their children.

I suspect that a lot of people who purchased this book would be delighted to earn $59,000 a year, but you may well have invested in this book hoping to find a way to earn much more. This is the point where you have to ask yourself which category you fall into: are you just looking for a way to make some extra money, or are you an entrepreneur with a desire to run a full-time eBay consignment business that can earn a six-figure income?

There is room in this business for both kinds of people. If you are approaching this as a hobby business or something to make a few extra dollars, then great—there is plenty of information in this book to help you. But, some of the information I will cover will apply only to those who want to develop this business to its full potential.

If you plan to grow your business beyond 50 auctions a week, you will need to dramatically automate and streamline your procedures and processes. You will need an efficient space to work in. For example, you can take photographs a lot faster if you have a permanent studio set up with lights, a tripod, and a shooting table. If you have to move furniture, set up lights, and move equipment every time you need to take auction photographs, this will be very time-consuming.

The same goes for shipping. If you have a permanent table in your garage or workshop with all your shipping supplies lined up and accessible, this process will go much faster.

There are several ways to increase your income:

- Increase your average selling price.

- Increase the number of auctions you launch.

- Decrease the time it takes you to launch an auction (allowing you to launch more auctions in the time you have).

- Charge higher fees.

- Lower your costs.

A smart business owner will take most or all of these steps. The secret to success and earning a large income is to constantly promote your business and innovate and improve your processes. Let's look at each of these strategies in detail.

Increasing Your Selling Price

To increase your average selling price, you will have to locate consignors with merchandise that will sell at a higher price. This could include jewelry, antiques, computers, medical and industrial equipment, and so on. The key to finding these higher-priced items is to proactively go out and look for them. The first step is to do some research to determine what goods are available in your community, who has them, and where they are located. Now you can set up a marketing plan to contact all of the potential consignors who have the high-value merchandise you are looking to sell.

Over time, as you develop your business, you will find yourself in a position to be selective. Once you have a good reputation in the community and with business owners, you will start to get referrals. Eventually, you will be offered so many goods that you will have a choice. You can either turn down those items that sell for low dollar values and concentrate on the higher-priced items, or you can hire someone to work for you to handle the day-to-day small stuff.

Launching More Auctions and Launching Them Faster

Anything you can do to decrease the time spent on each auction means you can launch more auctions. The more auctions you launch, the more money you make. Also, the more time you save, the more time you can spend finding higher-value goods to sell. Yes, "time" really is money. This means you need to automate: use systems and equipment to decrease the time taking photos and launching your auctions. In the preceding example we spoke of a complete auction cycle taking 30 minutes. The complete auction cycle consists of these steps:

1. Taking and uploading the photos

2. Writing the auction description

3. Launching the auction

4. Communicating with the successful bidder

5. Receiving payment

6. Shipping the item

Anything you can do to reduce the time spent on these tasks will drive profits to your bottom line, because you will be able to launch and manage more auctions. Fortunately a whole industry is devoted to helping eBay sellers manage and improve automation of auctions. We will cover automation in the next chapter.

At what point would engaging help be a good investment? Fortunately, I am married and my wife and I are both active in the business. Karen works full time every day answering e-mails, shipping products, answering the phone, and doing the myriad little tasks inherent in an eBay business. I take the photos, launch the auctions, work on the web site, and look for goods to sell.

You may not have that advantage. If you are single, or if your spouse works a full-time job, then you will need to hire some help. At first this may be as simple as hiring a local teenager to help package and ship your sales. Later you may want someone more sophisticated who can answer the phone, field questions, do simple bookkeeping, and eventually even launch auctions.

You will have to work out the economics. If you can hire someone for $8 an hour and it frees up your time so that you can make $30 an hour (or more), then this is a good investment. Take this to its logical conclusion. If you have the ability to find a continuous supply of people giving you merchandise to sell on eBay, wouldn't it make sense to hire as many people as you need to launch the auctions.

If you can pay someone $8 an hour so that you can make $30 an hour, then you should hire all the people you need—as long as you can find enough merchandise to keep them busy launching auctions.

Your primary job, and where you make most of your money, is finding people to give you goods to sell. Once you know how to launch an auction, the products will either sell or they will not. If they don't sell, your only loss is the eBay listing fees (unless you charge them to the customer). The key to growing a successful business is having a steady supply of goods to sell.

Let's do the math at the beginning of the chapter again, only this time we will assume you are launching 100 auctions a week. Using the same numbers, that would work out to a gross income of $1,594 per week. To do that, you would probably have to pay about $300 in wages. This leaves you a net of $1,294.50, or $67,314 per year. If you double this, then you are looking at an income of $134,628 per year. Now at this point you would probably have some other costs—rent, utilities, and so on—but conservatively, you could make about $120,000 to $150,000 with a few employees and a storefront or other commercial location.

If you are very good at finding merchandise that will sell for higher values than an average of $85, then your income will be that much greater. Once you start working with businesses and selling office equipment, medical equipment, and industrial merchandise, this becomes a very real possibility. You could also reach this level of income selling expensive art, antiques, and collectibles.

Your first priority should be to automate and streamline the processes you have: photography, uploading images, launching auctions, e-mailing buyers, and shipping and packing. The next step is to get help doing those things that are low-value to your time. Is your time better spent prospecting for new consignors, writing auction descriptions, or wrapping a cookie jar in bubble pack and standing in line at the post office?

Now don't go out and rent a storefront or commercial space next week. Remember, you want to start slow and avoid risk. The point we are making here is that this is a business you can grow to almost any size you want. It is all a function of how much merchandise you can find. Ultimately, it's your ability to find merchandise to sell that will allow you to reinvest in growing your business.

Charging Higher Fees

Another way to increase your income is to increase your fees. This is probably the most difficult strategy to achieve, but it can be done. The secret here is to be so good at what you do that you can command a higher price for your services. This will take time and very good references, but it is a goal you should strive for.

Another factor will be competition in your local area. Consignors seldom go looking for an eBay seller—they usually wait for someone to come to them. If there are other eBay Trading Assistants or active eBay consignment sellers in your territory, your ability to charge higher fees will depend largely on how aggressive they are at finding business. There are three other consignment sellers in my town and an eBay drop-off store about 12 miles away. Yet none of these sellers markets their business aggressively. Even the eBay drop-off store seldom advertises, preferring to rely on signage around the store to pull in business.

Lowering Your Costs

Cost control is something you should constantly strive for. Here is where good record keeping and business information come in. If you have set up your business with QuickBooks, you will have the ability to constantly analyze your costs. Once you know where you are spending your money, you can spot areas for cost reduction. Shipping is a good example. As your volume of business increases, you will be in a position to negotiate better shipping rates with UPS and its competitors. UPS rates for high-volume shippers are up to 50 percent less than for someone who ships only a few packages a week. You can also save money by purchasing your shipping supplies in larger quantities.

A major cost center is nonperforming merchandise. Every auction you launch that doesn't sell, or that sells for a very low final value, lowers your profit. You should keep very good records on the merchandise that sold versus those items that didn't. Over time you will see patterns and learn which merchandise to avoid. Anything you can do to increase your conversion rate (the percentage of auctions that sell) will lower your costs and put money in your pocket.

The key to understanding your business and controlling your costs is to understand, track, and manage your important business metrics. Table 11-1 shows the important metrics every eBay seller should track if they want to properly manage their business and their costs.

Besides tracking your critical business metrics, you will want to understand the elements that make up your total profit and loss. The two most important values here are your gross margin and your net margin. A traditional eBay seller who purchases merchandise for sale would calculate their gross margin as follows:

Gross merchandise sales	$22,000
Less cost of goods sold	– $9,200
Less eBay and PayPal fees	– $1,156
Gross margin	$11,644

Metric	Description
Average selling price (ASP)	Your ASP is nothing more than the average final value of all the items that sell. Do not calculate items that did not sell into your ASP.
Conversion rate (CR)	This is the percentage of auctions launched versus the number that closed successfully. If you launch 100 auctions and 62 of them result in a sale, then your conversion rate is 62%. Any CR over 60 is considered good on eBay. The top pros aim for 70 or better.
Gross merchandise sales (GMS)	GMS is simply your total sales for the period (week, month, quarter, etc.).
Non-paying bidder rate (NPB)	This is the percentage of your GMS that is not paid for by the winning bidders. NPB rates of 2–5% are common on eBay. Anything higher than 5% should be cause for concern.
Average commission rate (ACR)	Because commissions vary with the final value of an item and you may offer discounts to repeat consignors, it is important to know and track your average commissions over time. You should have a record-keeping program in Excel or QuickBooks where you enter every commission paid. You will want to add up these commissions at the end of each month and divide them by your GMS to get your ACR. It pays to track this number very closely, watching for any up or down movements or trends.
Fee to sales rate (FTS)	PayPal fees and credit card fees are pretty much a constant, but eBay fees can vary widely, depending on how you price your starting bids, special features used, the length of auctions you select, and how often you use reserves. You calculate your FTS by dividing your total eBay fees for the month by your GMS for the same period. If you sold $8,500 in merchandise over the month and your total eBay fees were $942, then your FTS is 11%.

TABLE 11-1   Critical Business Metrics

Your gross margin is your total sales less your direct selling costs. (The GM calculation would normally include your income from shipping in your GMS and the cost of your shipping as another item to subtract, but I have removed shipping for the sake of example.)

As a consignment seller, your model is a little different. Your gross income is determined by the commissions your charge. In a sense, you do not have any cost of goods sold. Your gross margin calculation would look like this:

Commission income	$12,400
Less eBay & PayPal fees	– $1,042
Gross margin	$11,358

Gross margin is just what the name implies: it is your gross margin before you remove all of the other costs related to your sales. Net margin (not to be confused with net profit) is your gross margin less all of your other costs related to running your business. These would include rent, utilities, salaries, employment taxes, insurance, advertising, travel expenses, and just about anything else you can think of except the income tax on the business's profits. That is how you get net profit as opposed to net margin. Net margin is your operating profit, and net profit is what is left after you pay the income taxes on your business income.

Calculating your business metrics and your margins may seem like a lot of work, but it really isn't. All of the information to calculate your critical metrics is available on your My eBay Page and in your monthly eBay Sales Reports. eBay calculates some of it for you and even presents it in a graphical format. All you have to do is transfer the information to a spreadsheet to perform your calculations and keep a record that you can compare from month to month.

Calculating your gross and net margins is an automatic feature of several accounting programs, such as QuickBooks. As long as you set the program up correctly to track your expenses, and you always use the business checking account associated with your business, you can print out very detailed reports at the end of the week, month, or quarter that will calculate and show all of your margins and more.

Chapter 12

Automate Your Auctions

This is probably one of the more important subjects in this book. If you plan to make any serious amount of money selling on eBay, you will have to automate some or all of your routine tasks. When I first started selling on consignment, there were plenty of eBay automation solutions—both web-based and offline software products—but there was only one consignment solution, the Liberty4 Software system from www.resaleworld.com. Today consignment selling is so hot, several companies have designed solutions and many more are racing to do so.

The Need for Automation

Once you have more than 20–30 auction listings online, you will need to develop an effective system for keeping track of them. Simply listing the items and sending a confirmation e-mail to the winners is not enough. For example, if a customer purchases one of your products and asks whether you received payment yet or not, you need to track down the item number and see if you have received his check. Other customers may want to know when the item was shipped or have other questions pertaining to auctions they won in the past. Consignors will want reports on their ongoing and completed auctions.

If you use a manual method now, you will want to automate as soon as possible. Selling the merchandise is only half the battle; you must keep track of multiple aspects of your business, or you will quickly find yourself lost and confused.

There are several areas of the auction process that can benefit from automation:

- Auction photography and image management

- Tracking inventory

- Writing descriptions

- Communicating with successful bidders

- Getting paid

- Shipping

- Posting feedback

- Consignor database and contact information

- Tracking commissions, fees, and consignor payments

Each of these tasks can be automated to some degree. You can't actually automate the taking of photos, but you can save time by using an advanced photo editing and uploading software program. You can also automate the storage and retrieval of the images used in your auctions with online auction management systems and offline software programs. These services fall into two major categories: auction software and auction management systems.

Auction Software

Auction automation software resides on your computer and communicates with eBay when you go online to launch auctions. If you are a do-it-yourself type of person, there are several auction management software programs you can buy.

There are over 25 different companies offering eBay management software. Two of the most popular come from eBay themselves. However, very few of them can handle the consignment part of the business.

- **Liberty4 Trading Assistants**   www.resaleworld.com

- **MarketBlast**   www.marketblast.com

Liberty4 Trading Assistants

The Liberty4 Trading Assistants software from Resaleworld is probably the most sophisticated system on the market, and at $495, the most expensive. Ed DiRuzza, the owner of Resaleworld, has been producing consignment store software for over 15 years and probably knows more about the industry than anyone else. If you are going to do high volume and/or operate from a storefront, then this system may make sense for you. The software is very robust and frankly takes a bit of training to use all the features. Ed offers a three-day training course at his facility in Orlando for around $300.

Liberty4 Trading Assistants features fast and consistent auction creation as well as the ability to track your consignors and pay commissions. Here are some of the standard features:

- User-defined screen layout

- Automatic title creation

- Built-in HTML editor

- Assign up to 20 photos per auction

- Edit and manipulate photos

- Set duration of auction, starting bid, and reserve

- Customize eBay features for auctions

- Twelve predefined templates or create your own

- Preview auctions before launching

- Set fixed or calculated shipping

- Delay launching of auctions

- Use eBay Store categories

Liberty4 Trading Assistants also tracks consignment business information, including the following:

- Unlimited mailing addresses

- Unlimited e-mail addresses

- Default auction account

- Splits/fees/commissions

- Attach notes and messages to accounts and transactions

- Transaction history

- Check/payout history

- Monitor auction status

Finally, it also features direct integration to eBay (for a monthly fee):

- Supports eBay or eBay Motors (Parts/Motor sports)

- Supports unlimited auction accounts

- Supports unlimited auction postings

- Posts auctions directly to eBay

- Keeps track of eBay category changes

MarketBlast

MarketBlast is a product of 4D Incorporated, a large business-to-business software company. The MarketBlast software with the consignment feature is a second-generation system. As of this writing, the software sells for $99, making it one of the most affordable solutions on the market. Although the eBay automation and integration is second generation, the consignment part of MarketBlast is fairly new. I have not personally used the product, but I saw the software extensively demonstrated and it appeared to work flawlessly. The parent company of MarketBlast, 4D has excellent resources and very deep pockets when it comes to developing software.

The product incorporates all the standard functions, such as auction templates, launching items in bulk, editing and inserting photos, and a very sophisticated customer relations management suite that sends automated end-of-auction and payment e-mails as well as automatic feedback posting based on parameters you create.

Table 12-1 provides a list of the various features in MarketBlast.

Feature	Description
Local database access	Allows you unlimited access to your information even when you're not connected to the Internet.
Advanced search	Search for any information according to any criterion or any combination of criteria.
eBay, eBay Motors, and eBay Stores support	Launch items to the eBay option of your choice.
One integrated solution	All options are integrated and can be used together without any extra expenditure.
Automatic application updater	The application updates itself automatically when a new version is available.
Context-sensitive help	No matter where you are in the application, context-specific help is just a click away.
Inventory Support	
Import	An inventory can be imported from any Excel spreadsheet, comma delineated text file, or database.
Auto-updating of quantities	Automatically update quantity levels when items are launched, sold, ended, etc.
Auto-alert when quantity reaches critical level	Automatically get an alert when the quantity reaches the minimum reorder level.
Individual item sales success	Track sales stats for each individual item, such as average days per listing or average fees per listing.
Inventory folders	Organize items into folders to easily track specific groups of items.
Smart inventory folders	Automatically group items when they meet certain criteria.
Global profiles	Create product templates to allow easy item creation.

TABLE 12-1   MarketBlast Features

Feature	Description
Sub-profiles	For each group of information, such as shipping, create a sub-profile to easily reuse this information over and over again.
Related items	Designate related items, which purchasers of this item may be interested in as well.
Consignment Support	
Manage consignors	Track all consignors' contact details.
Consignor history	Easily see all past transactions with a consignor.
Manage all fees to consignors	Easily track what is owed to each consignor.
Flexible consignor fees	Set up consignor fees according to base fees, eBay fees, percentage of sales price, and variable percentages based on sales price and maximum pricing.
Create mailing labels	Create mailing labels to send checks or marketing information to consignors.
Consignor folders	Group and subgroup consignors' listings.
Smart consignor folders	Smart-group consignors according to whatever criteria you choose.
Automatic e-mails	Automatically e-mail consignors on the status of their auctions.
Auto–success alerts	Automatically e-mail consignors when their item sells.
Auction Listings	
Over 100 auction templates	Differentiate your listings with the over 100 ad templates included.
HTML editor	Modify templates or create your own without knowing any HTML.
eBay fee preview	Choose your enhancement options and preview what your eBay fees will be.
Buy it now support	Allow bidders to buy your items immediately.
Flickr integration	Use Flickr.com as a storage area for your images. Flickr.com offers unlimited storage with bandwidth limits of 20MB/month (free) or 2GB/month ($24.95 per annum).
Use your own image server	Use your own FTP site or any FTP site for image storage.
Update your images from within MarketBlast	You don't need to know any other software. MarketBlast can automatically upload your images to Flickr.com or whichever image server you choose.
Free scheduling	Schedule your items to launch at any time at no extra cost.

TABLE 12-1   MarketBlast Features (*Continued*)

Feature	Description
Bulk launching	Bulk-launch items with one click.
Save a listing as profile	Customize your listing and then save it as a profile to ease future listings creation.
Update listings	Update your listing(s) without having to relist the item(s).
Automatically relist unsuccessful listings	Automatically relist unsuccessful items and save on eBay fees.
Duplicate your listings	Make up to 50 copies of your listings to ease new listing creation.
Listing reports to multiple formats	The various listing reports can be printed, or you can automatically create Excel or Word documents.
Customizable reports	Reports can be customized to capture whatever fields you wish to include.
Fixed-schedule recurring listing	Always launch items at your chosen times until you have sold out the available quantity.
Fixed-quantity listings	Always have an exact number of items listed, so that when one is sold, another is automatically listed.
Auto–price/quantity adjustments	Increase/decrease prices and quantities according to when items sell or don't sell.
Post-Sales Management	
Automatic WBNs	Automatically send winning bid notifications with your own customizable e-mail.
Shipping insurance	Specify whether shipping insurance is required or not.
Automatically send feedback	When a transaction is complete, feedback can be sent automatically.
Print mailing labels	Automatically print mailing labels.
Create invoices/packing slips	Automatically create and print invoices and packing slips, or save them as Word or Excel documents.
Second-chance offers	Automatically send second-chance offers to losing bidders.
Customer Relationship Manager (CRM)	
Send and receive e-mail	Manage all your e-mail communication from within MarketBlast, no need to use a third-party e-mail client.
Group your customers	Create folders and subfolders for your customers for even easier management.
Smart-group your customers	Dynamically group your customers by a single criterion or multiple criteria; for example, group those who bought the most by either quantity of items or dollar amount.

TABLE 12-1   MarketBlast Features (*Continued*)

Feature	Description
Automatic response to questions	Automatically respond to questions with customizable e-mails.
Smart drill-down of customer communications	Click a customer and send all e-mails to and from that customer.
Highlight deadbeat bidders	Highlight deadbeat bidders and automatically see if they bid on your items again.
Related items marketing	Automatically send an e-mail with related items to winning bidders.
Newsletters	Send newsletters to all bidders or any group of bidders you choose, with customizable details such as all current auctions, BIN prices, and closing schedules.
Spam management	Remove people who do not wish to receive your e-mails automatically.
Mailing labels	Create mailing labels for any group of customers.
HTML e-mails	Create attractive HTML e-mails.
Marketing e-mail templates	MarketBlast includes a number of customizable marketing e-mail templates.
Business Reporting	
Business trends report	See where your business is heading with the business trends charts based on GMS, ASP, listings, and fees.
Category trends report	Get a bird's-eye view of your business, with the sales by category, ASP by category, listings by category, and fees by category.
Built-in ledger	A built-in ledger tracks all incoming and outgoing payments to keep even the IRS happy. (Of course, always check with your own tax professional.)
Cash flow analysis	Forecast your cash flow with a what-if analysis.

TABLE 12-1   MarketBlast Features (*Continued*)

As you can see, MarketBlast is loaded with features to help you manage your auctions.

Auction Management Services

Auction management software resides on your computer, whereas an auction management service is a fully web-based application service. Personally, I prefer the online version, but I must admit that the Liberty4 Trading Assistants and MarketBlast software packages do almost everything the online companies do.

Here is a partial list of some of the services provided by a typical auction management company:

- Predesigned templates make your auctions look very professional.

- An HTML editor lets you type text into a box and have the system generate the HTML code for bold, underline, tables, bullets, etc.

- Prewritten e-mails are automatically sent out to your winning bidders at the end of the auction.

- You can schedule your listings to start at a specific time and date.

- You can create templates to use again and again.

- It will offer online inventory tracking and control.

- It will include a spell-checker.

- You can preview the listing before you submit it (always a good idea).

- It will offer inventory management and tracking (very important).

- You can print shipping labels.

- It will display hit counters.

- It will automatically post feedback for transactions.

- It will provide reports to help you analyze your business.

- It will set up a web-based store similar to eBay Stores where your customers are directed after completing the sale.

There are about a dozen web-based companies providing some level of auction management service. The most well known include Vendio, Andale, Marketworks, and Channel Advisor. However, only two web-based solutions include a feature to track consignment sales:

- **Mpire**   www.mpire.com
- **AuctionWagon**   www.auction.com

Both companies provide auction monitoring, hit counters, image hosting, automatic e-mails, and preformatted auction templates (you just type your text and insert your pictures). They both have a scheduling utility that launches dozens (or even hundreds) of auctions at one time and they provide online tutorials and customer service to help you get started. Let's take a look at each one.

Mpire

The Mpire site is easy for the novice to use, yet it provides all the services an experienced professional desires. Once you learn the features, Mpire's system is so easy you can create an auction in about a minute and then schedule a week's worth of auctions within about ten minutes.

Mpire also offers sophisticated image hosting and a way to place your photos and images effortlessly without being a computer genius or getting involved with your local ISP or service provider. Most important, their services give you the ability to perform market analysis, control your costs, and manage your inventory without tedious manual bookkeeping. The software can also be integrated into QuickBooks. This is a major plus.

Mpire is sectioned into modules. Each module has a specific function, but you can switch seamlessly between each of them—and they are all interconnected. If you enter data in one, it is automatically updated in the others.

Mpire Home Page

The My Mpire home page is a real-time business dashboard. You can track all of your listings, monitor your sales progress, and keep on top of your tasks and contacts with the click of a single button. It's a very clever solution modeled after the My eBay page that lets you spend less time compiling your data.

Listing Management

This page has three tabs that let you view all the items you're currently selling on eBay on a single page. The tabs allow you to switch from Auction-Style view to Fixed Price view to Store Listings view with the click of a tab.

The listing page is also where you access Mpire *Blueprints*. These are predefined routines that execute specific functions, from relisting your products to creating customized e-mail correspondence when certain business events (known as *triggers*) occur. And as your business grows or your processes evolve, you can change your *Blueprints* to keep pace.

Mpire's Listing Scheduler is free. You can create your listings in advance and launch them whenever you want. For example, you could launch holiday specials to post while you're having dinner. There's no limit to the number of listings you can schedule in advance. This is not only a time saver. eBay charges ten cents to schedule a listing in advance. If you are listing 100 auction a week, this saves you $10 a week, more than the cost of the service.

Smart Flow

Smart Flow is Mpire's name for its automated e-mail and customer relations management system. Sold items automatically move from your inventory to awaiting shipment, and buyers are automatically added to your customer relations management (CRM) database.

Financial Manager

I really like Mpire's financial management module. Mpire's financial reporting systems provide the tools to control and monitor your financial information and processes. Your financial reports are integrated with sales, inventory, and shipping and receiving functions. Plus everything can be downloaded into QuickBooks.

Consignment Manager

This module is the heart of your consignment business. Mpire's Consignment Manager makes managing all of your consignors fairly easy. You can set up an individual account for each consignor and assign any commission plan you wish. There's no limit on the number of commission plans you can use, including flat-fee, sliding scale, and eBay- or PayPal-based arrangements. Even complex plans can be customized and assigned to any inventory item.

Mpire's system keeps track of each consignor's items. From the summary page you can see how many items are ready to ship or are active and unsold. Mpire also keeps track of how much commission you owe your consignor at any moment in time.

You can create a professional-looking financial statement for each consignor for print out or to mail. Additionally, if your consignor takes PayPal, you can send them the statement and the payment at the same time.

AuctionWagon

AuctionWagon (www.auctionwagon.com) started as one of the first eBay consignment drop-off stores in southern California in 2002. The company developed its [G2] platform shortly after opening its second store. AuctionWagon's [G2] platform was the first system specifically designed for eBay consignment businesses. It provides the tools necessary to manage customers, inventory, sales, and shipping across the entire service spectrum.

Here is a list of its key features:

- Provides a complete eBay consignment auction solution.

- Manages inventory, payments, shipping, and check writing.

- Manages consignor payments and check writing.

- Prints contracts, barcodes, and inventory labels.

- Automates auction scheduling.

- Tracks bidder questions to auctions.

- Allows multiple users to access data simultaneously.

- Offers a task-driven interface.

- Includes an image hosting and seller info web site.

- Provides Integrated Photo editing.

- Is built on the [G2] platform.

AuctionWagon's system is not entirely web-based. There is a software application you must download in order to integrate with the G2 web site. This is an advantage, however, as you can create inventory items offline and bulk-upload them later.

AuctionWagon offers another service for the consignment seller that bears mentioning. If you are starting your business working out of your home and you would like to get started selling immediately, the company offers a program called the AuctionWagon Management System. It works like this: You take an item in on consignment, take the photos, and write a short description. You then e-mail this to AuctionWagon, which put the auction up and sell the item for you. AuctionWagon charges fees on a sliding scale, but most fees average 33 percent. AuctionWagon collects the payment from the buyer and tells you to ship the item. Once the buyer receives the item, the company pays you 20 percent of the final value, keeps 13 percent for itself, and then sends the balance to the consignor.

Of course, you are making less money with this system, but you are also doing very little of the work. As we have discussed earlier, one of the highest-value tasks you can perform is to find consignors with merchandise to sell. If you were making 33 percent margin on your auctions, you would easily spend part of that on overhead, eBay fees, and perhaps even an employee.

Auction management companies and software applications each have a personality, and I believe the choice is personal. One system I like, you may hate. Fortunately, most auction management and software companies offer a free trial or a money-back refund on the first month's service if you don't like them. If you are not comfortable using a system, don't hesitate to try another.

If you visit the web site I have set up for readers of this book (www.skipmcgrath .com/consignment), look for the tab that says Auction Management, where you can link to a table that compares the fees and services of over 25 software and system providers. Another great source of information to help you contrast and compare the various systems is Andy Gellman's Software Review at www.auctionsoftwarereview .com. Andy charges a small fee for his service, but this could save you some time and costly mistakes.

Chapter 13

Auction Photography and the Photo Studio

Reasonably good photography is essential to success on eBay. You don't have to be a professional, but in focus groups of eBay sellers, bad photos were the second highest complaint after poor packaging and shipping.

If you are going to be successful on eBay, it is imperative that you develop the ability to take good photographs. This will require an elementary photo studio consisting of a tripod, a neutral backdrop, and a few lights.

The only way to make money in the consignment business is with volume. This means you will be taking a lot of photographs. If you have the room, I strongly suggest you set up a permanent photo studio in your garage, basement, or any spare space in your home. Otherwise, you will find it very time-consuming and cumbersome to set up and take down your equipment several times a week.

Taking Good Photos

Here are some simple tips to improve your auction photographs. Don't overlook these, as they are very important to your success.

Camera Selection

I am often asked, "Which digital camera should I buy?" In my first book, *The eBay Powerseller Manual* (Vision-One Press, 2001), I attempted to recommend specific cameras and it brought nothing but grief. I was constantly answering e-mail from people with differing opinions. There are many good digital cameras on the market today, and almost all of them will work. I own a Nikon Coolpix 5000. Its ability to crop photos right in the camera is a real time-saver.

Olympus, Canon, Sony, Kodak, and others all have similar cameras. Just make sure your camera has a viewfinder and a preview screen, as there are times you will need both. A macro (close-up) feature is also important.

Finally, make sure there is a convenient way to upload your photos and some elementary software that allows you to crop photos, adjust brightness and contrast, and remove red eye. You shouldn't have to invest in Photoshop or some expensive image program to use a camera for auctions.

If you buy a Nikon, you can get a software program that allows you to plug your camera into a laptop computer and see your photos live on the laptop display as you shoot them. This can be a real timesaver, as you can catch bad photos before you upload them.

POWER TIP *Another way to see your photos as you shoot them is to set up an old television set next to your photography setup. Just run a video cord from the camera to the television as you are shooting, and you can see all of your shots "live" as you shoot them.*

Digital cameras are rated by the number of pixels they can capture and store. A 1-megapixel camera is far less expensive than a 5-megapixel model. You don't really need a high megapixel count for auction photos. In fact, you don't ever want to use the high-quality setting on your camera for auctions or uploading to a web site.

Most digital cameras today come with a low-resolution or e-mail setting. This is the setting you want to use. Dense (high-quality, high-megapixel) images take a long time to download. Even with high-speed Internet connections such as DSL and cable, it can take 20 seconds or more for several high-density photos to load. If someone is on dial-up (and 60 percent of the market still is), forget it. It could take up to three or four minutes for a single five-megapixel photo to load when someone opens your auctions.

You still may want to buy a high-megapixel camera for your family, hobby, or vacation photos, as high-density shots can be enlarged much more so than low-density ones. But just don't forget to set your camera on the lowest density setting when taking photos for auction or for uploading to your eBay store or web site.

Take Sharp Photos

The very first thing you should do is purchase a sturdy tripod. Unless you are shooting in bright sunlight, digital cameras are biased to shoot at fairly slow shutter speeds. This means that any unsteadiness on your part will slightly blur your photos. A tripod provides a steady platform and results in much sharper photographs. You will need a small tabletop tripod for close-ups and small objects, and a larger tripod for larger items. If you must shoot without a tripod, try to brace your hands or elbows on something steady.

Composition

Eliminate distracting backgrounds and unrelated objects in your photographs. If you are shooting an object in its natural setting, such as a computer sitting on a desk, clean up the area around the subject to remove distracting objects. Hide wires or bundle them up so that they show neatly. When you are about to shoot, look through the viewfinder past the subject at the background and see if there is anything that could distract from the photo.

A good way to eliminate distraction is with a neutral backdrop. A backdrop is nothing more than a curved piece of poster board, carpeting, or cloth suspended in a frame that you place objects on to photograph. The curve of the backdrop is important because it disperses the light and therefore the shadows.

POWER TIP   *Backdrops can be expensive. It is actually very easy to make your own if you can sew, or else you can hire someone to do it for you. However, there is also a large supply of used backdrops on the market. Just perform a search for "used backdrops" on Google and/or Craig's List, at www.craigslist.com. A source of new, inexpensive backdrops is at www.ezauctiontools.com.*

Get Close to Your Subject

The subject should fill most of the frame. Most digital cameras have a zoom lens that will allow you to fill the frame without getting too close. In addition to the overall view of the subject, you should use the macro setting to show close-up details that may be important.

Lighting

Digital cameras prefer static light to flash. Shooting outside on a cloudy day or in open shade on a bright day works fairly well, but you can't always control the weather or the time of day you have available to shoot. Therefore, you will need to purchase some artificial lighting.

You don't really need fancy professional lighting equipment. For small objects, a couple of gooseneck student lamps with at least a 75-watt bulb (100 watts is better) will work fine. For larger items you can buy the cheap clamp lights that will clamp onto practically any nearby object.

The reason you need two lights is to fill in shadows, which can be very distracting. Another way to fill in shadows is with a reflector. This is nothing more than a piece of white cardboard or foam-core that you place on the opposite side of your object to bounce some light into any dark areas.

You can also take very nice photographs using a north-facing window. Simply place your objects on the backdrop and photograph them using this soft natural light. Be sure to use a tripod for this light to get a sharp photo.

White Balance

All digital cameras except the very cheapest amateur models have a white balance adjustment. This refers to the color of light. Different lights give off different colors. If you shoot an object under a fluorescent light and then a regular household (incandescent) light bulb, you will see a big difference in the color. Cameras are set by default to the *daylight* setting, which is normal outdoor light and flash. There are separate settings for indoor fluorescent and incandescent lights. If you visit www .ezauctiontools.com, you can buy a daylight-balanced fluorescent bulb that stays cool and gives off perfectly balanced light for a digital camera. These light bulbs cost over $30, but they will last over 10,000 hours and give you a perfectly color-balanced shot every time.

Rather than reinvent the wheel, I would like to recommend you visit the web site of my good friends David and Ina Steiner. The Steiners run www.auctionbytes .com. When you get to the web site, you will find a series of free resources listed on the left side of the main page. Click the link that says Photo Tips. This will give you a simple, easy-to-follow tutorial for taking good auction photographs. It includes examples of the foregoing description.

Also available at AuctionBytes is a book written by David called *Snappy Auction Photos*. David is a professional photographer and videographer. *Snappy Auction Photos* is an excellent and inexpensive book that will help you make money with good auction photos. You can purchase *Snappy Auction Photos* at www.ezauctiontools.com.

Your Studio

The EZcube from TableTop Studio (available at EZ Auction Tools at www .ezauctiontools.com) is a ready-to-use tabletop photo studio. It's a translucent nylon box, as shown here:

You simply set your objects in the box and shoot with either outdoor sunlight or indoor studio lights shining in from each side. You will get almost perfect photos every time. EZcube sets start at around $55 and go up to about $300, depending on the size and accessories selected.

There are four sizes available:

- **Micro**   12" square

- **Small**   20" square

- **Medium**   36" square

- **Large**   55" square

There is also a model called the table-top portrait kit. It is not for human portraits, but it comes complete with portrait backdrops in varying colors so that you can easily put complementary or contrasting professional-looking backgrounds into your shots.

The EZcube products are available at www.EZAuctionTools.com.

As a consignment seller, you will be selling many different types of objects. You could be selling estate jewelry one day and a garden tiller the next. This presents a lot of challenges.

Jewelry and small shiny objects are notoriously difficult to shoot. There are two devices on the market that can really simplify this task and help you take good photos. The first one is the jewelry kit from EZcube. It consists of special lights and a dark plastic translucent platform to isolate the jewelry.

A somewhat better, albeit more expensive, solution is a device called the MK Photo eBox from MK Digital Direct at www.mkdigitaldirect.com. There are several models available, starting at about $700 and going up to over $1,500. This is how the professionals take those stunning photos of watches, jewelry, and other small items you see in magazines and catalogs. Be sure to visit the web site for a complete description. This is the way to go if you are going to be in the jewelry business.

Glassware and small shiny objects such as coins also present challenges. Both EZcube and MK Digital Direct offer specialized kits for these products.

Give some thought to props. If, for example, you are selling clothing, it might be a good investment to buy a store window mannequin or a seamstress's dummy to display the clothing on (unless your wife or daughter, or you yourself, can model the clothes). If you are selling products that work outdoors such as barbeques, garden tools, or accessories, then you will need an outdoor location with a clean backdrop to photograph these items against.

If you will be selling art or antiques, you might want to set up a larger backdrop of textured wallpaper to highlight the objects or use a small Persian rug to place the objects on. You will also need some dark cloth to highlight bright objects made of gold, brass, or silver.

Many items have difficult shapes to work with or can't stand up on their own. You will need supplies such as tape, fishing line, wax, clothespins, and other paraphernalia to help you mount or stand objects upright.

Make sure your studio is efficient. Photography can be a real time sink if you are not organized. You will also need to keep this area clean, as dust is a photographer's worst enemy.

Image Management

The other important consideration is production throughput, what you might call flow; picture-taking can be very time-consuming, so you want to streamline the process as much as possible. This means your studio or photo-taking area has to be somewhat permanent; you don't want to have to set up and take down your equipment every time you want to shoot. You should also keep it clean and well organized. Anything you can do to minimize the time spent taking pictures will be worthwhile.

You will need a system where you take the photos and upload them to a file that is tied to the auctions you plan to launch. For this you will need a good image management software program or an auction management service (such as Mpire) where you can upload images and store them in specific folders you can create. (See Chapter 12 on auction management systems.) If you prefer to store your photos on the web, there is a service called Flickr at www.flickr.com (see Chapter 12). Flickr is an online photo management and sharing application.

Photo Selection

Several years of research by eBay have shown that using good photographs can increase the number of bids an auction receives as well as the final values you achieve. In general, you should use more photos rather than fewer; however, don't put so many that they make your auction pages slow to load.

Be honest with your photos. Software programs such as Adobe Photoshop allow you to manipulate photos to remove blemishes and even change colors. If someone receives a product that is very different from the photo, they could be disappointed enough to leave you negative feedback.

As a consignment seller, you will be selling used goods. When selling something used, it is important to disclose any flaws, damages, or shortcomings both in your descriptions and in your photos.

Chapter 14

Set Up a Consignment Storefront

This is a very big step, and one that I would not take until you have already proved your ability to be successful and generate a steady stream of cash flow. On the other hand, if you have a proven business model, this is the step that could catapult your business into the big time.

What Are the Advantages of a Storefront?

The largest advantage of operating your business from a commercial space is instant credibility with your consignors. A storefront sends a message that you are a "real" business. When you visit a prospective consignor, you can show a photograph of your store in your presentation book; this will assure the person you are speaking with that you are a business that means business. Other business owners know the costs of rent, employees, and so on that come with a commercial location. When you have a storefront, you will be one of them.

Another advantage is a location where prospective consignors can drop off merchandise instead of your having to travel to them and pick it up. It also gives you the space to store merchandise until it sells, room for a photo studio, and a professional shipping setup. If you consider the cost of gas and the time spent going to people's houses or businesses to look at merchandise, a low-cost storefront operation may actually be a bargain in the long run.

Visibility is a huge advantage. If your store is in a good location, lots of people will walk by it, see your sign, and possibly drop in to see what you do. Others will see your store and tell their friends. You also have a location where you can advertise, receive mail, and get UPS pickups and deliveries.

A final benefit is that you get the business out of your home. I am not comfortable having employees come to my home to work. Besides, a burgeoning eBay business can really eat up a lot of space. Wouldn't it be nice to turn that extra room back into a guest room?

What Are the Disadvantages of a Storefront?

Once you move into a commercial location, you are a "real" business and you will have to deal with local and state governments. You will need a business license. You will have to pay employees a wage, and this means you will also have to pay for matching FICA taxes, workers compensation insurance, liability insurance, state disability insurance, and more. Every little government agency in the town, county, and state will be at your door looking for some kind of fee or another they can wring out of you.

A few days after you open your doors, the fire marshal will show up and inspect your location for first aid kits, fire extinguishers, and smoke detectors. You will undoubtedly fail this inspection. About an hour after the fire marshal leaves, you will get a visit from a company selling everything the fire marshal says you need. (For some reason I don't understand, these companies are almost always owned by the fire marshal's brother-in-law.) Another disadvantage to owning a store is you will need at least one very honest and very loyal employee who can run things in your absence. Finding, training, and retaining such a person can be very difficult. Until you do, you don't want to get the flu or go on vacation.

There is also some risk. You will have to sign a lease for a minimum of one or two years and then invest in signs, decorations, shelves, counters, furniture, and so on. This can be very expensive.

Owning a business with a retail store location has its plusses and minuses, and that is a decision you need to make. Ask yourself: Is the hassle worth the extra potential income?

What Kind of Store Should I Open?

As realtors say, "Location is everything." The location you select will determine the rent you pay. The more traffic that walks by the store and the better the commercial environment around the store, the higher the rent will be.

Depending on the nature of your business, you may not need a storefront in a high-traffic retail area. If you are dealing primarily with businesses and lawyers, you can get a location in a commercial area off the main street (see Figure 14-1).

FIGURE 14-1   An eBay drop-off store

This will be less costly. On the other hand, if you are seeking the consumer market, then you will want to be where you can get foot traffic and walk-ins.

Store Layout

You will want a counter near the front door, where you can deal with the walk-in public. This counter should separate the customers from the rest of the store. Remember, you are storing other people's goods and you are responsible for them until they sell and you get paid. You don't want a situation where someone can come in and browse through the merchandise you have up for sale. One shoplifting event can ruin your feedback if the item sells before you realize it is missing. You may also want to install a security system.

It is really helpful to have a computer with a monitor on the front counter that you can turn around to show the client. When someone comes in with an overblown idea of what their item is worth, you can look up the item in the closed auction listing on eBay and show the potential consignor what similar items actually sold for.

Next you will want to construct shelves where you can organize and store your merchandise until you ship it. The size and type of shelves will depend on what you are selling. (Stores such as Loews, Costco, and Home Depot sell various types of prefabricated shelving that is low cost and you can install yourself.)

Since you will probably have an employee to help you, he or she will need a computer and a place to sit. This should be near the front counter so that customers are seen when they walk in. You will also need a workstation for yourself.

Finally, you will want room enough to set up your photo studio and shipping table.

How Much Space Will I Need for All of This?

This depends on how large you want to grow your business. As a minimum, if it will just be yourself and one employee, you will need about 400 square feet. Personally, I would go for something closer to 700 square feet to give room for growth. Remember, if your business booms and you are stuck in a two-year lease, you will have to wait until it expires before you can expand.

Commercial Lease Checklist

Commercial leases can be very involved, but if you break everything down into simple parts, they are fairly easy to understand. Here is a commercial lease checklist that addresses some of the most common issues that occur when a store or commercial property lease is being negotiated.

After reviewing it, you should be in good position to understand what to look for in a property lease. Of course, before signing any real property lease, have it reviewed by an attorney who specializes in real estate. In the checklist that follows, the landlord is the "lessor" and you would be the "lessee." Using a checklist to anticipate problems and having the lease reviewed by your attorney will hopefully keep you from becoming the "screwee."

- **Nature and duration of the lease**   Determine the term of the lease, and when the lessee is entitled to possession. Is the lease to be a net lease? What are the duties of the lessor?

- **Rent**   In the contract, make sure that the amount of rent and when and how it is payable are stated. If the lessee holds over, what is the rent for this period?

- **Escalation clause**   Since most commercial leases contain a rent escalation clause, determine whether the escalation is keyed to actual increases in operating costs or it is keyed to some index.

- **Competition**   If the landlord owns other nearby space (such as other units in a strip mall), you may want to insert a clause that he will not lease to another directly competitive store such as a UPS store that acts as an eBay consignment front for AuctionDrop.

- **Renewal**   Is there an option to renew, and what is the term of each option? What is the rent for each renewal period? How must the option to renew be exercised?

- **Subletting**   Is the lessee entitled to sublease the property or to assign the lease? What is required before the lessee may sublease? This could be important if your business doesn't survive; you can sublet the space to mitigate the remaining time on your lease. On the other hand, if your business explodes, you may want to sublet so that you can move up to a larger space.

- **Space**   What the landlord considers rentable square feet and what you get in usable square feet of space can vastly differ. The location of a building's columns, doors, and windows can affect a tenant's total space requirements. Determine whether the lease provides an option for additional space. Are you given a right of first refusal when additional space becomes available? Can other tenants be moved when additional space becomes available so that your areas are contiguous?

■ **Taxes and expenses**   Determine who is responsible for the real property taxes. If the lessee is agreeing to pay only for increases, is there a stated maximum? Who pays for general maintenance and services? If it's the tenant, is the tenant free to contract with whomever he or she wants for these services, or must they be obtained from or through the lessor? Who is responsible for extraordinary or structural repairs or alterations?

■ **Construction**   Does the lessor warrant that the building conforms to all local laws and codes, and will the lessor reimburse the lessee for correcting any code violations? Does the lessee have the right to inspect before execution of the lease and before taking possession? Are there adequate parking facilities and other transportation facilities?

■ **Work agreement**   Space is rarely taken by tenants in "as is" condition, whether the building is new or old. The fitting out of the premises to mutually agreed-upon specifications is accomplished by a work agreement. A *work agreement* (sometimes called a "workletter") is a contract between the landlord and the tenant describing what is to be constructed, who pays for it and how, what the schedule for completion is, and who is responsible for delays and cost overruns.

■ **Zoning**   What zoning applies to the building, and is your intended use permitted? Are there covenants or restrictions on the property? Easements?

■ **Liability and insurance**   Who is responsible for liability insurance, and what are the limits? Who carries theft, fire, and other casualty insurance? To what extent does the lessor or lessee excuse the other party for liability for injury to persons or property? Lessees should scrutinize any hold-harmless provisions within the lease with great care. While you may be willing to reimburse the landlord for losses caused by your negligence, you would not want to hold a landlord harmless for damage caused by actions of the landlord. The provisions should indemnify the landlord only for harm caused by the lessee within the leased space.

■ **Termination**   What obligations are imposed on the lessee as to the condition of the property at the end of the lease term? Are ordinary wear and tear excepted from lessee's obligation to return property in good condition?

■ **Purchase option**   Does the lease give the lessee an option to purchase the leased property? What is the option price, and when and how must the option be exercised?

■ **Grace period**   Are there grace periods for default on rent or other conditions in the lease? What are the lengths of the grace periods?

■ **Enforcement**   Are damages specified for breaches of various lease conditions? Who pays attorney's fees for actions to enforce lease provisions?

■ **Lease commencement date**   It is not unusual for a lease to commence on a date based upon some external event, such as completion of improvements or upon the present tenant vacating. Once the commencement date has been established, the parties should sign an amendment setting forth that date as well as the starting date for payment of rent. This will avoid problems that may arise in the future, such as the expiration date and base periods for determining rent increases. Arbitration should be provided to resolve any dispute, or if a party refuses to sign the amendment. To avoid delaying tactics, a simple expedient is to provide that the losing party pays the arbitration costs, including legal fees.

■ **Representations and warranties**   The landlord may want the tenant to agree to disclaim any implied warranty or take the premises on an "as-is" basis without any landlord representations or warranties as to its condition or history. In either case, such a clause will impede the tenant from holding the landlord responsible for losses attributable to it. A tenant still wishing to lease the space on such a basis should at least request the landlord's specific representation as to any problem of which the landlord is already aware, and ask the landlord to have prelease tests conducted by an independent building inspector. Personally, I would not lease space under those conditions.

■ **Use restrictions**   Are there any limits on the kind of business you can conduct on the property?

■ **Improvements**   The tenant may wish to add "improvements" to the premises that might be of value to the tenant but not future tenants. Determine the extent to which the landlord will allow improvements.

■ **Right of entry**   It may be in the best interests of both landlord and tenant that the landlord be permitted entry to the premises on an as-needed basis, despite inconvenience to the tenant, even if a shutdown for repairs is necessary. The tenant should plan to cooperate in these situations.

■ **Legal compliance**   The landlord may want to include a provision whereby the tenant is obligated to comply with all present and future federal, state, and local laws, including future environmental laws, affecting the leased premises, tenant's business, or any activity or condition involving the premises; to change, reduce, or cease any noncomplying activity; and to install pollution-control systems, equipment, safety devices, and the like in order to comply. This is unlikely to affect you, but you will see it in most commercial leases.

Finally, take your time and look at lots of properties before making a decision. Every time I have made a mistake involving real estate, it was caused by impatience to find a space and get into it. Taking the time to see everything available in your area will pay dividends and prevent you from making a costly mistake.

Chapter 15

Fees and Costs

Cost control is one of the major challenges of any business. You can't control your costs unless you know what they are. This will be one of the most time-consuming of your non-auction chores, but probably the most important.

I strongly suggest you automate your record keeping with a system such as QuickBooks. The popular Quicken software is cheaper, but it's not really up to running a full-time business. You may also want to hire a part-time bookkeeper to do your quarterly taxes. There are a lot of complications to the tax code once you have employees that can result in fines if taxes are not filed and paid on time and in the correct amounts. Fifty dollars a month spent on a bookkeeper can free up your time for more productive work and keep you out of trouble with the state and federal tax people.

Costs of Doing Business

As I mentioned, you must know what all your costs are before you can control them. Here is a list of some of the business costs you will need to track:

eBay listing fees
Advertising
Labor (salaries)
Internet (ISP) fees
Rent
Payroll taxes
Telephone
Utilities
Benefits
PayPal fees
Credit card fees
Insurance
Final value fees
Office supplies
Travel/entertainment
One-time costs (deposits, furniture, computers, office equipment, etc.)
Money owed and paid to consignors
Automobile expenses
Loan payments
Banking fees
Shipping and postage

You may have more expenses than these. The best way to track your expenses is to open a business checking account, tie it to your QuickBooks account, and resist the temptations to use your business account for personal use (this really complicates your bookkeeping). If you need to take money out of the business for personal needs, take it as an expense reimbursement, salary, bonus, or dividend. Don't use the business account debit card to pay for a new blouse or the latest CD unless you plan to turn around and sell it on eBay. Keep receipts of all your expenditures. Don't forget to back up your financial and tax records if you keep them on a computer.

Cost Control

Running a small business is an exercise in watching pennies so that the dollars take care of themselves. The great thing about QuickBooks is that you can get a printout every month by category of expense to see where your money is going, right to the penny. You can also track your expenses month by month to spot trends. For instance, you notice that your telephone bills are increasing—is it time to shop for cheaper telephone service? If you see your eBay fees taking a big bite (you will), then you should look at how you are posting your auctions. Are you paying reserve fees? Are you listing your items above the eBay listing fee breakpoints? If you are paying special feature fees, are they working?

The point is that you won't know how to control your costs unless you know exactly what your costs are.

POWER TIP   *There is a popular myth that most businesses fail because they were underfinanced to begin with. In fact, most businesses fail not because they were underfunded but because they did not understand their cost structure from the beginning. By the time they discovered where their money went, the money was gone and it was too late to do anything about it. Keeping track of your costs and expenses will help you spot trends and problems in time to address them.*

Once you have systems in place to monitor and control your costs, you should go back to your business plan and adjust it using real numbers. Write down your financial goals and targets and measure your progress each month. You may find that over time, your projections were too low or too high. Once you have been running your business for a few months, you will get a better feel for how much you have to invest in advertising and promotion to drive business. Now you can make investment decisions with a greater degree of confidence than when you were just starting out and everything was based on estimates and guesses.

Advertising

In the chapter on marketing your business I pointed out that advertising for consignors could be one of your major business expenses. It is very easy to overspend on advertising. After all, everyone likes to see their name in print. The best way to control your advertising expenses is to test every ad very carefully. My rule of thumb is that I am looking for at least a 5-to-1 return on investment (ROI) on each ad dollar I spend. If I spend $200 for an advertisement, I expect it to bring in $1,000 in commissions and fees.

The other thing you want to be careful of is signing long-term advertising contracts until you have absolutely proved the viability and ROI of the advertising medium and your content.

POWER TIP   *Good advertising is all about benefits. If your ads do not clearly state or imply a benefit, they may be read but not acted upon. A good ad has four main components that you can remember with the acronym AIDA: Attention, Interest, Desire, Action:*

- *Attention   Captures the reader's attention with an arresting headline to get them to keep reading.*

- *Interest   Builds information in an interesting way, usually meaning that this must relate closely to the way that the reader thinks about the topic you are writing about.*

- *Desire   Relates benefits to the reader so that they will want what you are offering.*

- *Action   Tells the reader to call a telephone number or visit your store. Advertising that does not prompt action is a wasted opportunity.*

eBay Fees

We will cover the subject of eBay fees in Chapter 22. But in the area of cost control, one of the biggest expenses is paying eBay listing and feature fees for items that don't sell or have to be relisted several times before they do sell. There are several ways to reduce this expense or to turn it into extra income:

- Research items before agreeing to sell them to make sure there is a market for the product.

- Learn to say "no" to consignors with unreasonable expectations. If a consignor insists on a reserve or starting price that is higher than you think is reasonable, ask them to pay the fees up front as a nonrefundable charge.

- If a seller wants to use a reserve, get them to pay the reserve fee up front. The fee is $2 plus 1 percent of the reserve amount up to $100. Thus, if a consignor wants a $500 reserve on an item, you charge them 1 percent of $500, plus $2. If the item meets its reserve and sells, these fees are refunded to you. You then have the choice of refunding to the seller or just keeping the fees.

- Create a "value package." This is where you charge the consignor an upfront fee for some of eBay's extra services. For example, your value package could consist of

  - eBay Picture Service (supersize and gallery)—your cost, $1

  - Bold Listing—$1

  - Border—$3

  - Item Subtitle—$0.50

These items have a total cost of $5.50. You could charge your consignors anywhere from $6.95 to $9.95 for this "value package." You simply explain that this is a good investment on their part because these features tend to increase bids and final values by as much as 30 percent on eBay. Make sure your consignors prepay for these extra services. This way, even if the item doesn't sell, you have covered your fee costs and made a couple of dollars to pay for your time.

Employment and Employee Costs

When it comes to hiring employees, I would avoid hiring a friend or family member unless you are absolutely sure you can manage the relationship. I once hired a close friend and had to fire her. Because she was a friend, I kept her on longer than I should have, and when it came time to fire her, it ruined the friendship.

You will need to decide what you want an employee to do. When you are first starting out, I suggest you to hire someone to do the low-value tasks that free up your time for more important work. This would include taking photographs, packing and shipping, and perhaps sending out the shipping notice e-mails. Later, you may want to train a person to write simple auction copy and eventually launch auctions. Eventually, as your business grows, you may want to hire a highly skilled person who can interact with your consignors, do bookkeeping, and carry out general office manager work.

Another issue is motivating and keeping a great employee when you find them. Besides a competitive salary, employees expect benefits such as health insurance, sick leave, and vacations. They also expect to be recognized and rewarded. Hiring and training a new employee is always a time-consuming chore and entails some risk that the employee will not work out. Accordingly, you should do everything you can within reason to keep a great employee when you find them. Sometimes paying a little higher than the local scale for the skill level can save you a lot of money in the long run.

Finally, be sure to follow all the local, state, and federal labor laws. Not doing so can get you in a lot of trouble and cost you a fortune in lawsuit defense, higher insurance rates, and fines. The best resource is your local Department of Labor office. They have plenty of books and publications that explain the labor laws, safety regulations, and worker's compensation insurance issues. They can also supply you with all of the required posters and legal notifications you are required to post where employees can see them. These days, not getting sued or fined is a major cost-control strategy.

There are three ways to pay for labor: you can hire an employee, you can "lease" an employee, or you can hire an independent contractor.

Employee Leasing

Dealing with employees can be difficult and time-consuming. One answer is the concept of employee leasing. Using the services of a vendor to provide all or some of their employees for a fee has become an increasingly popular option for employers. These arrangements serve to provide employers an alternative to the traditional management and administration of the employee workforce. Employee leasing arrangements have been replaced with a new category of company that serves small businesses. These companies are known as *professional employee organizations (PEO)*. If you search this term on Google, you will come up with dozens of companies that provide this service.

The way a PEO works is that they actually hire your employees and rent or lease them out to you. You are responsible for their daily supervision, job performance, and management, including hiring and firing. But the PEO provides all of the nonmanagement employee services, such as taking care of payroll, providing benefits, and filing reports and forms.

Independent Contractors

An independent contractor is someone who works for you who is not an employee. You pay them an hourly rate or a fixed fee to perform a specified task. They pay their own taxes, benefits, and normal costs. This sounds like a good solution to the employee problem, but there are several drawbacks. The IRS has several rules regarding the employment of independent contractors.

First of all, they must be truly independent. You cannot treat them as you would an employee. A general rule is that you, the payer, have the right to control or direct only the *result of the work* done by an independent contractor, and not the *means and methods* of accomplishing the result.

The IRS requires you to file returns to report payments made to independent contractors during the year. For example, you must file Form 1099-MISC, Miscellaneous Income, to report payments of $600 or more to persons not treated as employees (e.g., independent contractors) for services performed for your trade or business. For details about filing Form 1099, go to www.irs.gov/forms. You can read the regulations and download a copy of the form from this site. If you use QuickBooks, this form can be automatically generated by the program.

You want to be careful to follow the rules as they relate to independent contractors, because if the IRS finds that you are paying someone to do work as an independent contractor who is really an employee, they can force you to pay back withholding taxes and fines.

Generally, if you hire someone to perform a specific task and they can come to begin the task and then go when the task is complete, then you can qualify and pay the person as an independent contractor. For example, suppose you hire a student to come in every day after school to package, address, and ship your merchandise. This is a specific task. You would have to pay the student a fixed rate per package or a set daily fee. Under this arrangement you would pay them the same fee regardless of how long they worked. If one day they shipped 40 packages and the next day only 10 packages, they would earn the same amount on a daily fee or a fee per package. When they were finished, they could leave. If they finished early, you could not ask them to stay and sweep the floors, stock shelves, or perform other duties that an employee might do.

You can also hire independent contractors to do specific technical tasks, such as take digital photos, update your web site, or come in and count inventory. A lot of small businesses do this today. They hire the minimum number of actual employees they need to accomplish the daily tasks of their business and then pay independent contractors for other services such as web site design, bookkeeping, and janitorial service.

Chapter 16

Organization and Record Keeping

We have already addressed the need to be organized and to keep accurate cost data. There is more, however. Your ability to keep good records and have them organized so that you can find them will be critical to your long-term success.

Getting Organized

Here is a list of the information categories you will need to organize, file, and control:

- Contact information on each consignor
- Consignor contract, payment receipts
- Merchandise in/out by consignor and buyer
- Tracking nonpaying bidders
- Merchandise storage (connecting the storage location with the auction)
- Shipment tracking
- Delivery confirmation
- Posting feedback
- Payments for auctions
- Image management
- Auction templates
- Personnel data on employees
- Insurance papers
- Warranties and service contracts
- Business expenses
- Tax documents
- Correspondence (e-mail and snail mail)

Tracking and storing this information will require you to organize both electronic and physical filing systems. Don't forget to back up your data frequently.

Pro Tip   Choose Investors with Care

If you are going to go into business with another person, I recommend you set up a simple corporation where you, or your family members, have at least 51 percent of the voting stock.

If you find an investor to invest in your enterprise, I would advise seeking professional investors, rather than family and friends. The problem with family and friends investing in your business is that you feel an emotional attachment to their money and pressures you would not feel if some stranger invested in your business. (See Chapter 18 on raising venture capital.)

There are exceptions to this, of course. If you have a wealthy relative who can easily afford to lose a few thousand dollars, that is one thing. But don't convince someone to borrow on their home, or their 401(k), to invest in your business. You will never forgive yourself if you lose their money. (This is the voice of experience speaking!)

We will talk about raising money and investing in your business in greater detail in Chapter 18.

Looking at this list, you may say, "Whoa, do I really want to get into this?" Only you can answer that question. If you are not an organized person, you should either forget about this business or hire someone to help you do it. Notice I said, "hire." Unless you are married to one, I would forget about a partner. Business partnerships seldom succeed and often lead to lawsuits at the very worst and losing a good friend at the least. I would never go into a partnership with a close friend or a family member unless it were my spouse.

Consignor Records

Among the things you will need to track are the goods consignors brought in, when they sold, how much they sold for, your commission, your costs such as eBay and PayPal fees, and when and how much you paid the consignor. If you are doing fairly low volumes and want to track this information manually, I would set up an Excel spreadsheet for this purpose. But at some time you are going to want to automate this function, as it can become very time-consuming. The software programs and online auction management systems covered in Chapter 12 can perform a lot of these tasks for you. Then, if you integrate with QuickBooks (see the next section, "Financial Record Keeping"), you can combine your consignor records with your financial records. This is really the best method to use, as it saves you time by not having to enter duplicate data.

If you are struggling with this task, I would suggest you get some help. All of the software solution providers and auction management companies provide different levels of support. Typically, this support is free for the first month and is then limited to e-mail support after that. However, most of the companies offer live telephone support as a paid option. These systems are so important to the long-term success of your business that the small amount of money you invest in getting support to set them up correctly will pay huge dividends in time and money saved later.

You will also need to sign a contract with each consignor. This can be a very simple agreement laying out the terms of your service, your fees, and how the merchandise will be returned or disposed of in the event it does not sell. Or, some consignment sellers go to the trouble of creating long, detailed legal agreements. If you are dealing with day-to-day consumers, you can get by with a simple contract, such as that shown in Appendix A. If you are dealing in the business-to-business world, your customers may demand a more detailed contract. In this event, I would start by taking the contract in Appendix A to your attorney to use as a starting point. Although attorneys understand contract law, few are familiar with the consignment business. Starting with an existing contract will save you time and money, as it gives your attorney a framework to work within and a quick overview of the issues specific to eBay and consignment selling.

One word of warning: although I have prepared hundreds of contracts over my lifetime, and I had a lawyer review the contracts in Appendix A, I suggest you still have your lawyer check it over to assure compliance with state and local laws.

Financial Record Keeping

A good bookkeeping system such as QuickBooks can easily organize your financial information and generate monthly reports to help track your finances and control your cash flow. QuickBooks can also easily generate the data you need to file sales tax reports and quarterly estimated tax statements to the IRS.

There are other programs besides QuickBooks on the market, such as MYOB and Peachtree Accounting Small Business software. The advantage of QuickBooks is that it has become somewhat of a standard for small businesses across the U.S. Most community colleges offer adult education classes on QuickBooks.

If you need help with bookkeeping, it is pretty easy to hire someone who is already trained on QuickBooks, while you may have to hunt to find someone familiar with Peachtree. The other advantage of QuickBooks is that many of the auction management systems such as Mpire and software programs such as MarketBlast and Liberty4 are set up to download their sales data into QuickBooks. PayPal and most merchant credit card accounts also include this functionality.

Any time you spend setting up systems and files to help organize and control your business will pay huge dividends in time and cost savings once your business is up and running.

Pro Tip   How to Avoid IRS Audits

Small businesses are ocassionally the target of IRS audits. The secret to making an audit painless is to have excellent financial records. The IRS position is "if you can't prove it, you can't claim it." Although I use QuickBooks for my recordkeeping, I hold on to every receipt, every cancelled check, and all sales, income, and expense records going back three years.

The other way to avoid IRS audits is to use a Certified Public Accountant (CPA) to prepare your taxes. CPAs charge a little more than a tax or bookkeeping service, but, statistically, tax returns prepared by a CPA are far less likely to be audited.

Chapter 17

Write Your Business Plan

Every business needs a plan. The most famous statement about business planning goes: "Those who fail to plan, plan to fail." This is an incredibly true statement. Running a business without a plan is like sailing a boat into uncharted waters. Running a business with a plan is no guarantee of success—your boat may still hit a sandbar, but you will have a plan for getting off the sandbar.

Your Business Plan

You don't need an MBA from Harvard to write a business plan. The essence of business planning is understanding what business you are in and your target market, setting your goals, setting out a list of tasks to get you there, understanding how much money it will cost and how you will spend it, and setting up contingencies if something doesn't go as planned.

Business Plan Basics

Let's look at some of the basic elements of a good business plan.

What Business Are You In?

This is where you describe your business. The key here is to focus. Focus on products, market, or geography—but have a focus. Don't start a business that will do anything on any given day.

Vision or Statement of Objective—What Are You Trying to Do?

You need to set out your objective in a few short sentences or paragraphs. This is where you describe your business and what you want it to look like a year from now. What will you sell or specialize in? How big will your business be? What is unique about your business, and what special strategies or markets will make it successful?

What Is Your Market? What Is Your Marketing Plan?

Where and how will you find your consignors? How will you advertise? Will you specialize, and if so, what will you specialize in? What goods will you look for, and how will they sell on eBay? Are you going after the individual market or the business market, or both?

Ask yourself, how much will I have to invest in advertising and promotion? What is my expected return? How much will it cost me to acquire a consignor?

What Resources Will You Need?

What will you need that you do not now have? Take into account computers, cameras, photo equipment, physical space, employees, office equipment, etc. How much will this cost? If you plan to hire employees, what will they do and how much will you pay them?

How Much Will You Need to Invest in Your Business?

This is where you create a cash flow plan. Lay out your first-year costs, month-by-month on a spreadsheet. Total them up by month. Now, project your sales and income month-by-month. At some point your income should exceed your costs. This is your "break-even point." Don't forget to calculate how much money you will have to take out of the business to live on. (See the sample cash flow projection later in this chapter. This example is for six months. You should do one for at least a year.)

There are two main categories of cost you must track. The first one is how much are you spending to attract consignors. At first you will have to estimate this. After a few months, you will want to measure this cost as shown by actual data. Once you know this cost, you will be able to analyze it and control it.

The second category is your selling costs. This includes your eBay and PayPal fees, Internet service, rent if you have a storefront, and so on. Once again, you cannot control your costs if you don't know what they are. Put another way: "You can't control something you can't measure." That is a quote from Meg Whitman, CEO of eBay, at a recent conference of investment analysts. Total all the expenses until you hit your break-even point and add 20 percent to it (for a safety margin). This is the amount of investment you will need to start our business.

What Is Your Growth Plan?

How will I grow my business beyond the first year? How large a business do I wish to build? Will I need more investment in the future? Where will it come from?

A business plan is nothing more than a map to follow, but as anyone who has ever followed a map over unfamiliar terrain can tell you, there are detours along the way that no map can predict. A map, or a business plan, is a snapshot in time. Landslides can change the terrain, and economic conditions can change your business plan.

Nevertheless, a map will keep you headed in the general direction with a destination in sight; a business plan will likewise keep you headed in the same direction with an outcome in sight. A landslide is just a temporary obstacle. Changing market factors or economic conditions may cause a slight change of direction or strategy, but the outcome should remain the same.

If you are starting small and plan to bootstrap your business, your plan may not need to answer all of these questions right away, but you should give some thought to all of these issues if you plan to grow your business beyond a part-time endeavor.

Your Financial Plan

The following table shows an example of a *simple* cash flow spreadsheet. The numbers are *invented* for purposes of example. Note that I have shown only the commission income, not the eBay selling prices. You will need to estimate and calculate eBay fees and PayPal fees from the number, starting price, and final value of the items sold. Notice that I have shipping supplies as a cost element. You should also estimate shipping charges that you collect from buyers on the income side.

Item	Jan	Feb	Mar	April	May	June
Income						
Commission income	2,000	2,500	3,000	3,500	4,000	5,000
Fee income	50	60	70	80	90	1,000
Subtotal	2,050	2,560	3,070	3,580	4,090	6,000
Expenses						
eBay fees	350	400	450	500	550	600
PayPal fees	250	300	350	400	450	550
ISP & web fees	35	35	35	35	35	35
Telephone	45	45	45	45	45	45
Rent	600	300	300	300	300	300
Utilities	30	30	30	30	30	30
Advertising	100	100	100	100	100	100
Shipping supplies	40	50	60	70	80	100
Office supplies	100	10	10	10	10	10
Miscellaneous	500	100	100	100	100	100
Salary	1,000	1,000	1,000	1,000	1,000	1,000
Subtotal	3,050	2,370	2,480	2,590	2,700	2,870
Net income	2,000	2,500	3,000	3,500	4,000	5,000
Net expenses	3,050	2,370	2,480	2,590	2,700	2,870
Net cash flow	−1,050	130	520	910	1,300	2,130

In this example, you have just over $1,000 in negative cash flow the first month. By the second and third months, your cash flow is positive, but not by very much. As you can see, each month looks a little better as your business grows, and by the sixth month you are earning a reasonable income. Don't be discouraged by this example; it is only that, an example to show you how to construct a cash-flow statement. You could get lucky and find a small business that wants to sell a $20,000 digital telephone switch your first month in business; your results would then be quite different. The idea here is to plan and know what the reality is if you don't find that big sale right away.

Once your business is up and running, it is a good idea to compare your actual numbers with your plan to see how you are doing. If necessary, you can adjust your plan monthly as you get a better feeling for the "real world" numbers.

Chapter 18

Invest in Your Business

If you are already selling on eBay and making money, you will not need very much money to start your consignment business. You will have to invest in advertising to find consignment clients, and you may need to buy greater quantities of shipping supplies, but other than a few small purchases, your investment will be minimal. Starting at this level, you should be able to bootstrap your business by reinvesting your profits back into your business. This is how most successful eBay consignment sellers started.

If, on the other hand, you plan to grow your business quickly, then you may need more resources, such as a commercial business location, photo studio equipment, or money for an employee.

If you prepared a business plan, you will have some idea of a budget and how much cash flow you can generate. The other factor to consider is your own need for income. We all need to eat, so you can't reinvest all your profits back into the business. Unless a spouse or parent supports you, you will need to take something out for yourself. This "personal salary" should be included in your cash flow and business plan.

What Sort of Investments Should You Make?

This really depends on how large and how fast you want to grow your business. Anything you can do to improve efficiency or reduce time and/or costs is usually a good investment. This might include hiring an employee to perform low-value tasks such as shipping, filing, and keeping records.

You may want to invest in a better camera or lighting, studio props, backgrounds, and equipment. Perhaps a faster computer, an extra computer, or DSL service could save time and increase efficiency. Another area for investment is advertising. Once you have learned to run an efficient business and have the ability to handle more auctions, you may want to increase your advertising investment to grow your consignment client base.

At the risk of repeating myself, please go slowly. Make small incremental investments and make sure they pay off before committing a large amount of money. Research, experiment, and test everything you do that requires an outlay of any substantial amount of money.

Raising Money for Your Business

If you wish to build a large eBay consignment business grossing over $250,000 a year, this chapter is for you. Building a business this size could take a sizable amount of capital investment.

Although it is possible to write a business and financial plan to raise money before you start a business, this could be somewhat difficult in the current investment environment. Instead, I recommend you start your business and run it profitably at a small level for a few months, to prove you have the ability to create a profitable business model and execute it. This will give you credibility with potential investors and make the job of raising funds much easier.

Most bankers and professional investors are far more willing to invest in an ongoing business than a startup. Once you prove the concept, it is just a matter of demonstrating the scalability of your business. (If I had X dollars, I could grow my business X percent.)

Types of Capital

Three basic types of investment capital are available:

- Retained earnings

- Debt

- Investment (venture capital)

Retained Earnings

All capital has a cost. The first one, *retained earnings,* is the profit from your business that you reinvest in your enterprise. You should do this whenever possible because this is the cheapest capital you will ever find. Also, the fact that you are reinvesting your own profits back into the company makes your business look more attractive to investors. Just be sure to keep track of this amount so that you know what it is.

Debt Capital

Debt capital is nothing more than borrowed money. The advantage of borrowing money is you do not have to give up any ownership in your company. The downside is that banks and commercial lenders usually require either collateral, or that you personally guarantee the business loans.

Debt is a good solution when you require only a small amount of money and, if you had to pay the money back personally, you could do it without losing your home or going into bankruptcy. For example, if you needed to borrow between $10,000 and $20,000 and for some reason your business failed, that is a small enough amount of money that a bank will work out a payment plan with you. If, on the other hand, you wanted to borrow $50,000 or more, most banks would immediately foreclose on the loan the moment you defaulted.

A good rule to follow is never borrow "risk capital." Risk capital is money that you are going to put at risk in an uncertain venture. If you have been running your consignment business successfully for several months and you just need money to expand, that is called "working capital," which is fairly easy to borrow. If you are starting a venture and need risk capital, I would advise finding an investor who will share the risk.

Besides a local bank, a good source of working capital for eBay sellers is GE Capital. GE lends money to eBay sellers according to a business plan. You can link to GE from the eBay Seller Central page, and they exhibit every year at eBay's annual convention, eBay Live.

Investment Capital

Investment capital is money that someone invests in your business in exchange for a share of the ownership or profits. These investors are usually professional investors, called venture capitalists. They put up the money in exchange for a percentage of the stock. In a startup business, they will sometimes demand 51 percent as a way of protecting their investment if it starts to go bad, but they usually construct a formula where you can recover ownership once their profits are secure.

As long as you are running the business according to plan and making a profit, they will pretty much leave you alone. But if you fall below plan and their investment looks to be at risk, they can step in and fire you and hire someone else to run the company. You would still own your part of the company, but you would no longer be in control.

This is not as bad as it sounds. Many startups are founded by entrepreneurs with a great idea, or technical and marketing expertise. But once they get the business up and running, they discover they don't have the ability to manage a complex enterprise. If this happens, the professional investors will usually suggest you step down as president and hire someone who is an experienced manager. They would want you to stay on and do the things you do well. You still own your stock, and if the business succeeds you could stand to become very wealthy.

Where to Find Capital

If you are seeking debt capital, the best source is usually a small local bank or community bank. Large banks, such as Bank of America or Citibank, seldom lend money to small entrepreneurs. Your own bank is the best place to start because they know you. If you now use one of the large money-center banks, you might want to change to a local community bank where you can develop a relationship.

Start by approaching the commercial loan officer of the bank. Bring your business plan and both personal and business financial statements. (If you are using QuickBooks, you can easily create a profit and loss statement and a cash flow statement.) Your business plan should show how you would use the funds you wish to borrow and how this investment will increase your sales and profits and give you the ability to pay back the money.

As long as your business is profitable and shows consistent cash flow, your bank will probably lend you the money. If you are not profitable, you shouldn't be borrowing the money.

Another source of capital once you have been in business at least one year is the Small Business Administration. The SBA will guarantee a bank loan for most businesses if you can show a track record. Unfortunately, they do not fund new startup businesses.

How to Find Venture Capitalists

Finding venture investors is a bit harder than borrowing money. If you need to raise over $250,000, then you will want to approach a professional venture capital firm. Visit your local library's reference section, where you can find a directory of professional venture capital investors. Start by writing them a short letter outlining your business, how much capital you are seeking, and what you plan to do with the capital. Do not send your business plan with the letter; instead, ask them to contact you if they are interested and then mail the plan.

Once you get the appointment, be prepared to make a short presentation that describes your business, your personal background and experience, and how you will use the money you are seeking.

If you are looking for a small amount of capital (such as $20,000 to $50,000), you should look for local investors. These people don't advertise, but they are out there. Sometimes they are local successful business owners with money to invest. They might also be retired business executives living in your community.

You find these people by networking. Ask your lawyer and your banker if they know any such people. Check with your local Chamber of Commerce or county development agency. Basically just start spreading the word around that you have a profitable business and are looking for investment capital to expand.

An online source for finding venture capital investors is vFinance Investments, Inc. (www.vfinance.com), a rapidly growing financial services company that provides personalized investment banking and brokerage services to more than 10,000 corporate and private clients worldwide. This site is a leading destination on the Internet for companies seeking capital, as well as institutional and high–net

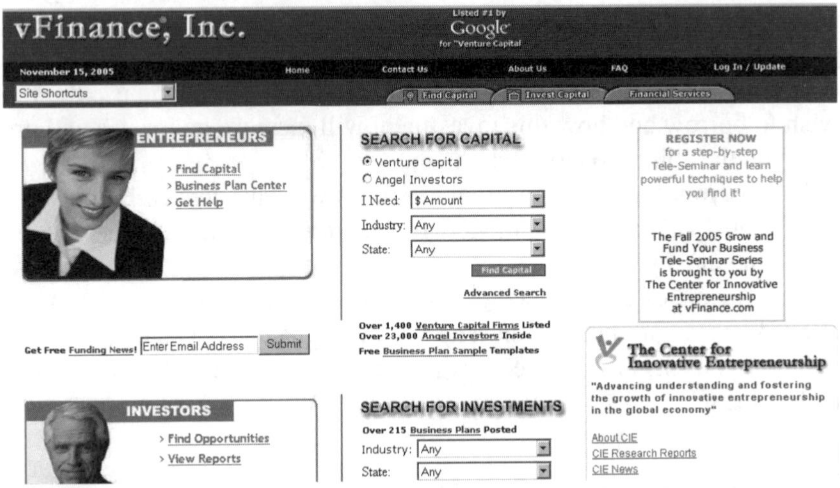

FIGURE 18-1   The vFinance.com web site with the fund-raising search box

worth investors seeking dynamic high-growth companies. It has a really neat feature, which is a funding search box (see Figure 18-1). You enter the amount of capital you are seeking, the industry, and your location and hit the Go button. A page will come up that asks for your e-mail address. You enter this and the results are e-mailed directly to you.

Each year, the site hosts more than one million investors and CEOs from over 50 countries. This huge audience creates a ready market for companies and individuals looking for investment capital.

Chapter 19

eBay Consignment Franchises

The first eBay drop-off stores opened in 2002. By early 2003 a couple of companies offered eBay drop-off store franchises. Today there are several.

The oldest and currently the largest franchise operation is QuikDrop at www .quikdrop.com. QuikDrop (see Figure 19-1) currently franchises over 100 locations around the United States.

Franchising Basics

Franchise fees from the various companies start at around $10,000 and go as high as $25,000 for QuikDrop. In addition to the franchise fee, the franchise companies have very strict rules about storefront design, signage, computer and photo equipment, and store location and layout. All this can be very costly. QuikDrop estimates that each franchisee will spend $15–25,000 on these items in addition to the franchise fee. In addition to the franchise fee, some franchisors charge an ongoing royalty or a percentage of sales.

This investment would get you professional management systems, training, signage, access to national advertising, branding, marketing services, and an accounting and management system. Franchising has several advantages:

- The logo, store design, product line, marketing materials, software, etc., are already done and tested. Franchise fees can sometimes be less than the cost to reinvent the wheel.

- Operational systems and software reduce your cost to run the store.

- Branding and proven advertising programs reduce the cost of customer acquisition.

- Most franchise companies have proven advertising materials, including preproduced newspaper, radio, and TV ads.

- Professional business advice and training can help you grow faster and become profitable sooner.

- When it comes time to sell your business in the future, a branded franchised business usually sells for much more money. Would you rather sell a sandwich shop or a SUBWAY sandwich shop? Franchises are easier to sell because they typically have an established price point that other locations have sold for and corporate backing for training and operational support.

FIGURE 19-1   QuikDrop Franchise page

In general a franchise can be a good idea for someone without business experience. If the franchise is well run and provides national and regional advertising, as well as ongoing support and training, then it can often be a good investment. There are plenty of good books in your local library about the ins, the outs, and the pitfalls of buying a franchise. It would probably pay you to do some research before taking a leap.

Here is a list of some of the companies currently offering eBay franchises:

- **QuikDrop**   www.quikdrop.com
- **AuctionDrop**   www.auctiondrop.com
- **iSold It**   www.i-soldit.com
- **The Online Outpost**   www.theonlineoutpost.com
- **Snappy Auctions**   www.snappyauctions.com
- **Sunshine Pack & Ship**   www.sunshinepackandship.com

QuikDrop is considered the most sophisticated of the franchise operations. The last one, Sunshine Pack & Ship, is an interesting concept that combines an eBay drop-off store with a pack and ship business. This is already being done by United Parcel Service with their UPS stores, which act as drop-off locations for customers wanting to sell merchandise on eBay. The PakMail franchise recently exhibited at eBay Live with a similar concept.

Franchise Checklist

Going into a franchise is something you should do very carefully. Once you explore the various franchise opportunities, be sure to get a copy of the contract before you put down any money or sign anything. Once you have a copy of the franchise contract, sit down with your attorney and review it. A franchise can cost anywhere from $10,000 to $40,000, so spending a few hundred or even a thousand dollars on an attorney is a good form of insurance. Some franchises may ask you to sign a confidentiality agreement before giving you a copy of the contract. That is usually okay, but even then you may want to show the agreement to your attorney. Once you have the contract, here is a basic checklist you should go through to help make a decision:

- Has your attorney studied the contract, and do you both approve it without reservations?

- How many years has the franchise firm been in business?

- Does your state have laws controlling the sale of franchises, and has the franchisor complied with that law to your satisfaction?

- Will the franchise give you an exclusive territory, or can the franchisor sell a second or third franchise in your territory?

- Can you terminate the franchise contract, and what will it cost you to do so?

- Does the franchisor have a reputation for honesty and integrity among its franchisees?

- Has the franchisor supplied any CPA-audited figures indicating net profits and operating costs of existing franchises that you can check with existing franchise operators?

- What can the franchisor do for you that you cannot do for yourself?

- Will the franchisor provide you with

  - Management and employee training?

  - Advertising and a PR program?

  - Help in obtaining credit?

  - A merchandising program?

  - Assistance in finding a suitable location?

- Is the franchisor adequately financed for the long term?

- Does the franchisor have experienced management?

- How much equity capital will you need to purchase the franchise and operate it until you achieve positive cash flow?

- Has the franchisor investigated you carefully to assure you can successfully run the business?

If you can get satisfactory answers to these questions, then you are most likely looking at a reasonable franchise opportunity. However, if you're in doubt about any of these issues, be sure to do the research and obtain the answers before you sign the contract.

Buying a franchise can give you a measure of security and, in most cases, improve your chances for success. Business surveys show that fewer than 20 percent of all new franchised businesses fail. This is in comparison to a 60–80 percent failure rate for all new businesses.

I believe it is inevitable that the eBay consignment business will grow into a large industry. It is a natural franchise opportunity. I suspect, however, that someone will come up with a formula enabling one to franchise this type of business for something less than $15,000, perhaps closer to $5,000. Perhaps one of my aspiring readers will be the first.

A Franchise Alternative

David Hardin is an eBay Platinum Power Seller who has sold on eBay under the name of Shoetime since 2001. In 2005 David started a company called eSAVz at www.esavz.com. eSAVz is not a franchise but sort of a "franchise-like" opportunity. They supply many of the same services a franchise company does, including branding under the eSAVz name, but without the upfront franchise fee.

Instead, they charge a low monthly fee to cover the costs of their training, support, and access to their software and systems.

Their services include:

- Reporting software

- A relationship with eBay

- Training materials

- Market expansion

- Territory protection

- eBay-certified training

- Team communication

- Dedicated support

- National advertising

- Provides leads

- Public relations

- Discount supplies

- Contact referrals

eSAVs is not really a franchise and does not give you the kind of support a franchise is known for, but if you already have some experience running a small business, it might be worth investigating.

Chapter 20

eBay Stores and Web Sites

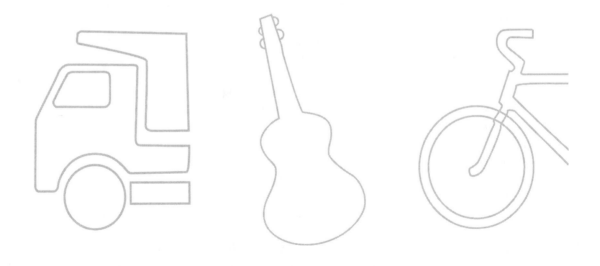

As a consignment seller, you will often be offered merchandise that, although it will sell, may not sell very quickly—or in the auction format. You may often get merchandise in large quantities of the same item. Selling the items in wholesale lots will turn your cash quickly but may not bring top dollar.

For example, a retailer is closing out a line of toy figures. He or she has 200 of the same item to sell. Instead of putting up 20 lots of ten or a Dutch auction for 200 items, you might try listing them in an eBay store on an e-commerce-enabled web site at a fixed price.

eBay Stores

eBay Stores is basically a fixed-price listing on eBay that runs for 30 to 90 days with a fixed *Buy It Now* price. You can list one item, or a quantity of items, similar to a Dutch auction.

There is a basic monthly fee of $9.95 to operate an eBay store. Just click eBay Stores from the eBay site map to go to a page where you can sign up for an eBay store. Launching at item into an eBay store works just the same as launching an auction. Most of the auction management services also support eBay Stores.

Customers can find your store in several different ways. eBay has created a Search eBay Stores link on the eBay home page that will appear as a standard search option. eBay also has a store directory and optional featured listings right on the main store page.

The other way customers find your store is from your auction title page. An eBay Stores link (with a red price tag) appears next to the seller's User ID and in a link under the seller's ID that says Visit my eBay Store (see Figure 20-1). When a bidder clicks this link, they are taken to a list of your auctions in the eBay store. If a seller clicks View Seller's Other Auctions, they will see a list of your active auctions and a list of your eBay store auctions.

Although the eBay store listings look just like an auction, bidders do not "bid" on items in your eBay store. The only way to buy is with the fixed Buy It Now price.

If you have multiple quantities of the same item for sale, or similar items for sale, you can drive traffic to your eBay store by mentioning it in your auction description. You might place a line such as this:

"If you do not want to wait until the end of this auction to receive your NFL Coffee Mug, you can buy it now from my *eBay store*." (The words *eBay store* would be a hyperlink direct to your store listings.)

Description (revised)

The Auction Seller's Resource
Visit my eBay Store: ⊞ The Auction Seller's Resource
Books

FIGURE 20-1   Screenshot of User ID with store logo

If you have similar items in your eBay store, you might say this:

"I have dozens of other sports collectibles for immediate sale in my eBay store. Please *click here* to view them." (The words *click here* would also be a hyperlink.)

The advantages of the eBay store are many. You can list items up to 90 days. The listing fees are much lower than for auctions. All of your ongoing auctions and your e-mails to customers can have a link to your eBay store. You can also submit your store URL to directories and search engines.

If you use an auction management service such as Vendio or Mpire, the service also provides a storefront where customers are directed after linking back to you for acknowledgment or payment. These listing are very low in cost, usually about five cents a listing. This is another good place to park slow-moving merchandise or large quantities of identical items.

eBay ProStores

In late 2005 eBay introduced the concept of eBay ProStores. Similar to Yahoo Shops or a stand-alone merchant web site with built-in e-commerce tools, ProStores are hosted on the eBay platform. The ProStores concept is the brain child of Chris Tsakalakis, the highly regarded manager of eBay Stores, and his team. Here is what Chris said about ProStores when they were introduced at eBay Live: "ProStores is an option for any eBay seller who is thinking about adding an additional sales channel to their selling strategy. ProStores offers full integration with both eBay and PayPal, and eBay sellers can use ProStores to create and manage their listings on eBay and in their ProStore online store. eBay buyers can go through a seller's ProStores shopping cart and secure checkout process to pay for their eBay purchases from that seller."

There are four tiers of ProStores, with monthly subscription fees ranging from $6.95 to $249.95.

ProStores Express

ProStores Express is a low-cost solution for individuals who wish to sell a limited number of different products online and provide secure online checkout for customers via PayPal. It provides two pages displaying up to ten products, which can be created using the setup and design wizards in as little as 30 minutes.

ProStores Business

ProStores Business is a customizable e-commerce solution for small businesses just starting out online. It includes unlimited pages and product presentations, domain registration and hosting, 50 unique e-mail boxes, 5GB of storage space, data transfer, 24/7 tech support, and Quickbooks integration.

ProStores Advanced

Designed for small- to medium-sized businesses that want to grow their sales and streamline operations with built-in merchandising, promotion, inventory management, and payment features, ProStores Advanced can support scheduled billing and products that have multiple attributes, such as size, color, or finish.

ProStores Enterprise

For medium to large businesses that want to integrate online sales with existing back-end systems, ProStores Enterprise enables drop shipments, affiliate marketing programs, and team coordination. You can also create customer groups and wholesale programs that reveal special pricing throughout the site.

ProStores does not currently support any type of consignment tracking; however, most of the auction management software companies and auction management services are working with eBay to integrate ProStores into their systems. Once this is complete, you should be able to integrate ProStores with services such as Mpire and software such as Liberty4 and MarketBlast.

Web Sites

You should consider having a web site. The obvious advantage of selling from a web site is that you don't pay any fees to eBay (or a service such as Vendio or Meridian) for sales made directly from your web site.

A quick and easy way to create your own web site is through CityMax (www.citymax.com). You simply select a template and color scheme; CityMax provides

FIGURE 20-2   CityMax web hosting

you with pages for which all you need to do is fill in the text and upload photos. You can design and launch a web site in less than one hour. CityMax is integrated with PayPal and eBay, so you can even put inventory on your CityMax-hosted web site and upload it to eBay from there (see Figure 20-2).

You can use PayPal's Web Accept service for a single product purchase or their free shopping cart to accept payments for multiple purchases at no monthly charge. You may eventually want your own custom-designed web site, but this is a great way to start. I would avoid the consumer web site services that offer free pages for families and hobbies, etc. They are not set up for e-commerce.

You don't need a professionally designed web site to begin with. All you need to start is a good, basic site with a shopping cart and the ability to accept credit cards. PayPal fills this need very well, although you may want to open a merchant credit card account to be able to accept credit card payments from consignors.

After setting up a web site with your products, you can use eBay as a free advertising tool for the new web page! I used to receive hundreds of hits each day just by featuring a link to my web site in my auction description. eBay, however, has changed its rules about linking from your auction page directly to a storefront or web site that offers items for sale.

You can still link from eBay to your web site, but you must use a little creativity. Every eBay user can create an About Me page. Now you can place a link with an invitation to visit your web site on your About Me page.

If you have a page with additional product photos, or product information, you can also place a link from the photo page to your web site. Another choice is to create a web page about your company and your products, but with no products actually selling on that page. Invite your readers to "click here" to learn more about your company and your products. On that page, you can now create another link to a page that actually sells the products.

Another advantage of having a web site is that you can use it to promote your consignment business. A lot of people will search the web for eBay sellers by location. If someone in your geographic area is looking to sell something on eBay, a web search should turn up your web site.

Chapter 21

Reduce and Control Your eBay Fees

eBay has several types of fees. To reduce and control your eBay fees, it is essential to understand how eBay calculates its fees. The various fees are categorized as *insertion fees*, the cost to post an item for sale, *final value fees*, the cost to sell an item, and *fees for additional listing options*.

eBay Listing Fees

eBay charges a basic fee to list an item on their site for sale. The listing fees are calculated on a sliding scale that increases with the listing price (starting value of the first bid). It is important that you fully understand the listing fee schedule as these fees can really add up if you are not careful. You also want to know the various levels where the fee increases. For example, if you were to start an item at $10, your listing fee would be 60 cents. By dropping your opening bid to $9.99—just one penny less—your listing fee is reduced to 35 cents.

Starting Price	Listing Fee
$0.01–0.99	$0.25
$1–9.99	$0.35
$10–24.99	$0.60
$25–49.99	$1.20
$50–199.00	$2.40
$200–499.99	$3.60
$500 and up	$4.80

Reserve Price Auction Fees

eBay charges a special fee in addition to the listing fee to place a reserve on an item you want to sell on eBay. However, this fee is refunded if the reserve is met and the item sells. No matter how high your reserve price is, the maximum reserve fee tops out at $100.

Reserve Price	Fee
$0.01–49.99	$1
$50–$199.99	$2
$100 and up	1% of reserve price (max. $100)

Final Value (Selling Fees)

You are charged a final value fee only if something sells. If an item fails to sell, you may relist it in the same category without paying an additional listing fee, but you will still pay the final value fee if the item sells.

Selling Price	Fee
$0–25	5.25% of the closing value
$25–1,000	5.25% of the first $25 + 2.75% of the balance over $25
Over $1,000	5.25% of the initial $25 + 2.75% of the value $25–1,000 + 1.50% of the remaining closing value

Optional Feature Fees

eBay offers several optional listing features designed to make your listing stand out and to place your listings where they will be seen by more potential bidders. Fees for these features are discussed in greater detail in the following table:

Feature	Fee
Home Page Featured – Single Item	$39.95
Home Page Featured – Dutch Auction	$79.95
Featured Plus (featured in category)	$19.95
Highlight	$5
Item Subtitle	$0.50
Bold	$1
Gallery	$0.35
Gallery Featured	$19.95
List in Two Categories	Double the listing and optional feature fees (except the home page feature, which is charged only once)
10-day Auction Duration	$0.40
Buy It Now	$0.05 for up to $9.99, $0.10 for $10–24.99, $0.20 for $25–49.99, and $0.25 for over $50
Listing Designer	$0.10

Controlling Your eBay Fees

Now that you understand eBay's various fees, let's take a look at how you can reduce them. Here are some tips:

Price your item's minimum bid at just below the breaking point in the fee structure. For example, if you hope to get $35 for an item, you would want to start the bid at $24.99 instead of $25. The same goes for setting a reserve price.

If you are selling at a Dutch auction, look at the final value fees to determine where to set your price. Setting your price just below the breaking point in the fee structure can save you considerable amounts of money over the long term.

The other major cost is listing fees for items that don't sell. eBay does allow one free relisting when at item fails to sell or to reach its reserve. You should always take advantage of this. I like to keep an eye on my sell-through rate (STR). The STR is the ratio of auctions launched to those closed successfully. If you launched 100 auctions and 60 of them closed with a winner or a Buy It Now, then your STR is 60 percent. This means that you are paying eBay listing fees on the 40 percent of the auctions that didn't end successfully. This is one reason you should be very selective when you accept merchandise from a consignor to sell. If an item fails to sell, you are still out the fee, unless you are charging the fees to the consignor up front. Even if you are getting the fees up front from the consignor, I would still be selective because it is a waste of your time and other resources to list items that don't sell.

Which Optional Fees Are a Good Value?

I always use the gallery fee ($0.35) because it is so cheap and there are people who will not buy unless they see a photo. Seeing your gallery images tells bidders there is a photo in the auction, and this can increase your hits. I rarely use the Gallery Featured option, however, unless I am selling something very expensive, and where the photo would definitely attract people to view the auction.

If I am selling an item with at least a $12 profit margin (or a $3 margin for Dutch auctions), I always use the Bold option. I use the Highlight option only if I am selling an item with at least a $25 profit margin ($10 for Dutch). The Bold option is a great value. eBay research shows that bold items achieve a 26 percent higher average final value.

List in Two Categories is a great value if you have the profit margin to support it. This feature will usually result in increased hits.

The Category Featured and Home Page features are really used only when you have a very expensive item or you are selling a large quantity of items with a large margin in a Dutch auction.

Fees are where eBay makes their money. They are also a major portion of your selling costs. Be sure to keep track of your fees so that you know how much you are spending.

If you visit the web site for this book, www.skipmcgrath.com/consignment, you will find a link in the products section to a company called ProfitCalc. This is an interactive program where you enter your item's costs and it calculates the fees for you using different starting prices, options, and so on. This excellent program will help you evaluate, reduce, and control your fees over time.

Chapter 22

Become an Auction Master

When eBay first started, there was only one type of auction. All auctions ran for a specific time and ended at a specific time. The highest bidder at the last possible moment was the winner. eBay now offers several auction formats:

- Standard auction

- Reserve price auction

- Dutch auction

- Fixed price BIN

- Private auction

It is important for the consignment seller to understand each type, as they all have a place in the larger eBay merchandising strategy.

Standard Auction

A typical auction-style listing works this way:

- The seller offers one or more items and sets a starting price.

- Buyers visit the listing and bid on the item during the online auction's duration.

- When the auction-style listing ends, the high bidder or bidders buy the item from the seller for the high bid.

eBay uses a system of proxy bidding. Let's say a seller started an item at $9. eBay sets the minimum incremental bid at fifty cents ($0.50). Now suppose you are a bidder and you decide you would be willing to pay as high as $14.50 for the item being offered. You would enter a bid of $14.50 and hit the button that says Place Bid. eBay would add fifty cents to the starting bid of $9, so the price would now show $9.50. No one else knows the top value of your bid; others see only the current bid. Now, another bidder comes along and bids $10. The bid price will rise to $10.50 (her bid + a $0.50 incremental bid from you), and he or she will get an immediate message that they have been outbid. If no one else bid, you will win the item for $10.50. As long as no one bids more than your $14.50 maximum, you will still be in the running.

If someone bids more than your maximum, you will receive an automated e-mail from eBay that you have been outbid. You can let it go, or you can go back in and place a higher bid if you still want the item at a higher price.

Reserve Price Auction

Some auctions have a reserve price, a hidden minimum price, on their item. This is done to allow a seller to start an item at a low price that is sure to attract attention, yet protect them from selling it at a price that's too low.

- Buyers are not shown the reserve price, only whether or not the reserve has been met.

- The seller is not obligated to sell the item if the reserve price is not met.

- The winning bidder must meet or exceed the reserve price and have the highest bid.

When you're bidding in a *reserve price auction (RPA)*, bid as usual, entering the maximum amount you're willing to pay for the item. Watch the label next to the current price to see whether the reserve price has been met. Until you see that the reserve price has been met, there have been no successful bids in the auction. Once the reserve has been met, the item will sell to the highest bidder when the auction closes.

If the maximum bid is the first to meet or exceed the reserve price, the effective bid displayed will automatically be raised to the reserve price.

Dutch Auctions

If you are dealing with businesses, you will often have the opportunity to sell large quantities of identical or similar merchandise. For example, a retail clothing store may offer you the opportunity to close out a large inventory of shirts. You would sort the shirts by size. If you had ten small shirts, six mediums, and seven larges, you would set up three Dutch *auctions*, each with those quantities. This is much more efficient and cost-effective than running an individual auction for each shirt.

A Dutch auction is used when you have several identical items for sale. You set the minimum price you are willing to sell for and specify the quantity for sale. The person who bids the *lowest for the last available quantity sets the price for all winning bidders.*

Dutch auctions can be difficult. Most auctions go to the highest bidder by price, but with a Dutch auction the highest bidders are assured of getting a quantity of the merchandise available but at the price of the lowest successful bidder. For example, you get a consignment of 24 inexpensive silver earrings from a retailer. You don't want to launch 24 separate auctions, and you don't think there is enough of a margin selling the earrings as a lot. You decide to put up a Dutch auction for all of the earrings. You start the bidding at $5 a pair. Here is how the bidding goes. Remember in a Dutch auction, you can bid on more than one item and there are only 24 rings available:

Bidder	Quantity Bid On	Amount Bid
A	3	$9.50
B	5	$8.25
C	3	$7.95
D	10	$7.50
E	1	$6.90
F	4	$6.00
G	3	$5.00
Total bids	29	

At the end of the auction, the 24 highest bidders, by *quantity*, would win the item for what the 24th bidder (by quantity) paid. In this example bidders A through F would each get as many rings as they bid on at a cost of $6 because this was the lowest price paid by the lowest successful bidder (Bidder F). Only 24 items were available. Bidder F would only get 2 earring sets, because although she was the lowest "successful" bidder, there were bids on 22 sets that were higher than hers. If this isn't complicated enough, eBay rules state that bidder F would not have to accept and pay for the two sets of earrings, because she bid on four sets. She could take them, but she is not forced to.

You cannot use reserves in a Dutch auction. Essentially your starting price becomes your reserve, because no one can bid below that.

There are several strategies you can use with Dutch auctions. If you are selling a large quantity, such as 100 of the same item, you can price them very low to attract bidders, but if less than 100 items are bid on, every one would get them for the same low price. Another strategy is to limit the quantity. Use a starting bid that ensures you at least break even and limit the quantity so that bidders drive the price up. Supply and demand works on eBay the same way it does in the open market. If bidders see too large a supply of an item, they are reluctant to bid very high. Thus, if you had 100 of an identical item, you might realize more money by running four separate Dutch auctions of 25 each over a period of a couple of weeks.

Dutch auctions can be an excellent way to dispose of low-value items. Just be sure to add enough shipping and handling fees to cover your costs. The downside to selling low-value items even in quantity is the extra time and handling costs you will incur per item—but if the volume is high enough, then the sale will still be profitable. One way to encourage multiple-item purchases is to offer free or discounted shipping to anyone who buys more than one item.

Fixed Price Listings and BIN

A *fixed price listing* is not really an auction. It is just a way to list an item for sale at a fixed price. You can do this in an eBay Store of course, but eBay Stores do not get as much traffic as the auction listing format.

The way you list an item for a fixed price is to set your starting price where you want it to be and then list your Buy It Now (BIN) price at the same price point. When someone places a bid, it instantly becomes a sale because the bidder hit the BIN price. A great strategy for using a fixed price listing is to launch two identical items at the same time, one at a low starting price designed to attract bids and one at a fixed price that will appear near it when someone does a search. This way the fixed price listing acts to establish a value in a prospective bidder's mind. And if one bidder is afraid they might lose the item, they will often hit the BIN item to make sure they get one.

Private Auctions

When a seller creates a private listing, a buyer's User ID does not appear in the listing or in the listing's bid history. Only the seller is authorized to view the buyer User IDs associated with that listing. This type of auction is typically used for items of an adult or sexual nature (sold on a separate section of the eBay site) and sometimes for expensive art and antiques to help protect the identity of wealthy bidders. In the second case, sellers also sometimes require bidders to prequalify themselves by e-mailing the seller to assure them they have the wherewithal to purchase an expensive item. Anyone who bids that is not prequalified has their bid cancelled.

Listing and Pricing Strategies

How you price your products to get that first bid will have a great impact on your final selling price and how often you convert your auctions. There are several options, and just as many theories as to the best way to price an item on eBay.

One school of thought says to start all items at $1 with no reserve to create excitement and bidding activity. Others say that you should always start bidding at your cost, because this way you cannot sell at a loss. And still others claim it's best to go ahead and start your auction at the minimum price you are willing to accept. Finally there is the strategy of using a reserve price auction, where you start the bidding at a low price but use a hidden reserve to ensure you do not sell an item too cheaply.

We will examine all of these strategies, but I can tell you now, there is no one correct answer. The truth is, it depends on what you are selling, the demand for the product, and what others selling the same or similar products are doing.

As a consignment seller, you have an obligation to the consignor to try to get the best price for the consignor's merchandise. You also have an interest, because the higher the final value, the more commission you will make. So anything you can do to increase the final value benefits both you and your consignment client. If you just put everything up on eBay starting at $1 with no reserve, most of the items will sell if there is a market for them, but some valuable items may end up selling at a ridiculously low price. This is not a good way to build repeat business from your consignors. If this happens too many times, word could get around and it could hurt your business.

Consignors often have overblown expectations or unreasonable ideas of what their item is worth. It is your job to research values and give your consignors an estimate of what you think the item will bring on eBay. I always like to underestimate what an item will bring. This way, if it doesn't bring a high price, you don't look foolish to the seller, and if it does, he or she thinks you are an eBay genius.

Reserve Price Auctions

As described earlier in this chapter, a reserve price is a tool sellers can use to stimulate bidding on their auction-style item while reserving the right not to sell below a price they have in mind.

Many sellers have found that too high a starting price discourages interest in their item, while an attractively low starting price makes them vulnerable to selling at an unsatisfactorily low price. A reserve price helps with this.

A reserve price is the lowest price at which you are willing to sell your item. If a bidder does not meet that price, you're not obligated to sell your item. You set your reserve price, as well as a starting price, when you list your item.

The reserve price is not disclosed to bidders, but they will be told that your auction has a reserve price and whether or not the reserve has been met.

I know power sellers who never use a reserve, no matter how expensive an item is. Of course, these sellers tend to offer popular items that almost always sell—digital cameras, computers, and so on.

I can't find the data anymore, but about two years ago someone did a survey and found out that over 30 percent of eBay bidders will not bid on a reserve price auction. As anecdotal evidence, I have seen hundreds of posts on the eBay message boards citing the same fact. No one likes reserves. Many people think they are somehow unfair. Millions of eBay buyers just have a negative emotional reaction to an RPA.

The only exception to this seems to be on eBay Motors, where people realize that the risk of putting a $60,000 Porsche up for bid with no reserve is simply too great. You will also find that people who buy artworks, expensive jewelry, real estate, boats, jet planes, and so on also understand the need for a reserve price.

The other issue for the seller to consider is the fees. As shown here, eBay charges a special fee for reserve auctions, but this fee is refunded if the item sells:

Reserve Price	Fee
$0.01–$49.99	$1
$50–$199.99	$2
$200 and up	1% of reserve price (up to $100)

When I was at eBay Live in Orlando, eBay threw a party for Titanium power sellers. I met one seller who does over $80,000 a month on eBay selling primarily consumer electronics. He sells items ranging from digital cameras for under $200 up to and including $5,000 Plasma TVs. He told me he used to use a reserve on anything worth over $500. After two years he did an audit and found that eBay reserve fees (and the higher listing fees) were costing him over $3,000 per month. He tried selling without a reserve fee for two months. In a few cases, he actually ended up selling an item for less than his cost, but his final bids on the more expensive items tended to be about 8 percent higher and his hit counters were showing a 12 percent increase when he added the letters "NR" (no reserve) to his auction title. Best of all, he was saving far more on his eBay fees than he lost selling the occasional item at less than cost.

The $1 No Reserve Strategy

The successful online consignment company, AuctionDrop, has a policy that all auctions must start at $1 with no reserve, unless you pay them a special fee of $19.95 to launch your auction. What is the reasoning behind this strategy?

Starting an item at $1 (or 99 cents) or any low number attracts attention and draws eyeballs to your auction. You need to get bidders' eyeballs to move from your auction title (headline) into your auction description to make a sale. The more bidders click your auction, the more bids you will get—and the higher your bids will be. Bidders look for action. The number of bids you have received is posted on your item description title page and in the search results. eBay has proved that active items (those with a high number of bids) get more bids. Therefore, getting the bidding started is crucial to realizing a high bid price.

Starting the bidding for an expensive item at a very low price is an excellent strategy, as long as you are selling a desirable item that is in demand. You would not want to use this strategy if you are selling an arcane item or something for which there is a very narrow market. The risk of its not being seen by enough people may be too great for something that is unusual or not an item that is popularly searched for.

List at Cost

Another popular listing strategy is called *list at cost*. Because you are a consignment seller, there is no "cost" per se, so you would list it at the minimum amount the consignor is expecting as long as the target price is reasonable. If it is too high, you just won't get any bids. Whenever I list at cost, I always place a Buy It Now price somewhat above what I hope to get for an item. The BIN price can help establish a value in a bidder's mind, and occasionally you will get an impulse buyer or a buyer who is looking for exactly what you are offering and doesn't want to chance losing out to another bidder.

Fixed Price Listing

As described earlier in this chapter, eBay also allows fixed price listings. This is where you set the selling price and the first person to bid wins the item. Fixed price listings are typically good for items with a well-established value or if you are selling closeout or overstock merchandise, for example, for a retailer.

Strategic Decisions

Now what does all this mean for the consignment seller? The strategy you use may depend on who your consignor is. If an important consignor (an estate attorney who gives you lots of business) gives you an expensive item that sells for a pittance because you did not use an RPA, then you might lose an important source of ongoing supply.

In the end it all comes down to your experience and judgment. To use, or not to use, an RPA can sometimes be a difficult call. Once you have completed hundreds of eBay auctions, you will gain the experience to make this call without losing sleep over it. Remember, the best way to establish a value in advance of selling an item is to research the completed auctions on eBay to see what identical or similar items have actually sold for.

Best Time to Launch Auctions

The best time to launch and end your auctions is a very controversial subject among eBay sellers. One of the keys to earning maximum bids for your auctions is to end your auctions during times of maximum activity on eBay. The more people online searching and browsing, the better your auctions will do. There are people on eBay at all times of the day. I rarely schedule auctions to end during the nighttime hours, but I always have items up for sale with a Buy It Now price and fixed price items in my eBay store. I am always amazed when I log on to my computer in the morning and find a sale that took place at 3 o'clock in the morning. Nevertheless, sometimes there are more people on eBay than others.

People, especially impulse buyers, tend to look for auctions ending within a few hours—or sometimes, even minutes—so they can bid live or snipe. Table 22-1 shows a calendar to help you pick the best days to end an auction.

Day	Value	Description
Monday	Fair	A lot of people surf eBay at work. After the weekend they need their "eBay fix." Lunchtime is the best time to end an auction on a Monday (or any weekday).
Tuesday	Worst	Tuesday statistically receives the lowest number of bids on eBay.
Wednesday	Poor	Wednesday is almost as bad as Tuesday, but not quite.
Thursday	Fair	Thursday is a good time to end an auction in the spring and summer because people who go away for the weekend will bid on Thursday before they leave.
Friday	Fair	Friday before 7:00 P.M. can be a good day for students and young people.
Saturday	Good	Weekend days are usually better than weekdays.
Sunday	Excellent	Sunday evening is the highest time of bidding activity on eBay. If your auction ends about 7:00 P.M. Pacific time, you will maximize your bidding activity.

TABLE 22-1   Auction Calendar

Remember, eBay times are Pacific coast time, three hours earlier than the East Coast.

As you can see, the auction duration you select is directly related to what day your auction will end. I personally prefer to launch my three-day and ten-day auctions on Thursday night so that they end on Sunday. An exception to this is holiday weekends when Monday is a holiday. A lot of people will be gone on Sunday, returning on Monday night. Also, be careful to avoid ending auctions when the time competes with other events such as election night, the Superbowl, or the World Series.

There are several exceptions to the ending rules. If you are selling professional items to businesses, then you want the auction to end during the business day (avoid Friday afternoon). If you are selling products that appeal to the elderly, they also tend to be at home all day and you might do better ending the auction on a weekday during the afternoon. Young people tend to buy in the early afternoon after school.

Another factor to consider when deciding how long and on what day to end your auction is where your auction will appear.

When a bidder performs a search or goes to the listing page for a category, they are given several choices on how to view the auctions. These are: *Time: Newly Listed, Time: Ending Soonest, Price: Highest First*, and *Price: Lowest First*. A buyer can select which listings to show in a drop-down box.

POWER TIP   *Different products do better or worse on certain days. Both Andale (www.andale.com) and Terapeak (www.terapeak.com) offer a feature that calculates the best day and time to launch an auction given the performance of similar items over the past 30 days. If you would like to see an interactive auction calendar, go to AuctionBytes at www.auctionbytes.com and click the Auction Calendar link to the right of the main page. AuctionBytes also does an annual survey of eBay sellers on best ending times. Just type* **ending times** *in the search box on the main AuctionBytes page to read the latest survey results.*

Another great resource is the eBay message boards. If you join the power seller message board, for example, you will see many posts on this subject and you can create posts to get the opinion of other sellers as well.

Other Considerations

There are other issues regarding ending times you need to be aware of. If you are launching dozens of auctions per week and all of them end on Sunday evening,

Pro Tip   Keep Your Customers Happy

Stan Shelley has run a traditional auction gallery in Hendersonville, NC for over ten years, specializing in fine arts, antiques, jewelry, rugs, and fine furnishings. In early 2005, his gallery started an eBay division, auctioning their customers' goods on eBay for the first time. Five months after starting, they are auctioning off over $10,000 a month on eBay, they're closing over 68 percent of their auctions, and their feedback is over 1,300 comments at 100 percent positive. They are so busy that when this book went to print they currently had over 1,500 lots awaiting listing on eBay.

Stan's advice: "When I got started, my research showed that almost all negative feedback for eBay drop off stores was due to poor post-auction management, so we have really emphasized good service in this area."

—Shelley's Auction Gallery, eBay username Shelleys_Yes

then you will have an impossible job answering e-mails, getting payments, and shipping on Monday and Tuesday. If you are a high-volume seller, you will need to spread your workload out over the week.

As a consignment seller, you will find that consignors expect you to get their items up as soon as possible. Therefore, you will be launching items almost every day of the week. Just be sure your auctions end at an appropriate time of day, no matter which day you select. I often find some great bargains on eBay by looking for auctions that end after midnight when very few bidders are on the site.

The other big issue is supply and demand. Yes, there are more people looking at eBay on Sunday evening, and for that reason most eBay sellers list their auctions to end during that time. If you do a search for a given product on a mid-week day such as Wednesday and perform the same search on Sunday, you will find many more items ending on Sunday.

Scheduling Your Auctions

As a consignment seller, you will find yourself working at all times of the day. Typically you will be meeting with prospective consignors in the daytime and launching auctions to end in the evening when most bidders are online. Therefore, you will need to schedule your auctions to launch at a specific time. All of the auction management companies and software systems we described in Chapter 12 have this functionality. If you are launching directly on eBay, eBay charges 10 cents for each auction you schedule. If you were to launch ten auctions a day for a month, this feature would cost you $30 a month. That is less than the cost of Mpire's auction management system and less than the cost of using MarketBlast software for a month. Both of these products allow you to schedule your auctions for free.

International Auctions

Certain types of merchandise sell very well on the various eBay overseas sites. For example, used medical equipment and printing equipment sell very well in India. Famous-name designer merchandise sells very well in Japan, Hong Kong, and other Far Eastern countries, and certain categories of collectibles sell very well in Europe. If you are selling something with international appeal, you may want to look at starting and ending times compatible with the time zone of the country or part of the world you are targeting. This can be problematic if your merchandise also has U.S. appeal, so you may want to try ending your auction at a time that may not be optimal for either market, but when people are awake in both time zones. For example, an auction ending at 6 P.M. Pacific Standard Time will end at 10 A.M. in Japan.

Chapter 23

Research: The Key to Profits

One thing about consignment selling you will have to adjust to is that you may sell all types of goods, including many that you are not familiar with or even know if they will sell on eBay. In the morning, you might launch an auction for collectible carnival glass, and in the afternoon, an old gentleman walks in with vintage tractor parts. A little later, someone calls you wanting to sell his or her mineral rock collection. Fortunately, there are plenty of research tools at your disposal. Taking the time to perform the research necessary to understand the market and the value of merchandise you are offered will pay dividends in several ways. First of all, you will not waste time and money accepting merchandise that probably won't sell, or listing merchandise at a price that is too high for the market. Research can also provide you with facts and information you can place into the item description that will help you sell an item. Finally, it will provide you with a realistic estimate of the value you can hope to attain.

Ask the Seller

Your first step is to ask the seller to tell you everything they know about the merchandise. What is it? Where did it come from? How old is it? Do they have any idea of its value? (Be careful about believing what they say—many people have an overblown concept of what their treasures are worth.)

Searching Online

There are several search options available to you. eBay has a very powerful search engine. Andale (www.andale.com) has a new research service that searches completed auctions and tells you not only what something sold for, but also the best time and day to list the item, the best category to sell it in, and other helpful information. This service has a one-month free trial. After that, it is $3.95 month. A newcomer on the block is Terapeak at www.terapeak.com. This is a very powerful search engine that can give you prices realized on eBay for almost any item sold during the past 90 days.

If you are researching antiques and collectibles, be sure to visit www.tias.com. TIAS is an online mall of over 15,000 antique dealers. You can search by product and see what other dealers are saying, and what they are charging for specific collectibles.

Curioscape is a power-search engine that can also help you locate dealers in specific antiques and collectibles including coins and stamps. They are at www.curioscape.com.

Kovels Online (www.kovels.com) has more than 12 price guides online. You can now search and browse through appraiser-approved actual prices for more than 450,000 antiques and collectibles! Establish values for your Federzeichnung vase or look at seven-year market trends for mass-produced items, like an Adam Depression glass plate or a Roseville Magnolia vase. Kovels also has an excellent yellow pages resource of antique and collectible sites and great articles on spotting fakes. If you are going to sell antiques and collectibles on consignment, this site is an absolute *must* resource.

There are over 3,000 price guides printed on coins, stamps, art, and various antiques and collectibles. Many of them can be found at your local library. If you live in a small town, your library probably has the capability to borrow from a major city or state library, so all of these should be available to you.

For general searches, my favorite Internet search engine is Google (www.google .com). Google is a very fast and powerful search engine. You can search worldwide or restrict searches to domestic hits, you can choose various languages, you can search for photos and images, and you will find tools built in for advance searching techniques.

The eBay Search Engine

You will probably use eBay's search engine more than any other. If you are trying to estimate an item's worth, I suggest you search closed auctions only. What something sold for is a more reliable guide than current bids on ongoing auctions.

Go to the Search tab at the top of any eBay page. When the search page opens, click the tab that says Advanced Search. This will take you to a new page where you can use the techniques described in the sections that follow.

Searching More Effectively

There are literally thousands and thousands of items listed at auction on eBay, and finding exactly what you are looking for can be a real chore. eBay's search engine is quite powerful, but to obtain the best results, should be used properly. Here are some simple, but powerful tips and tricks for searching eBay auctions and finding the item(s) you want. Remember: eBay's search capability searches only the auction listings; it does not search through the ad descriptions unless you check the Search Description box. Checking this box will bring up many more auctions—sometimes too many. Try searching titles only at first. Use a description search only if you can't find the item on the first try.

Locating Auctions That Include a Specific Word

If you want to find all auctions (ads) that include the word "watch" in them, you'd simply enter the word **watch** in the search field at the top of most of the listing screens and press ENTER. All listings containing the word "watch" would be displayed.

Narrowing Your Search

Since using a single word for your search can return too many results, you may want to narrow the search to get down to a more specific need. For example, suppose you are looking specifically for Timex watches as opposed to just any watches. Then use the AND keyword function in your search. In the search field, you'd enter **Timex and watch**. This would return a list of all results with both the words "Timex" and "watch" in them and exclude all that do not contain both words.

Narrowing Your Search Even More

If you are looking for auctions that include certain phrases, or words that go together in a specific order, try this: If you are searching for teddy bears, you can use quotation marks. The command you would use is **"teddy bear"**. This will return a listing of all ads with the phrase "teddy bear" in them. The word "bear" must immediately follow the word "teddy" for the listing to show.

Finding Listings with One of Multiple Words

If you are searching for auctions that have one of multiple words, you can use the OR keyword function in your search. For example, if you wanted to find all auctions that had the word "teapot" or "teacup" in their title listing, then you would enter **(teapot,teacup)** in the search field. This would return all listings that had either the word "teapot" or the word "teacup" in their listing. Make sure you type the parentheses, and don't put a space between the comma and either word. You can also include other keyword functions. For example **(teapot,teacup) +flowblue** will return all items that have "flowblue" and either "teapot" or "teacup" in the title. Note that there is a space between the closing parenthesis and the plus sign, but not between the plus sign and "flowblue."

Locating Listings with One Word, But Not Another

If you are looking for watches but are not interested in Timex watches, then you would use the AND NOT keyword function. In the search field, you would enter **watch -Timex**. This would return all results whose listings included the word "watch" but excluded the word "Timex." Note there is no space between the minus sign and the excluded word.

Third-Party Online Services

Two online research services are very popular with eBay sellers:

- **Andale**   www.andale.com
- **Terapeak**   www.terapeak.com

Andale

Andale is an auction management company that also offers additional services to users who choose not to sign up for their auction management service.

The two services are called What's Hot, a listing of the hottest items on eBay by category, and Price Finder, a research tool that allows you to enter an item into the Andale search engine and will come back with a listing of the highest, lowest, and average prices the item has sold for on eBay during the past 30 days. Andale charges $3.95 a month for this service.

Terapeak

Terapeak's service is similar to Andale's, except it provides much more detail as well as competitive data. Terapeak allows you to examine an item in four ways:

- As a general report
- By top sellers
- By listings
- By key ratios

At $9.95 per month, Terapeak is a bit more expensive, but you do get a lot more data.

Offline Research Tools

You will also need some traditional reference tools, such as antique price guides, books about collectibles, and other traditional reference materials. These books can be very expensive. You can save a lot of money by purchasing them at flea markets and secondhand bookstores. The prices will not be up-to-date, but that is okay, because you can always research the prices on eBay. The books are very useful in helping you identify what you have, get the correct names and spellings of unfamiliar items, and correctly date items. One of the best general books is *Kovel's Guide to Selling Your Antiques and Collectibles* (Crown, 1990). This book sells for over $25 new, but you can get a one- or two-year-old one in any secondhand bookstore for about $5.

Part IV

Building Your Sales on eBay

Chapter 24

Create Killer Listings

The success or failure of your consignment business will largely depend on how good you are at selling the merchandise you receive on eBay. Learning to take good photos and selecting the proper categories are key to your success. The most important factor, however, is your ability to attract potential bidders to your auction. Writing compelling auction titles and an item description that "sells" is thought by many to be the single most important factor that will increase your bids and sales.

Writing Dynamic Headlines

Successful sellers on eBay know how to write an item description (sales pitch) that instantly perks a bidder's interest and then draws them in after a few sentences. The first part of your eBay sales pitch is the auction title (a headline), which should be focused and catchy and should immediately draw a potential bidder to your auction. If you get them to click your auction, then you have won half the battle.

The auction title (headline) is the single most important item in your auction listing. An attention-grabbing or arresting headline has the power to get the "clicks." Remember, unless the potential buyer clicks your headline, your item description will never get read.

A headline is nothing more than a collection of words designed to stop your potential buyer's eyes from scanning and cause them to linger for a moment on your ad. To achieve this, your headline must

- Be compelling

- Be concise

- Imply a benefit or deliver intrigue

- Specifically mention a product the bidder is looking for

I recommend boldface titles at all times. Use hot-button trigger-words such as the following:

STUNNING	**SEXY**
BEAUTIFUL	**UNIQUE**
CHARMING	**SUPER-DEAL**
HOT-ITEM	**SECRET**
NEW	**PRECIOUS**
NEAT	**BEST-VALUE**
RARE	

I also suggest using all caps to make your title stand out above the rest.

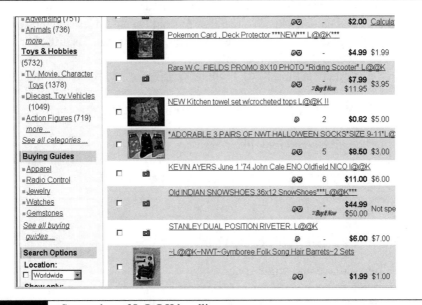

Screenshot of L@@K headlines

Do not use fancy symbols or other "cheesy" ways (such as L@@K) to attract attention to your auction. Such tactics immediately turn off potential customers and make your business look unprofessional or even ridiculous. See Figure 24-1 for examples of silly headlines with these symbols.

If you are new to writing headlines, try this next exercise with a few auctions to help you get the hang of writing great headlines.

Before writing your headline, sit down away from your computer with a pad of paper and brainstorm. First, write down the top three benefits. Next, write a one-sentence description of your primary customer. (This is the person you are trying to attract.) Do you have competitive advantages? If so, list them (price, quality, performance, etc.). Try writing at least five completely different headlines. Notice I said: "completely different." Don't write variations on the same headline. Now go back over your headlines. Which ones appeal to you the most? Take those two or three and start refining them. Eventually, you will emerge with at least two good headlines. You can either pick one or test them both.

You won't have to do this exercise for all your auctions. Once you do this several times, you will develop an intuitive sense of what makes a good headline. If you have a product that is not selling, then go back and do this exercise again. You may have fallen into a "headline rut," and doing the exercise will help sharpen your focus.

eBay limits your headline format, so you have to use some tricks in headlines to get attention. I call these tricks "White Space & Bold Face." Advertising professionals know that nothing attracts attention like white space. "Bold Face" is just what it says. It's designed to be bold and "in-your-face."

Let us say you are selling Keds Tennis shoes. You could run a headline like this:

NEW KEDS TENNIS SHOES - 50% OFF RETAIL

Or your headline could look like this:

*** KEDS ~ TENNIS SHOES ~ NEW ~ 50% OFF ***

Here is another example:

Unique Elvis Presley Collectible Watch

Or using boldface and white space:

~~ UNIQUE ~ ELVIS ~ COLLECTIBLE ~ WRIST WATCH ~~

You can see the difference. There is more white space to attract the eye, and the boldface helps to catch it. You can make your headlines bold by selecting the eBay Bold Title option. The cost is $1 and is one of the best values in the eBay fee structure. White space is also important in your item descriptions. We will cover this in the next section.

Keyword-Rich Headlines

Probably the most important tactic is to use the appropriate keywords in your headlines. Over 65 percent of eBay bidders find items by searching. They search by item name, brand name, size, color, style, and so on. A typical search might be for "Ralph Lauren polo shirt size medium," so it would be important to use the brand name and size in your headline. If you are selling anything with a model number, be sure to include that also. If someone performs a search for "Nikon D70 Camera" and your camera is listed as a "Nikon Single Lens Reflex Digital Camera," it will not come up in a search, or if it does, it will be at the very bottom.

Most important, make sure your keywords are spelled correctly. If you are selling a Staffordshire plate and spell it "Staffordshir," your auction will not come up when bidders use the eBay search feature to find items. eBay now includes a spell checker in its HTML item listing form, but it doesn't catch headlines. I like to type my headlines in a word processing document so that I can spell-check everything before I paste it into eBay or my auction management program.

I used to collect football cards when my kids were younger. I once saw a very expensive Terry Bradshaw rookie card at an auction (with no reserve and no bids) selling for a low starting bid. I had come across the card while browsing the football card category. When I looked closer, the seller (a new seller with low feedback) had spelled Terry's last name as "Bradeshaw." I could have stolen the card at a ridiculously low price. But, trying to be a nice guy, I sent the seller an e-mail pointing out his error and suggested he cancel his auction before he lost a lot of money. Instead of getting the card at an obscenely low price, I got an obscene e-mail in return telling me to place a bid or mind my own business. (He obviously never bought one of my books.)

Checklist for Headlines

Writing compelling headlines is one of the best ways to increase your auction hits and therefore bids. Here are a few things you should consider as you write a headline:

- Does it arouse curiosity?

- Does it use "action" words (now, buy, save, etc.)?

- Does it mention or imply a benefit (save money, lose weight, look beautiful, etc.)?

- Does it use a hot-button trigger word (unique, stunning, rare, etc.)?

- Does it mention a highly specific product (e.g., 1976 Ferrari Dino Matchbox Car)?

- Is it solution-oriented (does it solve a problem)?

- Does it state or imply a competitive advantage?

- Is it compelling?

- Is it provocative?

Your headline must meet the first test and should meet at least two of the other tests. If it doesn't, start over!

Selecting the Right Category

Proper category selection is one of the keys to maximizing your auction profits. Besides searching, the next most popular method eBay users to find products is by browsing the various categories on eBay to find what they are looking for.

Before listing your item in any category, follow these simple steps: First, browse through the eBay categories and write down the ones you feel are relevant to your product. You should be able to find at least two or three possible choices. Next, note the number of auctions currently online in each of those categories (it will appear next to the category name).

An average category has about 6,000 listings, so if there are more than those you may conclude that the category is *active.* If there are less than 2,000, you may consider it *inactive.* I consider categories with over 6,000 auctions to be *popular* and those with over 10,000 to be *most popular.* Some categories have over 50,000 auctions going at any one time. Using this ranking system, rate the categories that you have chosen for your product.

I recommend listing in the most active categories only because they get the most traffic. If you put your product in an inactive section of eBay, you may get few or no bids, even if you feature it. *Avoid categories with less than 1,000 auctions online unless your product is highly specialized to that category!*

Make sure the category you select is somewhat related to the item you are selling. With the growth of eBay, the eBay Safe Harbor Team is now vigorously responding to complaints, and they routinely scan headlines for items out of category. They will often move your item or cancel your listing altogether. You can usually get away with listing items in somewhat related categories, but if you repeatedly abuse the category selection, eBay will move or cancel your auction and threaten to suspend you as a seller.

List in Two Categories

eBay has a new feature called "List in Two Categories." If your item fits in more than one category, you can list in two categories for double the listing fee. Any special fees such as *bold, highlight*, or *category featured* are also doubled. If you select the Home Page Featured fee, this fee is not doubled.

Listing in two categories does work. eBay reports 22 percent more bids for items listed in two categories. Andale's research service show 11 percent higher final values when sellers list in two categories.

Most bidders (over 65 percent) find items by searching. Typically, a bidder first goes to the category of the item they are looking for, and then they do a search for the item within that category. Therefore, it is important to find the correct "general" category for your item. The advantage of listing in two categories is that you get the "searchers" in the main category and the "browsers" in the second category. However, because of the higher listing and special feature fees (Bold, Highlight, etc.), you have to make sure the items you are selling have enough margin to pay these fees.

POWER TIP *When a consignor brings me an item that I think will sell for over $200, I offer them my Auction Promotion Option. This includes Bold ($1), Subtitle ($0.50), and List in Two Categories (double the listing fees). I charge $10 for this option and explain that it is an investment in getting a higher price for their product on eBay. I find about one-third of consignors take this option when I explain it.*

eBay Specifics

A relatively new feature is *eBay Specifics*, a listing tool where you enter the specific details about a given item. Not every category has eBay Specifics available. This tool is used for commonly searched items such as clothing. Once you select something in a category such as Women's Jeans, a box will pop up when you are entering the item on eBay. It will ask you for the style, color, size, and condition (used/new).

If you perform a search for Women's Jeans on eBay, the search results page will come up with a box on the left where a buyer can select the size, color, and so on from a drop-down box. Now the buyer hits the search button again, and it will bring up only items with the specifics she is searching for. This is a great tool for buyers, but most sellers hate it because it means buyers have to click fewer auctions to find what they are looking for. Sellers believe this fact kills impulse bids that they used to get before this feature was introduced by eBay. So far, the evidence is only anecdotal, and eBay has never researched this particular issue.

eBay plans to expand *eBay Specifics* to as many categories as possible.

eBay is always changing and refining the categories. It is not uncommon to have a category change while an auction is ongoing. This can really be a problem if you tend to sell a lot of items in the same category and have your categories stored in your bulk uploader. You will launch an auction only to have it bounced by eBay because the category no longer exists. The only way to stay on top of this is to check the eBay announcement board frequently. eBay usually gives anywhere from three to five days notice before changing a category.

Chapter 25

Write Winning Auction Descriptions

The first goal of your auction description is credibility. Your auction description must inspire trust. If your item descriptions are too far-fetched, use wild or silly adjectives, or make outrageous claims, you will sow doubt in your readers' minds. Although the item description is basically a sales letter, it is important to find a balance between compelling copy and outrageous copy.

One way to inspire trust is to accurately describe your product, including any shortcomings. If a product has a flaw, mention it. If the product is new but the box is damaged, you should tell the prospective buyer about this. If a product is perfect except for a small scratch, tell the bidders and show them a photo of the scratch.

A big part of your sales pitch is the image or photograph you attach to your auction. Nevertheless, you should also provide an enthusiastic and energizing description that makes your potential buyer feel that he/she needs your product. The item description is your sales pitch.

Before you start writing the sales pitch, decide who you are writing to. If you are selling baby clothes to stay-at-home moms, your item description will be quite different than if you are selling a money-making product to entrepreneurs. Look at your niche market and try to picture your customers. What are their likes and dislikes? What are they looking for? How old are they, and what jobs do they generally hold? What are their hobbies and interests? What makes them tick? Do they have plenty of disposable income? Are they seeking quality—or a bargain?

A successful sales pitch appeals to the base instincts and self-interest of the customer. When writing a sales pitch, attention to psychology counts more than attention to writing style.

Appeal to the type of customer who will be viewing your auction. I recommend using some basic HTML coding to enhance the description, but I do *not* suggest giant letters and distracting objects such as blinking, animations, or more "cheesy" items in that regard (unless you are selling a really cheesy product).

Features Describe; Benefits Sell

A potential buyer wants to know what your product will do for him or her, and does not need a lot of useless distraction. Again, your item description must appeal to the profile of the buyer and promote a feeling of professionalism and trust in you as the seller.

The very first item in your item description should be a clear statement of precisely what you are selling. Here is an example: You are bidding on a slightly used Nikon F3 SLR camera with a Nikon 55mm F2.8 lens and a Tokina 35-80 F3.5 zoom lens, all in excellent condition with the following accessories:

- Leather carrying case

- Heavy-duty tripod

- Skylight filter for both lenses

- Remote cable release

- Cleaning kit

There should be no confusion about what the bidder is about to bid on. It is critical that this information be contained in the first paragraph of the auction. If bidders have to scroll through the whole auction to find out exactly what is included, you risk their clicking away and looking for another seller.

After the basic product description, you can put a few words to entice the reader to keep reading, but then you want to stop and fully describe the product. I like to list any specifications, sizes and weights, or features that help the reader understand what they are buying fairly early in the product description, usually before the third or fourth paragraph. This is where it is important to get good information from your consignor. Some products may be obvious, while others are not. The more information you can elicit from the consignor or research on the Web, the better, and more complete your auction description will be.

Next I like to talk about the product benefits. Words mean something. Use the power of words to convey the benefits the reader will enjoy when they buy your product. List the *benefits* of your product on a sheet of paper. Arrange the benefits in priority order (for your target customer) and place them beside your computer.

Now start writing about the first benefit and move on to the next. Keep writing about the benefits until you run out of benefits to write about.

Be sure to write about *benefits*—not only the product *features*. For example: "This lovely teddy bear has yellow eyes." That is a feature. "This *unique* teddy bear *will bring delight* to your child. *Her eyes will light up* and *she will squeal with excitement* when you tell her, 'I got it just for you, honey.'" The benefits are in italics.

"This *unique* bagel slicer *is rugged*. It *will not break*. Its foam-lined handle is *soft* and *will not slip*, even if wet, and *is sized* for a woman's hands." In this product description, "Foam-lined" is a feature. "Will not break," "will not slip," and "sized for a woman's hands" are benefits. You use features like "foam-lined" to describe benefits such as "will not slip."

A complete guide to writing winning advertising copy would be as long as this book. Rather than reinvent the wheel, we call your attention to the many good books in your local library on the subject of advertising copy writing and direct-response copy writing (which is what your auction description is). Here are some keys, however, that anyone can follow to write a good auction description:

- Organize your thoughts and information before you start writing.

- The goal of direct-response copy is to get people to act. Therefore, use action words and active verbs. (Understanding and using active rather than passive verbs is the most critical aspect of advertising copy writing.)

- Use short, simple words.

- The shorter the sentence, the better.

- If you write a sentence longer than ten words, follow it with a sentence of less than five words. Short sentences command attention. They should describe your most important benefits.

- Use short paragraphs and/or bulleted lists.

- Use pronouns: you, me, I, she, him, etc. "You" is the most powerful pronoun. Many of your sentences should begin or end with the word "you."

Remember: It is more important to express than to impress!

A word about the English language: If you cannot write well, get some help! You do not have to write like Hemingway, but you should write clearly and concisely.

Bidders notice misspelled words and tortured grammatical contortions. There are many people who can help. Ask your friends and family first. Visit your local community college. There are always English students looking to make a few dollars. Your copy doesn't need to be brilliant; it just needs to be readable.

Prepare your copy in a word processing program such as Microsoft Word that has a grammar and spelling checker. Then paste your copy into the auction template.

We already mentioned this in a previous section, but it bears repeating here: Over 65 percent of bidders use the Search feature to find items they are looking for. Make sure the keywords in your auction title are spelled correctly. If not, the search option will not bring up your auction, and you will get fewer bids. If you don't believe me, perform a search on the word "jewelry." Now perform a search using the spelling "jewlery." It is amazing how many people misspell this word. This is also a great way to find items on eBay that you can win at a low price because not many other bidders are finding the item.

Pro Tip   **Grading Items for Sale**

If you are selling antiques, collectibles, coins, used books, and so on, you should know the common terminology used by collectors to describe these items and how they are graded.

- **Mint**   This is the top grade for any item. It means the item is in new, original condition, such as a book that has never been read, or a toy that has never been played with. If the item is packaged or boxed, it is usually listed as Mint-in-box (MIB), Mint-in-package (MIP), or the like.

- **Near mint**   Just what it sounds like. Perhaps it is a book that was carefully read only once, or a coin that was never used but has been handled.

- **Very fine**   Now the description gets a bit subjective. *Very fine* primarily says the item is in premium condition and still highly worthy as a collectible. You often see descriptions such as "Mint item in very fine package," indicating that the item is mint but perhaps the package has been opened or had some wear and tear.

- **Very good**   Now we are dropping out of the top collectible categories. A *very good* item might be one that is in great condition for its age or use. An antique piece of furniture in very good condition may be a great piece. A depression-era glass pitcher in very good condition, however, may have minor chips or cracks, or a toy may have scratches in the paint.

- **Good, fair,** and **poor**   These words speak for themselves. You would only want a *good, fair,* or *poor* item if it is exceedingly rare or used to fill a hole in your collection. These items appreciate in value very slowly, if at all.

State the facts. After your descriptive selling copy, be sure to include important or relevant information, including:

- Model or part numbers
- Specifications

- Brand names/manufacturers' names

- Country of origin

- Packaging

- Size, weight, color, shape, etc.

- Age and specific condition

- History and provenance (if known—don't make it up)

Finally, tell the truth about any negatives, damage, or flaws. You can put a positive spin on any shortcomings, but be sure to mention them honestly. This will increase your credibility and trustworthiness, and the number of bids you receive.

Power Words and Emotional Appeal

You can't sell a diamond without the sparkle. Use the same hot-button power words that were listed in the preceding chapter. Words like "new," sexy," "secret," "bargain," "hot," and so on catch people's attention and work on their psychological hot buttons.

Other words that can create urgency and appeal work in descriptions but might not be appropriate for headlines. These would be words such as "fast," "easy," "simple," "free," "important," and so on. Just be sure not to exaggerate. Remember the first criterion is credibility. Even on eBay many people are still cautious and suspicious.

You should also make an emotional appeal to your prospective bidder. I like to do this by creating a little romance. You do this by using words to create pictures in people's minds. My wife sells expensive famous-designer goods on eBay from companies such as Burberry, Prada, Fendi, Channel, and Versace. After she describes what the item is, she tries to create a little romance in the customer's mind. Last year she had some great Prada handbags. Here is one of the lines from her item description:

"Imagine pulling up in front of New York's Tavern on the Green in your Jaguar and getting out holding your beautiful new Prada handbag. Everyone will know you are not worried where the next rent check is coming from."

Although my wife had bought the bags at an overstock price of 60 percent off retail, she ended up getting almost full retail on the entire collection by the time they had all sold. I am willing to bet very few of her buyers owned a Jag or even knew where Tavern on the Green was, but that is not the point. When they read her vignette, they created one in their own mind that matched their own circumstances, and it probably didn't involve driving up to Taco Bell in their Ford Taurus full of kids.

Here is another example. One of the products we sell on eBay is an expensive fire pit. After I describe all the features, I talk about the benefits, such as the spark arrestor, so that you don't get sparks jumping out when a burning log pops and the cutouts in the side that drive the smoke up and out so that you are not bothered by the smoke when you are sitting around it. Then I go on to describe what it is like to sit around the fire on a chilly evening snuggled up to my wife with a glass of Merlot in my hand.

Remember, the idea of creating a word picture is to help someone visualize using the product. Your picture doesn't have to match theirs—they will modify your word picture in their own mind to make it match their setting. If someone lives in an apartment and doesn't have a deck, they will imagine themselves taking the fire pit camping and using it in the woods or beside their RV—whatever their personal situation is.

You can't romance everything. If you are selling ink cartridges, there isn't a lot you can do. But almost everything else has some way to talk about it so that people can see themselves using it.

There are other motivators that appeal to people besides romance. These would include scoring a great bargain, a product's safety, or its environmental friendliness. Saving money is always a major motivator: people will often spend money in the hope of saving money. That is why the membership box stores like Costco and Sam's Club are so successful. People will spend $15 to buy a giant jar of mayonnaise because they reason that ten smaller jars of mayonnaise would cost $25 if bought individually.

All the romancing you can do with a product is based on the product's real or perceived benefits. Thus, understanding the benefits your product confers on the user is essential to creating any sense of romance or appealing to any emotions the customer might have. If I can't think of enough benefits, I will often do a web search for the product to see if I can find any advertising that others have done. You don't want to plagiarize the consumer advertising, but you can get ideas from it.

White Space and Boldface

One of the most frustrating things I see on eBay every day is auction descriptions in small type that just go on and on in one long paragraph.

I have actually seen auction descriptions that look like this:

You are bidding on a rare signed first edition of Dali by Dali. It had been translated from French by Eleanor Morse. What makes this book so rare is that Dali not only signed it but drew an erotic picture. The book was acquired at an estate sale on Eastern Long Island. The seller had an older friend who was Dali's secretary. The secretary had Dali personally sign the book back in 1972. While doing so, he did as only Dali could and added a personal touch. This book is guaranteed to be authentic. It comes with the dust jacket which is in poor condition. If one is interested in replacing the DJ, a Google search can provide a number of dealers selling a first edition of this book at a cost of less than $50. There is discoloration along the edges of the cover as shown in the photos. I have included a photo of the dust jacket and cover in three segments to show the binding, front and back cover. All three pictures in the photo are a little different size do to my inability to stay in the same spot after rearranging the book. A some pages have small bends at the corners, roughly a 1/4". Slight discoloration is also shown. When the book is held by the covers one can observe the glue adhering the book and cover has dried. A photo of this is included.

The type was very small, and the sentences all ran together with no paragraph breaks. This fellow was trying to sell a $1,500 signed art book with an original Dali drawing inside.

People tend to scan a computer page looking for something that grabs their attention. Instead of one long paragraph, use a series of short paragraphs, typically just three or four sentences each. Make lists, use bullets, and highlight important information with boldface type. Just don't overdo it. If every other word is in bold or all caps, you lose the impact.

By using short paragraphs and lists, you create *white space* in your auction. This makes it easier for people to scan the page to find the information they want.

If something such as a camera has a long list of specifications or features, break them up into several short lists by category and give each category a heading. For example, you might have the physical specifications (size, weight, etc.) followed by a list of the electronic specifications and then another list of the features.

The other major bid killer is reverse-out type, as shown in the following illustration. A reverse-out is when you feature white or light-colored type on a dark background. It may look artistically cool, but it is very difficult to read.

You are bidding on a Vintage Burberry Scarf in the original Burberry Plaid. The scarf is in excellent condition with minimal wear and no tears or holes.

If you are selling anything to people over 40, this is very important. As people age, their eyes need more and more light and greater contrast to see well. An older person will have a very difficult time reading yellow type on a black background. Type size is another factor. If you are selling body jewelry to teens, they can probably see the normal small-sized type that eBay uses as standard in their auctions.

But if you are selling products that someone older might want to buy, remember that most people over 40 need bifocals to read. If you want to increase the type size in your auctions, just start your auction description with the HTML command <font size +1>. Inserting this command in your auction description will increase the font size in your entire auction description.

Increasing Sales with a Call to Action

Salesmen have an old saying: "If you want to make the sale, you have to ask for the order." I have been in sales and sales management, and I can tell you that statement is 1,000 percent accurate. I cannot tell you how many times I have seen a salesperson go through a perfect product presentation and then end it with "Well, what do you think?" Would you take the time to write a perfect auction description and then add a last sentence that said: "Well, what do you think?" Wouldn't you rather end with something like this? "Don't be knocked out by a sniper. Place your best bid now so you can enjoy a sizzling steak on your new barbeque this weekend."

I always end my auctions by asking for the bid. This is known as a *call to action* in the direct marketing industry. Think of all the direct marketing pieces you have received in the mail over the years. Don't all of them end with something such as this? "Don't let this once-in-a-lifetime opportunity pass you by. Call now!"

The same thing is true in your auctions. I have tested this extensively. Whenever I add a call to action, my auctions experience almost a 20 percent increase in the number of bids and my final values average about 12 percent higher.

If your auction description is very long, you can actually put several calls to action in your auction. As you are writing about the benefits, use phrases such as "Don't miss out on this fabulous eBay bargain, bid now." Then, always put a final call to action again at the end.

If you have additional items up at fixed-price auctions or in your eBay store, you can also use a call to action to drive them there. When you do this, make sure you use a clickable link right in the call to action (see the example that follows).

Here is a list of some of the call-to-action phrases I have used in my auctions. With a little imagination, you can probably come up with many, many more.

- Don't lose out to a sniper—Buy It Now.

- Don't lose out to a sniper, place your best bid now.

- This _____ could be sitting in your home this weekend. BID NOW.

- You will be heartbroken if you lose this fabulous eBay bargain to another bidder. Place your best bid now.

- Don't wait for the bidding to end, <u>click here</u> to visit my eBay store, where you can buy it now.

- You might be busy when the auction ends, so just place your best bid now to win this fabulous _____.

Whatever call to action you decide to use, remember you can't make a sale unless you ask for the order.

How to Kill Bids

Why would you want to know how to kill a potential bid? So you won't do it.

I am continually amazed by some of the statements I see in auctions that seem designed by sellers to turn away bidders. For the past three years, I have been keeping a file of the ones I come across. Here is a list of the best—or should I say worst—policy statements I have seen in eBay auctions. All of these were taken from actual auctions. The spelling and grammatical errors are theirs, not mine.

- "If you are not going to pay then don't bid me. I will chase you down and find you if you win this auction and don't pay me."

- "Don't bid unless your feedback is at least 25. I don't deal with eBay cherries. I will cancel your bid if you have less than 25 feedbacks."

- "Yes I am making money on the shipping. What did you expect me to do, ship it at my cost."

- "please bid good price on my cd because I am very poor and need money bad and right away. i only take money order or put cash in evelope and mail right away and i will be nice to you in feedback and god bless you too if you are a nice person."

- "I ship this item I will wait 7 days for you to post feedbacks if you dun do it I will hit you with negative."

- "After the auction you can post positive feedback for me. If you do I will return it and if you post negative I will give you one two."

- "I only ship on Thursday. If your payment arrives after Thursday noon then you will have to wait a week until I ship again. If you dont like this then dont bid."

- "I charge the correct shipping cost plus a $5 handling fee to cover my time for wrapping and standing in line at the post office. Do not bid if this is not okeydokey with you."

- "I only take money order, cashiers check or Western Union transfer. PayPal is a screw job. They want to charge me a 3% fee on every deal. If you send a personal check I will just throw it away so please don't bother."

- "i am selling this as is just the way it is i do the best to tell you condition and so i do not want your bid if you do not agree it is as is and that is happy for you. please pay me very quickly and leave good feedbacks and i will do same for you."

- "My shipping policy: I ship everything by priority mail on Monday and Friday. I charge the priority mail rate plus $2.00 to pay for box and packing material. I don't guarantee anything. If you want insurance the extra cost is $5.00. I know it doesn't cost that much to insure a package but I have to wait in line and fill out forms at the post office and keep the forms until a claim is made and that is a big pain but I will do it for $5.00."

- (From the same seller) "My Returns Policy: No returns for any reason except if I send you the wrong item and then you need to send me a photo of what you received so I can be sure before your return it."

Whenever I see one of these statements, I copy/paste it into a file I have been collecting for the past two years. I also take a moment to check the feedback. Invariably the sellers who post these ridiculous statements have a high negative feedback rating themselves.

Chapter 26

Build Your Credibility to Build Your Business

In the last chapter we introduced the issue of credibility when writing your auction item description. But, building credibility goes further than just what you say. If you are going to build a large, successful eBay or Internet business, you will have to create an overall professional image. People will judge you in many ways. It starts with the look and feel of your auctions, how and what kind of photos and images you use, your writing style (both in your auction and your end-of-auction e-mails), and finally how you package and ship your merchandise.

Keep Your Auctions Clean

The look and feel of your auction is the first impression a potential bidder/customer has of you. When you launch an auction, you should give some thought to how it will look when someone clicks it and it opens. As we mentioned in the preceding chapter, the writing should be large enough for anyone to read easily. Short paragraphs with an extra space between them will create the white space necessary for someone to scan and then easily read. Next come your images. eBay and the various auction management software programs and online systems give you the option of placing your photos at the top, left, right, or bottom of your auction. If you know how to use HTML, you can also place images right into your description and have the text wrap around them. This last option, however, is very time-consuming and probably not practical if you are a consignment seller who launches large numbers of auctions for different products.

I prefer to put my photos at the top of the auction or on the left or right side. This way, the person sees the photo sooner than if they have to scroll all the way to the bottom of your auction. Using left or right placement toward the top of your description is probably the best because your bidder can see the photos at the same time they are reading your description.

Your photos should be clear and easy to view with close-up shots where necessary to see any important details. If you are selling new products, there are often professional (stock) photos available on the Web that you can download. It is okay to use one of these, but you should also show a photo of the actual product in or out of the box so that a potential bidder knows exactly what they are bidding on. If you are selling a new (unused) product in the original box (NIB) or an item that is new with tags (NWT), then show a close-up of the price or other information on the box or the tag. If your product has a designer logo or other well-known mark, then be sure to show that also.

Both eBay and all of the auction management tools available support the use of predesigned auction templates. Dozens of designs are available. It is important to pick one that is appropriate for what you are selling. eBay's Listing designer creates templates with product specific designs. Just select the product category you are selling in from the drop-down box and Listing designer will provide a template that reflects that product category.

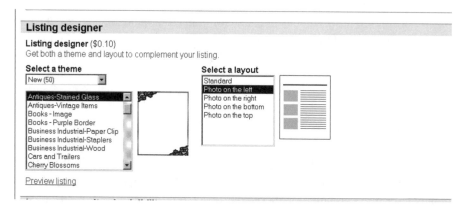

The various systems and software available on the market also allow you to create your own template. If you are selling one class or category of product, you will want to design a template that reflects the products you are selling. If you have an eBay store, eBay also allows you to design the look and feel of your store. Many sellers also sell on their web sites or through a Yahoo store as well as selling on eBay. If you do this, you should carry the same design theme through

Pro Tip

Business Builder Tips from the Cabana Girl, eBay Powerseller and Trading Assistant

- ■ Always include your phone number and e-mail in your auction and correspondence. It makes you "real," and the buyer instantly gains more trust in you.

- ■ Create a tag line. Mine is "The Friendliest Seller on eBay." You might choose "The Star Wars Vintage GURU" or "Your Favorite Ann Taylor Seller."

You can link to the Cabana Girl's auctions at www.thecabanagirl.com.

all of your sales channels. Now when a customer visits your different sales portals, they will see the same professional image. This will not only help brand your image, it will project the image of a professional, reliable business. This gives you credibility and tends to build trust.

Finally, avoid any gimmicks or images that detract from your image and your selling proposition. These include animated GIF images or banners, pop-ups, spinning dollar signs, dancing cartoon characters, and those irritating mouse-overs. People who are affected positively by these visual gimmicks are far outnumbered by those affected negatively.

Building Trust and Safety

The Internet has been plagued with fraud and fast-buck operators since its inception. Before the Internet, a lot of fraud occurred in direct-mail marketing, but the Internet has fast replaced that. With direct mail, a fast-buck operator had to invest quite a bit of money in printing and mailing pieces out to get a decent return. With the advent of the Internet and e-mail, anyone could reach millions of potential victims with virtually no costs involved. This simple fact, and the vast amounts of spam computer users receive every day, makes people naturally suspicious.

In focus groups, there are people who claim that they confine their business to only the most well-known e-commerce web sites such as Amazon.com because of the fear of being defrauded, being cheated, or just receiving less than they paid for. eBay has succeeded in creating a platform where millions of users feel safe making purchases, yet there are still a percentage of people who have an unsatisfactory experience on eBay. Out-and-out fraud is very minimal on eBay, as the organization does an excellent job of detecting and canceling the accounts of people who set out to cheat you out of money—although fraud does occur. One of my newsletter readers e-mailed me for help recently. He bid over $3,000 for a plasma TV on eBay from a seller who had a perfect feedback rating of over 100 comments. The seller asked him to send a certified check or money order, which he stupidly did. Once the check was mailed, the seller stopped answering e-mails, and of course, the TV never showed up.

A little investigation would have shown two things. Even though the seller had over 100 feedback comments, virtually all of them were from him buying, not selling. And when I clicked the auctions connected to the feedback posts, they were for very cheap items. When I pulled up the profile, the seller had only been registered on eBay for less than a month.

Basically, this seller set up an account, spent some money essentially buying feedback, and then launched dozens of auctions for expensive electronic items he did not possess and had no intention of buying for delivery. I spoke to the trust and safety people at eBay. They closed his account immediately and notified

Pro Tip   How eBay Can Help Local Stores and Small Businesses

The Front Room is one of the most unique small town antique shops you will ever find. A full-sized stuffed gorilla greets visitors who walk in, and every inch in the shop is chock full of memorabilia, collectibles, and everything from the weird to the normal. Pat Bruce has been selling on eBay for several years for his own account, but recently local people who know he sells on eBay started bringing him stuff to sell for them. Consignment selling now makes up a large part of his sales. Besides selling stuff for others, Pat teaches a lot of the local businesspeople how to get on eBay themselves.

Having a small business, an antique and collectible store, I find it hard to believe that most businesses have not ventured onto eBay with excess inventories, year-end stock, rare items, or just with what's on their shelves. My store is located in a semi-seasonal tourist area where business drops off 70 percent for about six months of the year. Without the income from eBay sales online, we would not be able to survive. In this town, many struggle to keep going over these months and instead of auctioning on eBay or opening an eBay store, their inventory gathers dust until the Christmas season, tourist season, or a large sale—too many times a "going out of business" sale.

There are thousands of stores and small businesses that could add $100-$1,000 a month (or much more) to their bottom lines with little time and effort, complementing their day-to-day sales and moving existing inventory that is just sitting there.

You don't have to own a collectible store to get into eBay. I have shown an electronics company, a book store, a kitchen supply store, a clothing store, and even a restaurant how to sell off unwanted inventory, fixtures, and outdated machinery.

Pat Bruce operates the eBay store, The Front Room in Anacortes. His eBay username is S.O.S.

the police. It turned out the credit card he used to register was false and his address was a Mailboxes Etc. box. They wouldn't tell me how many people he scammed, but they did admit it was several. Privately, another source at eBay told me this seller made thousands of dollars in the week or so that it took to uncover his scam and shut him down.

This type of story gets a lot of publicity. Even though literally millions of transactions each month go perfectly well on eBay as opposed to the tiny handful that are crooked, the perception exists that the fraud is worse than it really is.

Besides out-and-out fraud, the other thing that happens more often on eBay is running into a lazy or shoddy seller or sellers who either grossly or subtlety misrepresent their merchandise. This can take forms ranging from sellers who don't disclose slight shortcomings in the product up to those who sell out-and-out fakes and knock-offs.

eBay Trust and Safety Tools

eBay, and their online payment subsidiary PayPal, offer several tools to help buyers determine if they are working with an honest seller. When you register on eBay, you have to put up a credit card to verify your identity. The problem is that there are plenty of phony and/or stolen credit cards floating around. There are even Internet sites where you can buy credit cards. They are preloaded with a fixed amount of money like a store gift card, and look just like a normal Visa card. The problem is that you don't need to show ID to get them but they are good enough to get you registered on eBay.

Understanding the limits of credit cards, eBay came up with a system to ID Verify members. ID Verify establishes your proof of identity so that others may trust you as their trading partner. The process takes about ten minutes to complete and involves updating your information over a secure connection and answering a few questions. When you're successfully verified, you will receive an ID Verified icon in your feedback profile. eBay charges $5 for the service.

Here is how it works: When you click the ID Verify link in the eBay site map, a page come up where you enter your personal information. Then eBay pulls a credit check on you. They use the information in the credit check to send you an e-mail that asks you to verify certain items of information such as the account numbers on your mortgage or installment loan. Once you supply three correct pieces of information, eBay will place the ID Verified icon next to your username in all of your auctions.

The other service that marks you as a trustworthy seller is PayPal's Verified User tag. If you are not already verified, there will be a link on your PayPal account balances page to click to start the process. You fill out a form giving PayPal the name and account number of your primary bank account. PayPal then makes two small deposits to your bank account—usually a very small amount, under twenty cents. Once PayPal e-mails you that it has made the deposits, you call your bank and determine the date and the amount of the deposits and inform PayPal via an online form on its web site. If your information is accurate, PayPal will put the words PayPal Verified next to your name. Buyers will see this as they are about to pay you money.

PayPal offers eBay buyers who pay with PayPal a buyer protection program. But there is one catch. To use the buyer protection program, the seller must be PayPal Verified. Therefore, buyers who want this protection must look to see if you are PayPal Verified.

Third-Party Trust and Safety Tools

There are other trust and safety tools available to the eBay seller. The two most recognized are SquareTrade and buySAFE.

SquareTrade

You can access SquareTrade at www.squaretrade.com.

The SquareTrade program is somewhat similar to eBay's ID Verify, but they also insist you meet other standards and agree to dispute mediation.

All Seal Members must have their identities and/or contact information verified as a prerequisite to being approved for the Seal.

SquareTrade uses a range of tools to ensure that they verify the contact information and/or identity of each Seal Member. These tools include (courtesy of SquareTrade):

- Third-party databases (e.g., Equifax)

- A physical letter in the mail with a unique code, which the Seal Member has to receive and return

- A requirement to fax a utility bill or other official documentation identifying the applicant and their contact information

- For businesses, a Dun & Bradstreet number or an IRS Employer EIN

All applicants have to meet strict criteria to become SquareTrade Seal Members, and then they must continue to abide by these criteria to retain their Seal. These include:

- ■ **Continued good selling practices**   Members' feedback has to remain strong.

- ■ **Passing checks triggered by any changes in selling practices**   SquareTrade has around 30 checks that run automatically on all Seal Members, to highlight any potential areas for concern (e.g., a Seal Member who was principally a buyer in collectibles and now becomes a seller of high-value consumer electronics items is at once flagged).

- ■ **Approval by a dedicated compliance group**   A dedicated compliance group monitors and investigates every single escalation event for every single Seal Member. Based upon its investigations, it may decide to suspend the membership.

- ■ **Continued participation in resolution of disputes**   SquareTrade reads the transcripts of every single case filed against a Seal Member. If the Seal Member does not participate in good faith to resolve a valid dispute, SquareTrade may decide to suspend their membership.

SquareTrade's dispute resolution and mediation service has handled over 500,000 disputes. It is the preferred online dispute resolution service of eBay, Elance, and the California Association of Realtors.

buySAFE

The other popular online trust and safety tool is buySAFE, which is essentially a bonding service. Once you qualify for its program, the company will automatically place a seal on all of your auctions. This seal tells prospective bidders that you are bonded up to the amount of money specified. Depending on the volume of your auctions, how long you have been on eBay, and your credit score, the buySAFE bond will vary from $5,000 up to $25,000. The bond is underwritten by a major insurance company.

When a buyer clicks the buySAFE seal, they are taken to an information page about the seller as shown in Figure 26-1.

So this brings us back to trust, credibility, and professionalism. New eBay users may make the mistake of buying from a bad seller, but experienced eBayers are far more careful. When I am about to buy something that costs over $50 or $100, I usually take the time to check the seller's feedback and to look at their user profile. I determine if they are ID Verified and PayPal Verified.

If I am considering placing a bid on anything more expensive, I take the time to really examine the seller's feedback, I read the auction description very carefully, and I look for the buySAFE or SquareTrade seal.

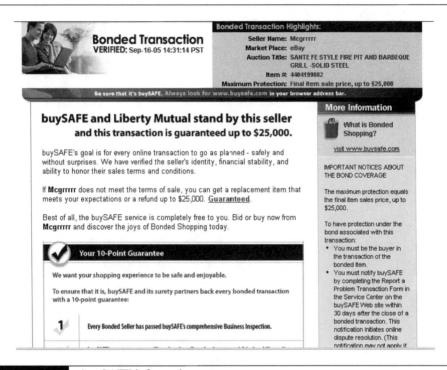

FIGURE 26-1   buySAFE information page

If you decide to sell expensive goods, such as $900+ digital cameras or $1,500 laptops, then the small cost to enroll in the SquareTrade and buySAFE programs is well worth it. buySAFE has performed research that shows conclusively that sellers offering items over $1,000 in value realize a 17 percent greater sell-through rate and achieve on average 4 percent higher values when enrolled with the service.

eBay is a business that directly rewards honesty, sound ethical business practices, and professionalism. Any time spent on building a professional image will add to your sales and profits.

Chapter 27

Give Superior Customer Service

Customer service falls into two categories: consignors and eBay bidders and buyers. You will need to do a good job with both categories.

Consignor Service

Your consignors are the lifeblood of your business. If you live in the suburbs or a small town, word of mouth will be essential to the growth of your business. But no matter where you live, you want to develop a reputation as a professional business that provides good service. Excellent customer service consists of three key elements:

- Practice excellent communications.

- Have fair, clearly stated business policies.

- Under-promise and over-deliver.

Good communications consist of such things as having a written agreement where everything is spelled out so that there are no misunderstandings or confusion. Answer all e-mails and return phone calls quickly. Your consignors will call frequently with questions such as: "My auction has been up for six days and there are no bids. What is wrong?" Remember, these people know little about eBay and how it works. You will have to answer each question patiently—even the stupid ones.

Always be clear and unambiguous in your communications with your consignors. If you say you will do something that is a change from your written agreement or not included in your agreement, then take a few minutes to put it in writing so that there are no misunderstandings later. Give your consignors your e-mail address and be sure to respond to their e-mails promptly. This will cut down on phone calls.

Although your contract should contain all of your business policies, a lot of people will just glance at a contract and sign it. It also helps to have your policies explained in a small brochure or a FAQ sheet that you can give to your customers when they leave an item to sell.

If you commit to do something by a certain time or date, then do it. If you can't keep your promise for some reason, it is essential that you communicate with your customer, explaining that you will not meet your deadline and why.

Be very careful about estimating what something will sell for. If you say something such as "I think your art glass vase will sell for somewhere between $100 and $200," you can be sure that the only number the person will remember is "$200." It is always better to underestimate what you think something will sell for. This way, if they get more they think you are nothing less than an eBay genius.

One business policy you must always adhere to is taking possession of the merchandise. This is critical! Imagine this scenario: A well-dressed gentleman contacts you with 12 nice pieces of Roseville pottery that he wants to sell. You agree to sell them, but he says he wants to keep the pieces until you do. You reluctantly agree because he looks like such a nice, honest person.

Now, Roseville pottery is a very hot seller on eBay. You put up seven-day auctions and all the pieces sell, bringing a very nice price. You call the gentleman up and ask him to bring the pieces, and he tells you that his daughter called him and talked him out of selling the pieces because she wants them to remember their mother by. Now you are looking at contacting 12 about-to-be-very-upset successful bidders and letting them know you can't deliver. Some of them will have already paid you via PayPal using the instant payment feature. You will have to return the money, and you will be out the PayPal fees. Next, you will have to apply to eBay to get your final value fees back; they could be substantial on a couple thousand dollars worth of sales. Finally, at least one or two of these bidders (and maybe more) are sure to leave you negative feedback. Not what you need when you are trying to build your business.

Here are some ideas that will help you convince the consignor to leave the product with you:

- Emphasize to the consignor the importance of having good photos of the items and that you have a professional setup to get good photos.

- Explain that potential bidders are going to be asking questions about the merchandise, and that you will need it so that you can look at it and answer those questions quickly and accurately. You don't want to have to call the seller every time someone asks a question and try to come up with an answer over the phone.

- Explain that you will be researching the item so that you can write the best possible headline and description and that you need it in your possession for easier research.

- Show the consignor your insurance certificate and your surety bond (if you have one).

- You can also make the consignor more comfortable by giving them their copy of the contract. Show the seller any testimonials you have and, if necessary, give them the names and phone numbers of two or three satisfied customers.

In the end, if the consignor won't let you have possession of the item during the selling process, walk away from the deal. It's very likely they aren't the type of person you want to deal with in the first place. Not having actual possession of the item exposes you to risks that you just don't want to take.

Occasionally you will come across items that are just too large to take possession of. If this occurs, you want to create a separate contract that requires the consignor to keep the item in good and safe condition while you are auctioning it and require them to post a nonrefundable fee as a "good-faith deposit" that the consignor would forfeit if they fail to deliver the item.

eBay Bidders

Always answer a bidder's and/or buyer's e-mail as quickly as possible. Whether the customer is praising your product or complaining, whether he is offering his input or asking a question, he or she deserves an answer—particularly on eBay, where feedback really counts!

Respond quickly and be clear in your communications with eBay bidders and buyers. If I have auctions running, I check my eBay messages at least three times a day and always a few minutes before I have auctions ending in the event there are any last-minute questions from a bidder.

If you fail to answer e-mails, you may receive comments such as "unresponsive seller" or "ignored my repeated inquiries" in your feedback file. You will also earn yourself a poor reputation and lose respect in the online trading community.

My recommendation: Keep your answers short, courteous, and to the point. Provide all relevant information and be friendly, but don't get bogged down in long e-mail conversations back and forth, and don't let the customer lead you on an irrelevant tangent. Your time is money.

All of your business policies as they relate to shipping, payment, posting feedback, and so on should be written in a clear, yet friendly style. You want to convey your policies, but you don't want to list a set of rules that turn people off. It is also helpful to explain why you have certain policies. For example, if you only ship with priority mail, you might want to say something like this:

> *We use priority mail for all shipments under five pounds. Priority mail costs less than UPS and includes free boxes and shipping materials, so we don't have to charge you for those or build in a handling fee.*

Create a classy signature file for your e-mails that inspires confidence in you as a seller and looks professional. Finally, I strongly recommend creating a folder in your e-mail program entitled "prewritten messages" in which you have template messages already created to answer common questions, such as

- When was my item shipped?
- Did you receive my payment?
- How long does shipping take?

Customize your prewritten messages to fit your particular product, as you will notice very similar questions and comments from customers as time passes.

It is much easier to send out a prewritten e-mail than to write a specific answer to each inquiry. However, make sure that it doesn't sound as if you are using a form e-mail, and add a personal touch when possible. Use the person's name if you know it, or their eBay username if you don't. Always give your name. When considering e-mail as a customer service, you must balance time, efficiency, and courteousness to maximize your working potential.

Amazingly, giving out your telephone number can save you lots of time. I started listing my phone number in my e-mail signature. Sometimes a phone call could clear up an issue in much less time than it took to send several e-mails back and forth. Also, the fact that you list your phone number really enhances your credibility and reduces suspicion.

One advantage of the auction management services we discussed earlier is the prewritten personalized e-mails that are automatically sent out to each buyer. Other specific messages, such as a payment reminder or a request for a shipping address, can be sent with a simple mouse click. The few dollars you spend per month for these services will save you hours each month composing and sending repetitive e-mails.

Remember, your reputation for customer service exists both offline and online. Offline, you will want to build a reputation in your community as a reliable and professional businessperson, someone who is friendly and a pleasure to do business with. Online, you will want to build a high positive feedback rating with hundreds of glowing comments about your service.

Chapter 28

Business Policies to Build Your Business

Every eBay auction has a place for the seller to enter information that is standard for each auction. Some of the standardized information sellers enter include their shipping policy, return policy, warranty information, and occasionally a money-back guarantee. Let's take a look at these.

Shipping Policy

eBay users are very aware of shipping costs and shipping policies. Shipping issues are one of the leading causes of negative feedback posts. These can range anywhere from "I never received the item" to "item was poorly packaged and broken" and the occasional "He charged me $13 to ship an item that only cost him $3 to ship."

The best defense against receiving negative feedback for shipping-related issues is first to pack and ship professionally and always use a tracking service, and second to spell out your shipping policy very clearly. More importantly, in your auction description, you should actually direct the reader to your policy with words such as "Please read my shipping policy very carefully."

Your shipping policy should be very clear. It should contain the method by which you ship, how soon you ship after payment, how you charge for shipping, if you charge a handling fee, and if you provide or offer insurance.

There are three ways to charge for shipping on eBay: offer free shipping, charge the actual rate with or without an added handling fee, or charge a fixed rate.

Free shipping is possible only when you can receive enough margin to absorb the cost. There is no question that free shipping can help you get more and higher bids, but the bids may not always be high enough to cover the additional cost. The ability to offer free shipping relates to the size and weight versus the selling price. If I am selling a very expensive postage stamp or baseball trading card, then I can afford free shipping. The steel fire pits I sell weigh 55 pounds and are the maximum size that can be shipped by a shipping service. If I offered free shipping on those, I would have to raise the price from $249 to over $300.

A lot of eBay sellers prefer to charge the actual shipping cost. If you use USPS, eBay has made this very easy by offering a USPS shipping calculator that you can paste into your auction description. A potential bidder who is concerned about the shipping cost can plug his or her ZIP code into your calculator and determine the shipping cost before actually bidding. You can also add a handling charge to the calculator that will automatically add a fixed percentage to each calculation.

The last method is fixed-price shipping. In fixed-price shipping you calculate the shipping charge to a preset destination. For example, I live on the West Coast, so I precalculate the shipping cost to a point midway across the country, such as Chicago. Now if I ship past Chicago, I lose a little money on the shipping, but when I ship to someone closer, I make money. This way, it averages out.

This is the method I prefer, although many large power sellers use calculated shipping. The advantage of a fixed shipping rate is the ease of finishing the transaction and getting paid. If you use calculated shipping, the buyer gets an end-of-auction notice that they have won and then they have to contact you for the shipping charge. You answer them, and then they send the payment. This extra communication adds to your workload, slows down getting paid, and can often confuse the buyer. There are automated systems that will send an e-mail to the buyer that will allow them to calculate the shipping and then pay by PayPal. This works well with experienced buyers, but new eBay users seldom use them. I know one seller who uses this method, and he states that only about half of his auctions go through automatically. In the other half, there is a back-and-forth communication with the buyer before payment is affected.

Whichever method you use, be sure to spell it out clearly in your auction description. If you include a handling charge, you should also tell the buyer. I believe it helps to explain why a seller uses a handling charge. In my auctions I have a statement that says: "We add a $2 handling charge to the shipping cost. We use only new, high-quality boxes and packing materials to make sure your item arrives safely. The handling charge is necessary to cover the cost of these materials."

Sellers will more likely accept paying extra charges if you make a case for them than if you just make a statement such as "We add a $2 handling charge to each item."

The last item in your shipping policy is when you ship. I use the following statement in my shipping policy:

We ship the same business day your payment arrives. Our cut-off time for shipments is 2:00 P.M. Pacific Time. Otherwise, it will go out the next business day. We ship via USPS priority mail with delivery confirmation. This typically takes two to three business days to most locations. We will send you an e-mail when we ship your purchase with the delivery confirmation number and a link to the USPS web site, where you can track your shipment.

Notice that we ship every business day. Because we use priority mail for most of our shipments, we can even ship on Saturday. Priority mail is fast, offers tracking, and gives you one extra day per week to ship. People like getting their purchases quickly, and this usually shows in their feedback posts.

There are many large eBay sellers who ship only on specific days. Yes, this is more efficient, but I don't recommend it. Look what can happen when an auction closes on Sunday evening and you ship on Tuesday and Thursday. The buyer may not get the payment off until Tuesday, and it arrives after your cut-off time. So you ship on Thursday, and it takes four business days to get there. If you are shipping priority mail, the seller will get their item as early as Tuesday. But if you use UPS, it will be the following Wednesday, that is, a total of ten days after the end of the auction. When I buy something on eBay and it takes an overly long time to get to me, I don't bother to leave neutral or negative feedback, I just don't leave any feedback at all.

The chance to sell a customer an additional item is important to any eBay seller's profitability. Part of your business plan should be to build a loyal and happy customer base so that you can sell them additional items later both on and off of eBay. Why make a buyer's first experience less than thrilling?

Payment Policy

The advent of PayPal has made receiving payment very safe and fast for most auction sellers. Although PayPal is responsible for over 75 percent of all auction payments, that still leaves the other 25 percent.

As with shipping, it is very important to spell out your payment policy in advance so that there is no misunderstanding.

Here is the payment policy I use in my auctions:

We accept and prefer PayPal. We also accept major credit cards, personal checks, money orders, bank cashier's checks and Western Union BidPay. If you send a personal check for any item over $25, we will hold your check until it clears unless you have an eBay feedback rating of at least 99% with over 25 feedback comments.

If you are new to eBay and have questions about our payment policy, please e-mail us through the Ask Seller A Question link at the top of this page. We will be glad to assist you with your transaction.

Why do we not hold checks for sales under $25? When you write a check with insufficient funds, your bank charges you a service fee of between $20 and $25. Most people know this and are hesitant to write a bad check for such a small amount of money. We have had thousands of transactions over the past six years, and hundreds of them have been paid by check. To date, we've only had four bad checks. Two of them were made good, and both buyers reimbursed us for the $20 fee our bank charged. In only two instances did we ship merchandise to buyers who paid with a bad check and fail to get reimbursed.

With the advent of PayPal, we now get fewer checks and money orders than we used to, but we still get three or four a week. If the amount is for a large purchase, the first thing I do is check the buyer's feedback. If the buyer has a high positive feedback rating and has been on eBay at least a year, I will usually ship the item immediately for sales up to a couple hundred dollars. If the buyer has a low or spotty feedback rating, then I inform them we will have to wait for the check to clear. Tracking the check clearance can be a real pain, which is why I err on the side of sending the merchandise whenever I can.

Return Policy

The next most important piece of information buyers look for is your return policy. Your return policy is largely determined by what you sell. If you are selling product returns, seconds, or almost any used goods, including books, records, CDs, and DVDs, you will want to explain that these items are sold *AS IS WITH NO RETURNS*. This will usually be the case for consignment sellers. Most buyers will accept this if you fully and completely describe the item you are selling, including a full description of any flaws or shortcomings.

With mechanical or electrical items, you need to let buyers know if you have plugged the item in and it works or if you don't know whether the item works or not. There is one large power seller on eBay who sells nothing but consumer electronic returns and warranty returns. He has a large boldface disclaimer in his auctions that he buys these returns by the pallet load and just cannot test each item and that you are taking a chance when you buy it. His policy is absolutely no returns. Despite the warning, he sells hundreds of items a month. However, his feedback rating is terrible. I think it was in the eighties the last time I looked.

Even though he warns people in large, bold letters that they may be getting an item that may not work, and he states this again in the end-of-auction e-mail, giving them a chance to back out, a lot of buyers still leave negative feedback comments. What is really amazing is that people actually lie and leave posts such as: "Seller promised new & delivered broken item in opened box."

Whenever I sell a used item, I use the following return policy:

I have done my best to accurately and faithfully describe this item and will stand behind it. If you receive an item that is not exactly as described, please contact me before returning the item. I promise to work out a solution to your liking.

The reason I suggest a work-out is so that I don't get automatic returns. If I did make a mistake, I will of course accept the return for a full refund. But many times you can work out an alternative solution. If the buyer believes you made a good-faith mistake, they still may want to keep the item if you make a gesture such as refunding their shipping charge.

When I am selling new merchandise I am more liberal. After all, if someone is buying something that is NIB or NWT, that is what they expect to get. If a buyer contacts me and says there is something wrong with their item, I will almost always ask them to return it for an immediate refund.

My return policy for new merchandise is as follows:

Your complete satisfaction is my top priority. Please inspect your purchase carefully when you receive it. If there is anything wrong, please contact us immediately and we will ensure you get an immediate replacement or a refund if a replacement is not available.

Notice that I do not automatically offer a refund. There are people out there who suffer from buyer's remorse. This is seldom a problem with small purchases, but there are a handful of buyers on eBay who get on the computer late at night after a few glasses of wine and go on a bidding lark. Later, when the bills come due, they start looking for ways to back out.

Chapter 29

Promote Your Auctions
with Special Features

eBay offers several ways to promote your auctions. Most of these cost money. In the last chapter we showed you the cost of these promotions in terms of their related eBay fees. In this chapter we will examine which ones work and look at their potential return on investment (ROI). It can be tempting to use the eBay promotions all the time, but as with anything else, it pays to test. Just because eBay says a certain promotional tool will increase your sell-through rate or final values, that does not make it so.

eBay's research numbers are an average taken over thousands of auctions. Not every auction achieved the desired result. With any average there are auctions that perform very well and others that did poorly. You won't really know if a certain promotional tool works for your specific product unless you test it. If you are selling a highly specific product in a fairly small niche, people will find it by searching and you may not need any promotional tool at all beyond perhaps the 35-cent gallery listing.

Keyword-Rich Titles

We already covered this in Chapter 25, but I wanted to reiterate the importance of keyword-rich titles. Given that over 65 percent of eBay buyers find items to bid on by searching, keyword-rich titles are simply the single most important form of promotion—and they are free!

eBay Subtitles

A *subtitle* is just that, a second title that appears in slightly smaller print just below your auction title on the eBay search results page. A subtitle can provide descriptive information on your item that buyers will see when browsing categories or viewing search results.

A subtitle allows you to provide additional information, which may not fit in the title field but would be of interest to potential buyers viewing a list of items.

The words included in the subtitle are not searchable when buyers conduct a basic search. However, the subtitle will be searchable if the buyer searches in titles and descriptions, although eBay bidders seldom do this, as it brings up too many results.

You may wish to add a subtitle to your listing if you want to provide additional information about your item beyond what would fit in the title or to pique the interest of potential buyers by providing them more descriptive information on the item. I find that subtitles also make your listing stand out somewhat from the other listings around it.

The subtitle can contain additional information about what you are selling—accessories included, benefits, and so on. The eBay fee for the subtitle is 50 cents.

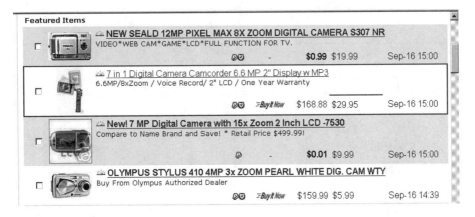

Bold, Highlight, and Border

A bold listing is nothing more than showing your auction title in boldface type to make it stand out. eBay's own research has shown this feature to increase final prices by an average of 25 percent, at a cost of $1. As long as you have an item that will sell for over $10, this is the single best promotional tool in terms of ROI. I use the bold option in almost all of my auctions.

Highlight is similar to bold in that it makes your auctions stand out. When you select this option, it places your auction title within a pink highlight band. Highlighting costs $5. However, if you use highlight without bold, it can be somewhat difficult for the bidder to read your title, so in effect this option costs $6 when you add the bold.

Border is simply an option that places a border around your auction. This option costs $3.

I am not a big fan of border or highlight. eBay hasn't announced any research statistics on this feature, which tells me it probably doesn't work that well or they would have. At $3 for Border and $5 for Highlight, I would probably not use it unless I was selling an item I expected to reach at least $100 and one that had a high closing ratio. Figure 29-1 shows an example of listings that contain bold, highlight, and border features. Note that some contain all three.

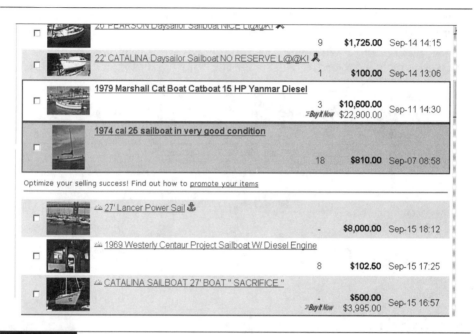

FIGURE 29-1   Bold and highlight listings

The eBay Gallery

The eBay gallery, shown in Figure 29-2, is the option to place a small thumbnail photo on the search results or browse page next to your auction title. At $0.35, this is the least expensive promotional tool. Almost everyone uses the gallery, and many

FIGURE 29-2   eBay Gallery listings

eBay bidders will not click an auction unless they see this photo, so I consider it mandatory. eBay's research shows that a gallery photo increases bids by an average of 11 percent.

Featured Plus

Whenever an eBay user performs a search or browses a category, a list of items featured in that category comes up first. This is a high-performing tool, but unfortunately it's a bit expensive at $19.95. (This feature was formerly known as Category Featured.)

I use this only on very high-priced items to make sure they get the visibility. Featured Plus is also very useful for Dutch auctions, where you may be selling a lower-priced item but you are selling a large enough quantity to offset the cost. The performance of this tool is impressive, as eBay reports that Featured Plus items are 28 percent more likely to sell and have an average 12 percent higher final value.

Super (Home Page) Featured

The Home Page Featured auction is the most expensive promotional tool, at $39.95 for a single item listing and $79.95 for a Dutch (multiple items) auction listing. Home Page Featured auctions rotate onto the eBay home page. It is important to point out that eBay does not guarantee either that it will rotate through or the time it will happen. Home Page Featured is a bit of a crap shoot, but it does work most of the time.

I once had an auction ending on a Thursday night where my item rotated onto the home page about an hour before the auction ended. I got over 250 hits in that last hour, and the item sold for almost double what I normally received.

Other Features

The other features eBay offers are 10-day Duration, Listing Designer, and Gallery Featured.

The 10-day Duration option costs 40 cents. I always use this option if I am paying for any of the other features (except bold and gallery) because I want to extend the life of the auction to amortize the cost of the special feature, such as Home Page or Featured Plus, over a longer period.

Listing Designer is nothing more than the ability to use predesigned templates when you are listing your auctions using the eBay *Sell Your Item* form. If you are using your own template, or one that is served up by an auction management company, these are not available to you. But if you are creating your listings directly on eBay, this is a nice feature and it only costs 10 cents.

The Gallery feature is the option to have your image featured in the gallery section of the eBay home page. When you choose this option your item will appear in the special Featured section above the general Picture Gallery.

At $19.95, I have never used this option and eBay has never released any research statistics on it. The only use I could think of for this feature is if you were selling a visually stunning product such as a painting, an expensive antique, or a beautiful Persian rug.

Chapter 30

The Consignment Seller's Web Site

It seems that everyone has a web site these days. I was at the supermarket one day and I grabbed a carton of eggs. As I placed them in the basket, I happened to notice a web site URL on the egg carton. I turned to my wife and said, "Good Lord, why would I ever visit an egg company's web site?" Purely out of curiosity, I looked up the web site when I got home. You couldn't buy eggs from the web site. You could find no nutritional information, no recipes, and no instructions on all the ways to cook an egg. There was just a picture of the farm, an About Us page, and contact instructions. I guess this company heard that everyone had to have a web site, so they created one.

If you are in some form of online business, I think it is safe to say that you will need a web site and that yours will have to contain more useful information than my local egg farmer. Most people do not have the programming and design skills to build a web site, and right away they think of the cost of hiring a designer and then someone to host and maintain it for them. That is how I started with my first web site six years ago. I was lucky—my son was a budding web site designer and managed to do a pretty nice job for me. The world has changed, however. I built my last two web sites myself using the services of one of several companies who have created a new industry: template-based web sites. Let's look at how this works.

Do-It-Yourself Web Site

There are over a dozen companies today that specialize in providing predesigned web sites that you can build yourself with absolutely no knowledge of programming or HTML. Some of the more popular ones are

- **CityMax**   www.citymax.com
- **Register.com**   www.register.com
- **RegisterFly**   www.registerfly.com
- **Bigstep**   www.bigstep.com
- **Homestead**   www.homestead.com
- **Network Solutions**   www.networksolutions.com

The first two, CityMax and Register.com, are the largest and most popular. I have used Bigstep in the past, and although it is workable, I wasn't that impressed with the ease of use. Currently I use CityMax, and I have been very happy with it

FIGURE 30-1   CityMax home page

(see Figure 30-1). CityMax charges $19.95 a month, or $16.95 a month if you pay annually. You can create and register a unique URL (web site name) for $8.95 a year.

In my opinion, CityMax is simply the easiest and most powerful web site builder available. You can literally have a basic web site up and running live on the Internet in just 20 minutes. CityMax is packed full of powerful features, many of which are unavailable on other technologies. These include:

- An e-commerce-ready shopping cart with up to 500 items

- 20 POP e-mail accounts in your domain name

- A text editor: you enter plain text and the editor creates the HTML

- Over 1,000 preformatted template designs and 2,000 stock photos

- Templates with over 20 color combinations each

- A capability to upload custom logos or your own images

- Autoresponders

- Message boards

- A newsletter function

- Catalogs

- Coupon support

- A custom feedback form: visitors can give you feedback on your services and operations

- Integration with eBay and PayPal (this feature alone makes it most useful for the eBay consignment seller)

You will find creating and updating your site a breeze. Most changes require only a click of your mouse, and editing text is just like typing a letter with an editor that looks just like Microsoft Word. If you can use a mouse, then you can make a great web site.

CityMax currently hosts over 170,000 web sites. They have excellent customer support, and they are the only service I have found that is directly comparable to a custom site built by a professional web development company.

All of the do-it-yourself web site companies operate basically the same, but the devil is in the details. Having tried several of the services, I have found CityMax simply the easiest to use, and the most inclusive for the price.

You start by selecting a design from one of over 1,000 preformatted templates (see Figure 30-2). Once you select a design, you choose a layout such as navigation bars on the left or top, images on the left or right, etc. You then choose an image from their stock photos as your image across the top, or you can upload an image, if you have one, from your hard drive. Next you choose your pages: home, about me, contact us, etc. Once this is done, you create a URL. At first your URL will be yourname.citymax.com. But if you pay the $8.95 to register *yourname* as your URL, CityMax will register and assign it to you, and you can drop the *.citymax.* This takes about two business days to complete.

Now you are ready to start. You simply select a page, for example, your home page. Hit a button at the top of the window that says Edit Page, and up pops the HTML editor shown in Figure 30-3.

Now you simply enter your text much as you would in a Word document. You can select text color, bold, italics, and so on. There is also a Browse button to upload photos. When you are finished with your home page, you can select another page that you have already created to start writing copy, or you can go on and create new pages.

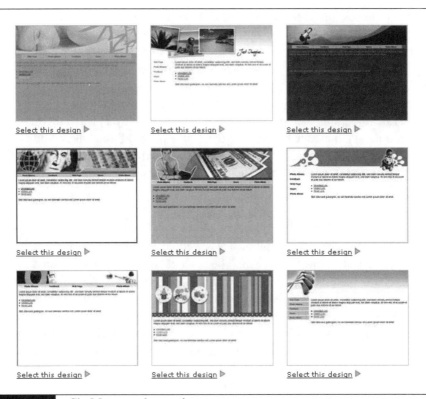

FIGURE 30-2   CityMax sample templates

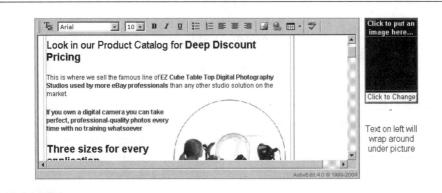

FIGURE 30-3   HTML editor

One of the best features of CityMax is its product catalog and e-commerce-enabled shopping cart. As a consignment seller, you will be selling on eBay, but there could come a time when you acquire a large amount of similar merchandise that you cannot auction all at once. In this case you could create a shopping cart and place the merchandise on your web site, where you can list it with some of the popular shopping search engines such as Froogle or Shopping.com.

Other neat features include a guestbook where people can leave their contact information and a message board. There is also a photo album where you can store up to 500 photos. This could work as a place to store photos with a unique URL if you are using a software program such as MarketBlast that requires web storage.

Marketing: If You Build It, Will They Come?

When you open your consignment business, people are naturally going to ask you if you have a web site. Now that you do, you can put your web site URL on a business card, on flyers, in classified ads and newspaper ads, and so on. You can also promote your web site to various search engines and index sites. Many communities have a web site, where local businesses can link from. The town I live in, for example, has a web site operated by the Chamber of Commerce. It contains all sorts of information and links to local resources as well as a listing of local businesses. For $25 a year, I can also buy a small ad box on the Business Resources page that describes my business and provides a link to my web site.

CityMax also offers several ways to promote your web site. If you click the Tools button at the top of your management page, it will take you to simple instructions on how you can enter your keywords and meta tags. Once this is done, CityMax will automatically submit your site to various shopping indexes such as Froogle and Shopping.com. Next click the button that says Make Money. This will take you to the page shown in Figure 30-4, where you can submit your site to Google, Yahoo, and other major search engines as well as sign up for $50 worth of free keyword advertising on Google.

Don't expect traffic your first day. Although some of the smaller search engines will index your site within a week or so, it can take up to 30 or 40 days for the larger sites such as Google, MSN, or Yahoo to find your site.

When you are submitting your site and coming up with keywords, remember you are trying to attract local business. Don't spend time and money tweaking your search engine submission to have lots of hits from Moose Jaw, Alaska, and Zimbabwe unless you have actually located your business there.

FIGURE 30-4   CityMax Search Engine submission page

What Should I Put on My Web Site?

Your web site can serve several purposes. First, it should describe your business. Tell them what you do. I would set up your home page with a short description of your business, where you are located, and exactly what it is you do. This is a good place to make your sale. You might want to create the following list of benefits right on your home page (for this example, we will call your business *FastSell*):

- ■ **Convenience**   We do all the photography, writing, listing, e-mail and phone call answering, payment processing, packing, and shipping.

- ■ **Experience**   We are experienced eBay sellers. We know how to avoid nonpaying bidders, scams, and phonies—and most of all, how to get the highest bids for your goods.

- ■ **Maximum return**   Your goods will be exposed to 45 million eBay buyers. This ensures that you will get much more than you would at a local auction or by selling your valuable goods to an antique dealer or secondhand shop.

■ **eBay feedback rating** A good feedback rating is imperative to bidder confidence. On eBay, sellers with a high feedback rating like ours (1000+) sell more merchandise at higher prices than new sellers.

■ **Privacy and safety** Selling things on eBay requires private information about the seller, including such things as bank account numbers. FastSell does not post any of your information. Only FastSell's information will be shared with eBay and the buyer. No one will know who the actual seller is.

Next, you want to explain the process. For example, you could create a list like this:

1. Bring your goods to the FastSell store located on Highway 20 across the street from Wal-Mart.

2. I will inspect your product and let you know if it is acceptable for sale.

3. Our staff will take photos of your product, research the best eBay category, and write and design a professional auction ad.

4. We will upload the auction to eBay on the best day and time of day for your specific product.

5. When your item sells, we will collect payment from the buyer first, and then we will professionally package and ship the item.

6. We will take out a percentage of the selling price (see our sliding fee schedule) along with shipping and handling charges and mail you a check.

7. If your product does not sell the first time, it is relisted for free. If your product does not sell the second time, either it can be picked up or we will deliver it to the Kiwanis Thrift Shop or the Salvation Army.

At the end of this list there should be a link that says, "Click here to see our fee schedule." This would take potential consignors to a page that explains both your fees and your sales policies. In addition to your commission and any fees, be sure to set out your standards and a list of things you won't sell (guns, TV descramblers, stolen merchandise, and other items prohibited by eBay). Also, set your value and size requirements in terms such as this:

FastSell only accepts items weighing less than 100 pounds and that will sell for a value estimated at over $50. Items must be able to be shipped by UPS or the U.S. Postal Service.

Next, you can create a page called What Sells on eBay. You don't want people bringing you tons of junk that won't sell. On this page you can list the kinds of items you are looking for. Another page can contain links to your actual auctions so that people can see what you are selling. This is also good for your consignors, as they can watch you auction their stuff off. This way, they aren't calling you every day.

Chapter 31

Bring It All Together

How large you want your business to be and how fast you want it to grow are a product of your desire, the time you can devote to the business, your talent, and how well you apply the lessons you learned in this book and from your experience. One of the largest sellers on eBay, a Titanium power seller from New York City, got started selling surplus and overstock shoes for department stores and distributors in the greater New York area. His first year he had one account and sold over $190,000 worth of shoes. Three years later he is one of the top 20 sellers on eBay. He has six employees and a large warehouse, and he estimates he will gross over $4 million in 2005. He started his business with a computer and a digital camera and about $1,000 in cash.

In the introduction to this book, I said there are many type of sellers who might buy this book. Some are already existing eBay sellers, frustrated with the difficulty in finding merchandise to sell. They are looking at the consignment model as a way to add to or grow their business. Others may be looking to start a small eBay business to make some extra money, while others are looking to start and grow a large sustainable business that can earn thousands of dollars a month. I have tried to provide the tools and techniques to support any of these three business models.

Whichever type of seller you are, you will still have to master the techniques of marketing your services to find consignors and selling on eBay in a productive and efficient manner to maximize your sales and minimize your costs.

Whenever I do a seminar, I am often asked questions along the lines of "What are the keys to success in the consignment business?" and "Can you give me a step-by-step plan for success?" Sometimes the questions are posed in the form "What is the real secret to success on eBay?" The questions are often posed differently, but they usually boil down to one of these three. If you are like most people, you may have a variation of the same question, so let me try and answer them here.

What Are the Keys to Success in the Online Consignment Business?

If you ask a real estate person, "What is the secret to success buying property?", the standard answer is location, location, location. In online consignment sales, it's marketing, marketing, marketing. Almost anyone can learn how to sell on eBay. There are dozens of books on the subject, including several by myself, and, in fact, over 600,000 people like you and me sell on eBay every day. I have met many of these people in my seminars and at eBay Live, where we exhibit each year. eBay sellers come from all walks of life; they represent all ages from those barely 18 to septuagenarians. They also represent the educational spectrum from high-school dropouts to those with Ph.Ds.

The usual eBay seller has the constant challenge of sourcing products at a price that can be sold at a profit. With all the competition and growth of eBay, this becomes a daily challenge. The consignment seller has a similar challenge. You have to be on the constant hunt for consignors to supply you with product. This is where your marketing comes in. Marketing is most successful when it is highly targeted. Therefore, you will need to decide what type of merchandise you want to sell and where to find the consignors that have that type of merchandise.

If you are going after the retail consumer market, you may need a commercial location to attract retail traffic. After that will come advertising. Fortunately, advertising venues for the consumer market are plentiful: everything from newspapers, radio, flyers, and direct mail to billboards like those used by AuctionDrop in the San Francisco Bay Area.

If you want to target bankruptcy and estate attorneys, your advertising outlets are more limited. It would be too expensive to pay for a newspaper advertisement that is based on the entire readership when your target market makes up only a small percentage of that readership. You will want to look at direct mail, networking, and advertising in local trade journals.

The same is true if your target market is the business-to-business community. Small business owners, purchasing managers at corporations, and bankers are more efficiently reached by networking, direct contact, and highly targeted advertising.

No matter which market you target—and you should target a market as opposed to trying to sell everything for everyone—you want to make sure your marketing efforts and advertising dollars are focused on your target. Otherwise, you are just wasting money. The same goes for your personal efforts. Finding a consignor with thousands of dollars worth of merchandise to sell is one of the highest-value tasks you can perform. If a consignor gives you $20,000 worth of goods to sell and you make a 15 percent commission, that is $3,000 gross profit. If you can hire someone to take photos and upload them, wrap and ship packages, and perform other day-to-day chores for $8–10 hour, that will allow you much more time to go out and find those $20,000 consignors.

The same is true of automation. Not spending money on auction automation and a bookkeeping system means you have to spend it hiring someone to do the work or do it yourself, which takes time away from your high-value tasks.

Can You Give Me a Step-by-Step Plan for Success?

The answer is yes, well, sort of. Everyone's plan is going to be different. Someone with a lot of money to invest and five years of experience selling on eBay will have a much different plan than a new seller who is trying to bootstrap their business. I can, however, list the elements that are necessary in every plan:

- The first step is to make a personal assessment of yourself. What are your strengths and weaknesses? What are your assets? How much money do you have to invest in this business? How much time can you devote to it? Understanding your own personal capabilities and the resources you can devote to the business will help assure you that your plan is realistic.

- The next step is to try to figure out what you want to do. What kind of business do you want to be in? What is your target market? Do you want to specialize or be a generalist? Are you going after the retail market or B2B? Knowing where you want to go is the first step in any plan.

- The next step is to figure out what you don't have. What resources, equipment, and professional assistance will you need to get your business off the ground? After you make a list, now make a plan for obtaining them.

- Next are your goals. Because you now have a clear understanding of what you have, what you need, and where you can get it, you are now in a position to set realistic goals. This is not a place to be vague. If you can't measure something, you can't control it. Your goals should be specific in terms of sales; income; the number of auctions you can launch; and your targets for ASP, GMS, and profit.

- Once your goals are set, you are ready to design your marketing and sales plan. At this point you want to stop and do some research into the media available for your target market, the costs, and the projected return. Advertising plans are always a guess at first, but once you start seeing results from the various media you try, you will be able to revise your plan and your budget.

- Last, you want to prepare a detailed cash flow plan. Businesses fail every day because they run out of money. Sadly, many of them were on the verge of success when the funds ran out. If they had just planned a little better, they could have made it over the hump and continued to grow and prosper. Be as realistic as you can with your projections, and keep some money in reserve for the things you can't foresee. As you gain experience, you also accumulate real data. Be sure to revise and update your plan every month for the first few months until you are sure you are operating with accurate numbers. After that, you should still look at both your business plan and your cash flow at least quarterly.

Now that you have a plan, use it. It doesn't make sense to do all that work, set the goals, and then allow yourself to be pulled off in another direction.

What Are the Real Secrets to Success on eBay?

This one is easy. There are none. Almost all of the information, strategies, techniques, and methods used by eBay sellers have been reported, written about, and discussed in numerous books, newsletters, TV stories, and seminars. A technique that one power seller considers his secret to success is derided by another power seller as a rookie mistake. I was having lunch one day with four of the largest power sellers on eBay; all were Titanium, and between them they sold over $25 million a year on eBay. I asked one seller, what was the best way to list an item on eBay? He replied: "I list everything at 99 cents, no reserve." One of the other sellers agreed with him in part, but the other two disagreed vehemently, kicking off a heated discussion that went on through dessert. One person's *secret* is seen by others as just another opinion.

I have been a member of PESA, the Professional eBay Seller's Alliance, and I attended their first meeting in New York in 2003. PESA, originally called the eBay Elite, represents most of the top 500 sellers on eBay (see Figure 31-1). Our members account for over $1 billion in annual gross merchandise sales on eBay. I have had the opportunity to engage in workshops and meetings and long discussions with many of my fellow members, and their opinion is the same as mine. There is no one secret to success on eBay; success comes to those who master the basics and execute them. The other theme you always hear is to run your business like a business.

What are the basics, and what does it mean to run your business like a business? Let's take a look:

- ■ Set up and organize your business like a professional business, because it is. If you take shortcuts and try to operate on the cheap, you will never be taken seriously. The Internet is still a scary place for some folks. Take the time to brand your business: create a look and feel that your customers can relate to and that creates a sense of confidence.

- ■ Time is your most precious resource. Anything you can do to automate functions and get others to perform simple operational tasks will free you to do the management and creative tasks that will build your business.

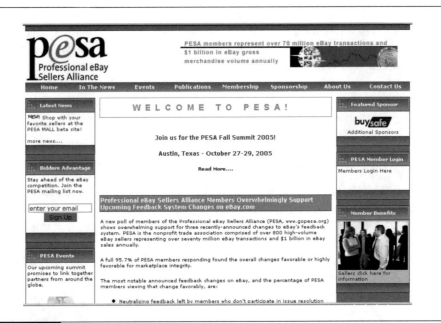

FIGURE 31-1   PESA membership guidelines

- Every listing is a reflection of you and your business. Each listing should look professional and contain good headlines, good photos, and item descriptions that are accurate, that are complete, and that *sell*!

- Establish sales, payment, shipping, and return policies that are both friendly and yet support your business model. Don't be dictatorial. eBay is a community built on trust. If you trust others to do right, they usually will. The percentage that don't is quite small, and you should treat it as a cost of doing business.

- Build and preserve an excellent feedback reputation. Feedback is the window through which others see you. You can have great products, perfect product descriptions, and great product photos, but if you have a lousy feedback score, your business will suffer. Great feedback is built by providing great customer service. Treat every customer as you would like to be treated and you will always have a high score.

- eBay is one of the most competitive marketplaces on earth. Study and stay on top of your competition constantly—and be prepared to react to changes in the marketplace.

■ Experiment – Test – Innovate. Experiment with new tools and software when they become available. Test different listing and pricing strategies, new products and sales strategies. Innovate constantly. Always look for new ways to solve old problems.

■ Don't be afraid to ask for help. There are plenty of resources for the entrepreneur (see the web site that comes with this book at www .skipmcgrath.com/consign). Amazingly, the best source of help is other eBayers. Your direct competitor may not want to help you, but there are plenty of others who will. A post on the Power Seller Message Board will bring dozens of responses. Once you are a power seller, you will have access to the Power Seller Support hotline and e-mail support box.

Well, maybe there is one *secret to success* on eBay. If I had to say, it would be: Do it all and do it right!

I'll end this book the same way I end e-mails to my customers: Good luck on eBay!

Part V

Appendixes

Appendix A

Sample Agreements, Forms, and Letters

You should always conduct your business in writing. A well-written agreement sets out the responsibilities of both parties and prevents disagreements caused by confusion or lack of communication.

On the next page is a "sample" agreement. I asked my attorney to take the extra time to write it in clear, understandable language, not legalese. This agreement (contract) will work very well in most states. Local laws and laws regarding auction selling and consignments can vary from state to state. I am not an attorney. Although this agreement was created by an experienced contract attorney and will work well in most places, I strongly suggest you take the time to have it reviewed by a local attorney.

Be sure to tell him or her you just want it looked over for any egregious errors and that you want the final agreement to be simple and readable. Otherwise, an attorney may spend hours on research and writing and hit you with a huge bill. If you are a member of a legal service plan, such as American Express Legal or PrePaid Legal, their basic service usually includes a "no-cost" contract review.

There is another issue to be concerned with. Some states have laws that you must be a licensed auctioneer to sell goods for someone on eBay. Other cities and states have laws requiring consignment sellers to send the local police photos and serial numbers of goods they sell. One way around this is to operate as a "service business." Basically, you are providing computer services to people who want to sell their own goods on eBay. This is how the QuikDrop franchises operate.

After the basic consignment contract below, I have also added the QuikDrop contract if you live in a location that is regulated differently. QuikDrop gave us permission to share this contract with our readers, and you may use it freely— simply change the name QuikDrop to the name of your company. Nevertheless, I would show it to a local lawyer, just to make sure everything works with your local regulations.

Notice that the agreement says that you take responsibility for the safekeeping and delivery of the goods. To do this, you must actually take possession of the consignor's merchandise. This is crucial. Do not attempt to sell something for someone else on eBay unless you take physical possession of the goods.

This may not be practical if you are selling large industrial equipment or a jet airplane. In these cases, I would get a lawyer to draw up an agreement to protect your rights and to make sure there is a penalty if the consignor does not follow through if you sell the goods. In these instances, you may want to get a deposit or have the consigner put the ownership in escrow until the items are sold.

Consignment Agreement

CONSIGNOR NAME: _____

ADDRESS: _____

TELEPHONE: _____ E-MAIL: _____

Your Company Name Goes Here, Consignee, accepts the goods on the attached *Consignor Inventory Form*, to sell on eBay to the highest bidder under the terms and conditions listed in this contract and documents attached hereto.

1. Consignor warrants that he or she is the sole legal owner of the property to be sold. (If property is jointly owned with another person, both persons will have to sign.) Consignor further warrants the description of the item(s) and any representations made about the item(s) is/are true and correct to the best of his/her knowledge.

2. Consignor agrees to pay a listing fee of three dollars ($3.00) for the first item consigned and a fee of one dollar ($1.00) for each additional item. This fee is non-refundable whether an item sells or not. *(This is the language you want to use if you charge fees in addition to your commission.)*

3. Consignee agrees to be responsible for the loss or damage and safekeeping of the items and will ensure they are packed and shipped properly to the eventual buyer.

4. Items with a final value in excess of $200 will be shipped insured. The insurance premium will be deducted from Consignor's value after commissions. Insurance charges are $1.90 per one hundred dollars of value or part, thereof.

5. Consignor agrees to the fee schedule that is attached hereto, as part of this contract. Any special fee agreements or changes must be in writing and initialed by both parties.

6. Consignee will retain possession of the merchandise until the goods are sold and delivered to the final purchaser or returned to the consignor. Consignor agrees to leave the items with consignee for a period of at least 15 business days during which time they will be listed on eBay for a three-, seven- or ten-day period for sale.

7. Once an item is listed on eBay, it will run the full auction course until it is sold to the highest bidder. If consignor demands return of the property prior to the end of an auction, or the 15-day period, he will pay a withdrawal fee of $25 per item. **Consignor may not withdraw an item after it is sold, or within the last 24 hours of the auction under any circumstances.**

8. Once an auction has ended with a successful sale, the property may not be withdrawn and will be delivered to the highest bidder upon receipt of payment.

9. Should the winning bidder fail to pay for the auction, the property will be offered to the next highest bidder. If this bidder does not accept the item, it will be returned to the Consignor or put up for auction again at the consignor's option.

10. If consignor's property fails to sell within the 15 business day period, consignor agrees to pick up the item within five business days or pay actual shipping and handling charges to have the item returned. Otherwise, unsold items will be donated to a local charity.

11. All items are sold without a Reserve Selling Price unless the consignor agrees to pay the non-refundable reserve fees and the additional listing fees in advance.

12. Once an auction is completed, and payment is received, the merchandise will be shipped to the buyer. Upon safe receipt by the buyer, Consignee will effect payment of proceeds, less fees to the Consignor. If a buyer rejects an item of merchandise due to misrepresentation, payment will be refunded to the buyer and the item of merchandise will be returned to the Consignor.

13. Both parties agree that any disputes arising under this agreement will be settled by binding arbitration according to the rules of the American Arbitration Association.

14. This agreement is signed in, and will be interpreted in and subject to, the laws of the State of _____. (*Insert name of your state.*)

Fee Schedule

Non-refundable Listing Fee: $3.00 for the first item and $1.00 for each additional item

Optional Selling Fees

Bold Fee: $2.00

Reserve Price Auction: $3.00 + 1% of the Reserve Value. The 1% fee is refunded if the item sells.

Commission Schedule

Final Value	Commission
Under $300	35%
$301–$500	25% of the amount over $300
$501–$20,000	10% of the amount over $500
Over $20,000	Negotiated amount

Category Feature Fee: $19.95 (recommended for items estimated to sell for over $250)

Homepage Feature Fee: $49.95 (recommended for items estimated to sell for over $1,000)

Consignor Inventory Form

Quantity	Item Description	Reserve

Remarks:

_____

_____

_____

_____

_____

Consignee: (*Put your name or your company name here.*)

Signed at (City)_____ (State) _____

Accepted and agreed to this _____ day of _____, 2006.

Consignor:

Name: _____   Name: _____

Signature: _____   Signature: _____

Once your auctions are completed, create a form like the one below in Excel to calculate your fees and the net payment to the consignor and send it to the consignor with the payment.

Qty	Item Description	Final Value	Selling Commission	Special Fees	Total Fees	Net to Consignor

Final Value _____   Less total fees _____

Net Paid   _____   Date _____

Alternate Non-Consignment Contract

In some cities and states, there are regulations that make it difficult or onerous for consignment sellers to operate. This contract is designed to avoid those regulations by setting out a relationship whereby you are providing a "service" and there is no consignor/consignee relationship.

This contract was developed by the QuikDrop Corporation (a franchisee of eBay storefront sellers). QuikDrop has graciously allowed us to provide this contract to our readers for their unrestricted use. **Simply replace the word QuikDrop with your company name throughout the contract**. After that, simply have it reviewed by your attorney for local compliance. You will also want to change the fee schedule in paragraph 4 to match your fee schedule.

Terms and Conditions

1. **Services**. By signing this Agreement, you authorize Quikdrop to provide the following services in accordance with the terms and conditions of this Agreement, to (i) receive and store the Goods listed on the reverse side of this page (the Goods), (ii) list, offer, and sell the Goods on eBay, (iii) deliver the Goods to the buyer, if any, and (iv) collect the sales price from the buyer, deduct Quikdrops' sales fee, and forward the remainder of the sales price to Seller in accordance with the "Services" below.

2. **Binding Bids**. Seller is obligated to complete the transaction with the highest bidder upon the listings completion, unless there is an exceptional circumstance, such as (a) the buyer fails to pay for the Goods or (b) Quikdrop cannot authenticate the buyer's identity.

3. **Unsold Goods**. Should the Goods fail to sell within ten (10) days of being listed on eBay, Seller hereby authorizes Quikdrop to re-list on eBay or dispose of such unsold Goods ("Unsold Goods") as Seller indicates on reverse side of this page.

4. **Payment to Seller**. As consideration for the Services, Seller agrees Quikdrop will be entitled to collect a sales fee ("Sales Fee") according to the following formula: forty percent (40%) of the first $200 of the sale price for which the Goods are sold ("the Sales Price") plus thirty percent (30%) of the next $300 of the Sales Price plus twenty percent (20%) of the remaining Sales Price over $500 plus any eBay charges incurred in the process of listing the Goods. Following receipt by Quikdrop of the Sales Price from the buyer, Quikdrop is authorized by Seller to deduct the Sales Fee from the monies received and forward the remainder to Seller at the address listed on this page, within fourteen (14) days from the date of receipt of the Sale Price.

5. **Bailment Relationship**. The relationship between the Seller and Quikdrop is that of a bailor and bailee in which the bailor (Seller) deposits his personal property (Goods) with the bailee (Quikdrop) for the purpose of listing and selling the Goods to third parties through eBay. Nothing contained herein will be construed as creating any agency, partnership, or other form of joint enterprise between the parties.

6. **Title and Risk of Loss**. Title and risk of loss for the Goods remains with Seller until such time as the Goods are delivered to a carrier for delivery to the buyer. Title and risk of loss will not transfer to a Quikdrop at any time. Title to Goods shipped will pass directly from Seller to a Buyer.

7. **Seller's Warranty of Goods**. Seller warrants that (i) Seller has all the necessary rights and authorization to produce and distribute the Goods and to permit Quikdrop to offer, sell, and deliver the Goods to any third party, (ii) the Goods and the rights granted under this Agreement do not infringe upon the proprietary rights of any third party, and (iii) the description of the Goods is truthful, accurate, and complete. Seller represents and warrants that description of the Goods and the Goods will not: Be false, inaccurate, or misleading; Be fraudulent or involve the sale of counterfeit or stolen items; Violate any law, statute, ordinance, or regulation (including, but not limited to, those governing export control, consumer protection, unfair competition, antidiscrimination, or false advertising); Be defamatory, trade libelous, unlawfully threatening, or unlawfully harassing; Be obscene or contain child pornography or otherwise be adult in nature or harmful to minors.

8. **Breach**. Without limiting other remedies, Quikdrop may immediately remove Seller's Goods listings from eBay, temporarily suspend, indefinitely suspend, or terminate the Services and refuse to provide future Services to Seller if (i) Seller breaches this Agreement, (ii) Quikdrop is unable to verify or authenticate any information Seller provides to Quikdrop, (iii) Quikdrop believes that the Seller's actions may cause financial loss or legal liability for the Seller, Quikdrop's users or Quikdrop stores, or (iv) Quikdrop suspects that Seller (by conviction, settlement, insurance, or escrow investigation, or otherwise) has engaged in fraudulent activity in connection with the Goods, Quikdrop, or eBay.

9. **Indemnity**. Seller agrees to indemnify and hold Quikdrop and (as applicable) Quikdrop's parent companies, subsidiaries, affiliates, officers, directors, agents, and employees, harmless from any claim or demand, including reasonable attorneys' fees, made by any third party due, connected to, or arising out of Seller's breach of this Agreement, or Seller's violation of any law or the rights of any third party.

10. **Warranty Disclaimer**. QUIKDROP PROVIDES ITS SERVICES "AS IS" AND ANY WARRANTY OR REPRESENTATION AS TO THE SERVICES, EXPRESS, IMPLIED, OR STATUTORY. QUIKDROP SPECIFICALLY DISCLAIMS ANY IMPLIED WARRANTIES OF TITLE, MERCHANTABILITY, FITNESS FOR A PARTICULAR PURPOSE, AND NON-INFRINGEMENT. SOME STATES DO NOT ALLOW THE DISCLAIMER OF IMPLIED WARRANTIES, SO THE FOREGOING DISCLAIMER MAY NOT APPLY TO SELLER. THIS WARRANTY GIVES SELLER SPECIFIC LEGAL RIGHTS AND SELLER MAY ALSO HAVE OTHER LEGAL RIGHTS THAT VARY FROM STATE TO STATE.

11. **Waiver of Consequential Damages**. IN NO EVENT WILL QUIKDROP BE LIABLE TO SELLER FOR ANY INCIDENTAL, CONSEQUENTIAL, EXEMPLARY, INDIRECT, SPECIAL, OR PUNITIVE DAMAGES ARISING OUT OF THIS AGREEMENT OR ITS TERMINATION, REGARDLESS OF THE FORM OF ACTION (INCLUDING NEGLIGENCE AND STRICT PRODUCT LIABILITY) AND IRRESPECTIVE OF WHETHER QUIKDROP HAS BEEN ADVISED OF THE POSSIBILITY OF ANY SUCH LOSS OR DAMAGE.

12. **Liability Cap**. Quikdrop's liability, and the liability of its employees and suppliers, to Seller or any third parties in any circumstance is limited to the greater of (i) the agreed upon value of the applicable Goods, as stated on the Reverse Page, or (ii) $100. Some states do not allow the exclusion or limitation of incidental or consequential damages, so the above limitation or exclusion may not apply to Seller.

13. **Release**. Seller releases Quikdrop and eBay (and Quikdrop's parent companies, officers, directors, agents, subsidiaries, joint ventures, and employees) from claims, demands, and damages (actual and consequential) of every kind and nature, known and unknown, suspected and unsuspected, disclosed and undisclosed, rising out of, resulting from, or in any way connected with the Services. If Seller is a California resident, Seller waives California Civil Code #1542, which says: "A GENERAL RELEASE DOES NOT EXTEND TO THE CLAIMS WHICH THE CREDITOR DOES NOT KNOW OR SUSPECT TO EXIST IN HIS FAVOR AT THE TIME OF EXECUTING THE RELEASE, WHICH IS KNOWN BY HIM MUST HAVE MATERIALLY AFFECTED HIS SETTLEMENT WITH THE DEBTOR."

14. **Terms**. The terms of this Agreement will commence upon the effective date and, unless terminated earlier in accordance with the terms of this Agreement, will continue until all Goods accepted for listing by Quikdrop under this Agreement are sold and delivered, returned to the Seller, or disposed of in accordance with Section 3, but in no event more than 60 days from the Effective date. This Agreement may be terminated by Quikdrop without notice, for any reason or no reason, at any time.

15. **Survival of Certain Terms**. The following sections will survive the termination of this Agreement for any reason: Reverse Page, 3, 5, 6, 7, 8, 9, 10, 11, 12, 13, 15, and 16. All other rights and obligations of the parties will cease upon termination of this Agreement.

16. **General**. This Agreement will be governed in all respects by the laws of the United States of America and in the state of California as such laws are applied to agreements entered into and to be performed entirely within California between California residents. All notices or requests will be in writing and will be sent by facsimile, or recognized commercial overnight courier. Notices will be deemed received upon receipt of written confirmation of transmission when sent by facsimile, or signing for receipt of delivery if sent by overnight courier. Notices will be sent to the parties at the address set forth in the signature block, below. The failure of either party to require a performance by the other party of any provision hereof will not affect the full right to require such performance at anytime thereafter; nor will the waiver by either party of a breach of any provision hereof be taken or held to the waiver of the provision itself. In the event that any provision of this Agreement will be unenforceable or invalid under any applicable law or be so held by applicable Court decision, such unenforceability or invalidity will not render this Agreement unenforceable or invalid as a whole, and, in such event, such provisions will be changed and interpreted so as to best accomplish the objectives of such unenforceable or invalid provision within the limits of applicable law or applicable court decisions. This Agreement and the exhibits hereto, constitute the entire Agreement between the parties with respect to the subject matter hereof. This Agreement supersedes, in the terms of this Agreement govern, any prior or collateral agreements with respect to the subject matter hereof with the exception of any prior confidentiality agreements between the parties. This Agreement may only be changed by mutual agreement of authorized representatives of the parties in writing.

Consignor:

Name_____

Signature _____

Consignee (*Your company name goes here.*)

Signature_____

Dated on _____ at _____City/State_____

Sample Auction Report

Here is a list of items that recently sold at a large auction house in Seattle. I then used the Search Closed Auctions feature on eBay and Terapeak's research service (www.terapeak.com) to find identical or very similar items that sold on eBay. You should perform the same analysis yourself at a local auction house in your own location. Be sure to list a wide variety of items and concentrate on those things that are easily available rather than rare or unusual items.

Item	Local Selling Price	eBay Final Value	% Difference
Tennessee Mossman Flat Top Guitar	$490	$745	52%
Signed Stickley Dining Chair (fair condition)	$190	$466.05	45%
1901 PCGS MS-64 Gold Liberty Eagle Coin	$945	$1,475	56%
Nikon F2 Camera, Body only (good condition)	$105	$241	43%
John Steinbeck, Of Mice and Men, 1st edition (good condition)	$85	$98.03	15%
Used Dewalt 18V Cordless Hammer Drill	$45	$72.03	60%
Tiffany Art Deco Sterling Salad Set	$2,150	$2,655	22.9%
Wallace Sterling Carving Set	$1,650	$1,822.07	10.4%
Seth Thomas Glass Domed Clock	$285	$346.05	21%
Complete Set of Nautical Quarterly (good to excellent condition)	$365	$788.01	115%
Totals:	**$6,310**	**$8,702.24**	**37%**

Sample Sales Letters to Prospective Consignors

Here are samples of several letters you can use to contact attorneys, business owners, charities, and others who are prospects for your consignment business.

I have included the body of the letter only. Your letter should be on letterhead and look like a professional business letter.

Whenever possible, you should research the specific names of business owners and send them a personal letter. You should type the letter but hand address the envelope because this will help distinguish it from junk mail.

When you don't know a name, you can address it to Dear Business Owner or Dear Storeowner. As for attorneys, I would always send it to an individual name. These are easily found in the Yellow Pages.

Letter to an Estate and/or Bankruptcy Attorney

Brewster Hamilton, Esq.   March 1, 2006
150 Main Street
Suite 550
Anytown, PA 20601

Dear Mr. Hamilton:

On-line Consignment Sales provides a professional eBay selling service to the legal community in western Pennsylvania. We handle estate sales, bankruptcy sales, and the liquidation of distressed merchandise.

Most law firms traditionally use local auction houses for these needs. You may, however, want to explore the opportunity provided by eBay, the world's largest online auction, to realize consistently higher prices than those offered by local auctioneers.

eBay currently has over 65 million registered users in the U.S. and over 85 million worldwide. Over $200 million worth of merchandise is sold on eBay every week. At this moment, there are over 12 million items listed on eBay, and the eBay site will receive over 50,000 page views in the time it takes to read this letter.

Goods and merchandise sell on eBay at values far in excess of what could be realized at a local auction house. As an example, I recently attended a sale at a major auction house here in Pittsburgh. I compiled a list of items and what they sold for. I then researched what these same items sold for on eBay during the past 30 days. Please see the enclosed report for the results.

On-Line Consignment Sales will handle all aspects of your mandated auctions, including creating and launching the auctions, receiving payment, and packaging and shipping the goods. Your client's goods are not shipped until payment is received.

I have a ten-minute, fact-filled presentation that will demonstrate the benefits to you and your clients of selling on eBay. I will call you early next week for an appointment. If you have any questions or would like to speak with me sooner, please call me directly at 505-555-1111.

Sincerely yours,

Harrison Ford
On-Line Consignment Sales, Inc.

Letter to Local Business Owners Outlining Your Services

Dear Sir or Madam:

On-Line Consignment Sales, Inc. is a local company providing an eBay online auction venue for northern Virginia businesses. We handle all aspects of selling your surplus or obsolete merchandise or equipment on eBay, the world's largest auction site.

If you are not familiar with eBay, please review the enclosed information. The advantages of selling on eBay are many:

- We can launch auctions within 24 hours of receiving the merchandise. You do not have to wait weeks for an auction house to schedule their next auction.
- Millions of potential bidders from all over the country, and the world, will see your goods and bid on them–not just the few dozen that attend a local auction.
- The higher number of bidders will guarantee you receive **top dollar** for your goods.

On-Line Consignment Sales, Inc. will handle all aspects of selling your goods on eBay, including taking photographs of your merchandise, creating and launching the auctions, receiving payment, and packaging and shipping the goods to the buyer.

Please review the enclosed material. I have a ten-minute, fact-filled presentation that will demonstrate the benefits of selling your merchandise on eBay. I will call you early next week for an appointment. If you have any questions or would like to speak with me sooner, please call me directly at 505-555-1111.

Sincerely yours,

Annie Smith
On-line Consignment Sales, Inc.

Letter to a Retail Storeowner

Dear Sir or Madam: (*Use the storeowner's actual name if you have it.*)

Are you tired of selling your overstock and surplus merchandise to a closeout dealer for pennies on the dollar?

(*Your company name here*) is a local company that helps retailers sell their excess inventory directly to end users on eBay, the world's largest auction site. We charge a modest fee for our service, which includes photographing the merchandise, launching and monitoring the auctions, receiving payment, and packing and shipping the product.

If you are not familiar with eBay, please review the enclosed information. The advantages of selling on eBay are many:

- Even after paying our modest fees, you will net far more for your goods than from a closeout dealer or wholesale auctioneer.
- We can launch auctions within 24 hours of receiving the merchandise.
- Millions of potential bidders from all over the country, and the world, will see your goods and bid on them–not just the few dozen that attend a local auction.
- The higher number of bidders will guarantee **you receive top dollar for your goods**.

Please review the enclosed material. I have a ten-minute, fact-filled presentation that will demonstrate the benefits you will realize from selling your merchandise on eBay. I will call you early next week for an appointment. If you have any questions or would like to speak with me sooner, please call me directly at 505-555-1111.

Sincerely,

Your Name
Your company

Letter to a Charity

Dear Sir/Madam:

Is your organization looking for a unique way to raise funds with no investment on your part? Sell On Line (SOL) is a local company that helps charities raise money on eBay, the world's largest auction site.

Here is how it works: You contact your members and regular donors and ask them to donate something of value that you can auction off on eBay. We do all the rest.

We charge a modest fee for our service, which includes photographing the merchandise, launching and monitoring the auctions, receiving payment, and packing and shipping the product.

The advantages of selling on eBay are many:

- Even after paying our modest fees, you will net far more for your goods than you would at a flea market or tag sale.
- We can launch auctions within 24 hours of receiving the merchandise.
- Millions of potential bidders from all over the country, and the world, will see your donated goods and bid on them–not just the few dozen that attend local sales and events.
- The higher number of bidders will guarantee you receive top dollar for your donated goods.
- Your donors can take a tax deduction based on the value of the goods or what they reach on eBay–whichever is higher.

Please review the enclosed material. I have a ten-minute, fact-filled presentation that will demonstrate the benefits you will realize from raising money on eBay. I will call you early next week for an appointment. If you have any questions or would like to speak with me sooner, please call me directly at 505-555-1111.

Sincerely,

Brian O'Brian
Sell on Line, Ltd.

Appendix B

Advertising Posters

The illustrations on the following pages are examples of advertising posters you can use to promote your business. Each of these posters is available as an Adobe Acrobat PDF file that you can download from the resource page for this book at www.skipmcgrath.com/consignment. Simply download the posters, customize them with your business and location information, and have them printed.

If you are a registered eBay Trading Assistant, you can download flyers and advertising posters with the eBay TA logo from the eBay *Trading Assistant Resource Page*.

Would You Like to Sell on eBay
but Don't Know How?

We can sell for you. What sells on eBay? Pretty much anything! Art, antiques, collectibles, real estate, retail goods, industrial equipment, and automobiles are just a few of the many categories of eBay goods. eBay is the largest shopping site on the Internet with over 50 million registered users.

We offer eBay consignment services for individuals, businesses, nonprofits, churches and charities, individuals, and governments and estates.

- ❖ We take high quality digital photographs of your items
- ❖ Write the description and launch the auction
- ❖ Handle all communications and questions with bidders and buyers
- ❖ Collect payment and handle all financial transactions
- ❖ Professionally package and ship the item to the buyer
- ❖ Provide escrow and insurance services when needed
- ❖ Arrange for appraisal services if required
- ❖ Pay the owner

All you do is provide the items and we do the rest

Selling effectively on eBay requires knowledge of sales and marketing strategies unique to the eBay marketplace. Our experience, established credibility, and reputation on eBay is a big advantage. This can be a huge challenge for beginners.

We are registered eBay Trading Assistants and
Gold eBay Power Sellers

Company Name

Address   e-mail address

Phone Number   Web Site URL

Pro Tip   eBay Fact Sheet

Almost everyone has heard about eBay. However, there are still plenty of people who have little or no idea about how big eBay is and how many people use it. Here are some facts you can use in your presentation materials and when discussing eBay with prospects. eBay statistics change every year so you will need to update these figures occasionally.

- eBay is the third most visited site on the Internet.

- eBay has hosted over 6.4 billion auctions since its beginning in 1995.

- eBay has over 65 million registered users in the U.S. and over 85 million users worldwide.

- eBay is a global enterprise with eBay sites in 26 separate countries, including China and India.

- eBay North America receives over 12 million page views per day.

- In 2004, eBay members transacted $26 billion in annualized gross merchandise sales (GMS, the value of goods sold on eBay). eBay estimates this number will exceed $35 billion in 2005.

- On any given day, there are more than 22 million items listed on eBay across 27,000 categories.

- People come to the eBay marketplace to buy and sell items in multiple categories, including antiques and art, books, business and industrial goods, cars and other vehicles, clothing and accessories, coins, collectibles, crafts, dolls and bears, electronics and computers, home furnishings, jewelry and watches, movies and DVDs, music, musical instruments, pottery and glass, real estate, sporting goods and memorabilia, stamps, tickets, toys and hobbies, and travel.

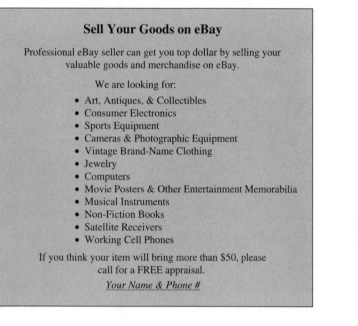

FREE APPRAISAL COUPON

Professional eBay Power Seller will sell your expensive art, antiques, and collectibles on eBay for a small fee. Bring this coupon to our store for a free appraisal to determine what your valuable items will bring on eBay, the world's largest electronic marketplace.

Your name, address, and phone #
Web site, URL, & e-mail

**Stop Selling Your Treasures
at Garage Sale Prices**

Our eBay professionals can get Antique Roadshow prices
for your valuables on eBay, the world's largest electronic
marketplace.

We take the photographs, create an eBay listing, track the
auction, collect the money, and package and ship the item
to the customer for one small fee. You are guaranteed top
dollar by exposing your item to 45 million potential
buyers.

Call today for a confidential FREE appraisal
Name & Phone #

Appendix C

Resources and References

As an eBay seller, you will find yourself constantly in search of useful information and resources to keep you up-to-date with changes, increase your skills, and help you find new tools and techniques. This appendix contains several resources both on and off eBay that you may want to examine. Many of these links you will want to bookmark in a special "eBay Resources" folder in your browser favorites.

To save you time, the web page created for the users of this book at www.skipmcgrath.com/consignment has all of the URL resources listed with direct, clickable hyperlinks.

eBay and Consignment Selling Online Resources

Following are some online resources that provide support and information for eBay sellers and online entrepreneurs.

News and Information

Power Up is eBay's monthly newsletter for power sellers; however, you must subscribe, as it does not come automatically once you achieve power seller status. You can subscribe to Power Up at http://pages.ebay.com/sellercentral/newsflash.html. It contains news of category changes, free listing days, and other special promotions, as well as top searches and product hot lists.

The Solutions Directory at http://cgi6.ebay.com/ws/eBayISAPI.dll?SolutionsDirectory features eBay and third-party software and services designed to improve your productivity on eBay. Each software application listed in the Solutions Directory is technically compliant with eBay.

eBay's Seller Central at http://pages.ebay.com/sellercentral/index.html has two very useful and important links: Best Practices and Advanced Selling. Best Practices list selling techniques related to research, listing, pricing, using special features, and merchandising, as well as many others. The link to Advanced Selling from Seller Central will take you to a page where eBay lists several resources, including inventory sourcing, promotional opportunities, data and research, and seller education tools.

Terry Gibbs is an experienced eBay power seller who has been selling on consignment and for his own account for several years. His web site at www.iwantcollectibles.com offers a very nice, basic e-Book on the consignment business, as well as other eBay selling tutorials.

You can find the guide *How to Open a Consignment Shop* at www.consignment-shop-store.com. This book is more about a traditional offline shop, but it contains some valuable business guidance that could be helpful to your success.

The Auction Seller's Resource at www.SkipMcGrath.com is my primary web site, where you can subscribe to the eBay Seller's News and access dozens of free articles and resources for eBay and web site sellers.

Another good site for auction sellers to keep up with news on eBay is www.auctionbytes.com.

Escrow Services

Escrow.com at www.escrow.com is eBay's preferred solution provider for escrow services. Escrow.com protects both buyer and seller by acting as a trusted third party during the transaction and managing the payment process from start to finish. Escrow is ideal for transactions over $500 because it provides added protection. Services are provided by Escrow.com, a fully licensed escrow provider. If you require escrow services, I strongly urge you to use Escrow.com. There are dozens of phony escrow companies advertising on the Web that are complete scams.

Authentication and Grading Services

The eBay Solutions Directory offers a list of companies that can render opinions on an item's authenticity and provide grading services. You can find it at http://pages.ebay.com/help/community/auth-overview.html.

Business Plans

Bplans.com offers help and guidance in writing a business plan. This is more for those of you who need a professional business plan to raise money. Visit www.bplans.com.

BizPlans offers sample business plans, business planning software, and various business start-up guides from Palo Alto Software at www.bizplans.com.

The American Express Small Business Resource web site offers free information and tutorials about writing business plans and raising financing: http://home3.americanexpress.com/smallbusiness/tool/biz_plan/index.asp. This is a long URL to type, but this is very worthwhile information.

The U.S. Small Business Administration has a great web site at www.sba.gov/starting_business/planning/basic.html. The web site has free resources on writing a business plan and links to pages where you can get information on SBA loans and grants and other help financing your business.

All Business, Inc., at www.allbusiness.com, is a great small business resource web site. They feature daily blogs and weekly newsletters on topics of interest to entrepreneurs. This is another location where you can download tons of free forms and templates. Here is a partial list of some of the useful information they offer:

- Confidentiality and nondisclosure agreements
- Consultants and independent contractors
- Domain name purchase agreements
- Employment policies and termination
- Letters of intent
- Promissory notes and loan agreements
- Protecting ideas and information
- Raising capital
- Real estate leases
- Venture capital agreements

Raising Money for Your Business

Angel Search by *Entrepreneur* magazine can help you find high net worth (over $1 million) individuals in your ZIP code area: www.entrepreneur.com/services/detail/0,4679,299461,00.html.

Another feature from *Entrepreneur* is a venture capital locator. Some of the searches are free, and detailed searches cost just a few dollars. Go to www.entrepreneur.com/services/detail/0,4679,299462,00.html.

How much money will you need to start your business? Here is an eight-step business cost and cash flow calculator. It's free and online at www.bplans.com/common/startcost/index.cfm.

GE Business Services is a division of General Electric Capital, one of the largest commercial lenders in the country. GE Business Services has a program for eBay sellers called the GE Premier Line of Credit, an unsecured credit program with interest rates as low as 5.75 percent.

GE also offers a secured credit line (inventory financing) for eBay sellers who sell new, nonperishable consumer goods, purchased directly from a manufacturer or wholesale distributor.

For those who qualify for secured credit, GE Business Credit Services pays the manufacturer or distributor invoices while providing the business with flexible repayment terms. GE Business Credit Services can also provide qualified eBay sellers other financing solutions, depending on the business's needs. You can get more information and apply for a loan online at their web site, www.gebcs.com.

Consulting

eBay and Elance have teamed up to bring you access to thousands of freelance professionals ready to help with your business needs. You post your project online and review the bids as they come in from various consultants. Once you see an acceptable bid, you can contact the consultant and pay for the services through Elance. Elance uses a feedback system similar to eBay, so you can get an idea about the quality of a consultant's work before you start. Projects include logo design, About Me and eBay Store design, and search engine optimization services.

Legal and Tax Advice

Unfortunately, we all have to pay taxes. Many occasional eBay sellers get away without reporting their eBay income, but as a professional seller you just don't want to take the risk. Legal advice is also something you may find yourself in need of. Here are a few resources that I have used in the past that you could find useful.

Taxes

Keeping good records and paying your taxes correctly and on time is crucial to the long-term success of your business. You are going to want a good CPA to help you out. There is, however, a great free resource on taxes and a place to download tax forms for free that I use all the time. It's the Motley Fool Tax Center at: www.fool.com/taxes/taxcenter/taxcenter.htm. Another great tax resource is from Diane Kennedy, a CPA who specializes in working with eBay sellers, at www.taxloopholes.com.

Here is a web site where you can link to the web sites of the various states to get information about sales tax and to register for a sales tax number: www.aicpa .org/yellow/yptstax.htm.

Legal Advice

LLC Legal at www.llclegal.com/index.shtml gives low-cost online legal advice.

Product Safety

It is against eBay regulations and the laws in many states to sell a product that has been recalled by the Consumer Product Safety Commission. Here is a web site where you can see if a product is subject to a recall: www.cpsc.gov/cpscpub/prerel/ prerel.html.

Online Fraud Resources

The National Internet Fraud Information Center provides the most complete web site available to connect to resources to fight and report Internet fraud. You can find those resources at www.fraud.org/info/links.htm.

Suggested Reading

A number of books and training resources are available to help you develop your Internet marketing and eBay skills. I have listed some of the best ones here:

eBay PowerSeller Secrets: Insider Tips from eBay's Most Successful Sellers by Debra Schepp and Brad Schepp (McGraw-Hill/Osborne, 2004). Debra and Brad Schepp interviewed dozens of top eBay sellers to gather information for this excellent selling guide.

How to Do Everything with Your eBay Business by Greg Holden (McGraw-Hill/Osborne, 2005—now in its second edition). This best-selling book shows new and aspiring eBay sellers how to do everything from finding products to sell and opening up an eBay store to expanding to international markets and offering unparalleled customer service.

The 7 Essential Steps to Successful eBay Marketing by Janelle Elms, Phil Dunn, and Amy Balsbaugh (McGraw-Hill/Osborne, 2005). This value-packed yet affordable guide offers hundreds of easy-to-implement, highly effective ways to attract the maximum number of bids and keep customers coming back for more.

eBay QuickSteps by John Cronan and Carole Matthews (McGraw-Hill/Osborne, 2004). This is a full-color, highly illustrated guide showing newbies how to get up and running with every aspect of the eBay site.

The Internet Marketing Course by Corey Rudl. This is the oldest and most comprehensive Internet marketing training program available today. It is available on the Web at www.marketingtips.com/tipsltr.html.

The Official eBay Bible by Jim "Griff" Griffith (Gotham, 2003). Griff is an early eBay employee who now hosts eBay Radio. His book is the official eBay reference text.

The Complete eBay Marketing System by Skip McGrath (Vision-One Press, 2003, Revised 2005). This is my complete basic-to-advanced seller's guide. You can order it from my web site at www.skipmcgrath.com.

eBay Consignment Business Operations Manual by Skip McGrath (Vision-One Press, 2005). This is a complete business manual structured along the lines of a franchise operations handbook for running an eBay drop-off store consignment business. The manual is available at www.skipmcgrath.com.

Appendix D

Consignment Startup Checklist

It occurred to me as I was writing this book that we covered a wide variety of subject areas, so it might be helpful to create a sort of "checklist" for an eBay consignment startup.

Every business is different and it would be impossible to create a perfect checklist for every situation and eventuality. Therefore, you should consider this list simply a starting point. Use this list to create your own checklist, which will help you stay on track as you start down the path to consignment success.

1. Figure out what type of business you want to be in. Are you going to specialize in a certain field, such as antiques and collectibles, business to business, retail closeouts, or will you be a generalist?

2. Set some goals, both short and long term, and *write them down*. Make your goals specific. If you can't measure them, you can't control them.

3. Make a list of your resources and a list of your needs (hardware, software, office supplies, shipping supplies, second computer, camera, photo equipment, etc.).

4. Sit down and work out a budget for your business (eBay listing fees, equipment, software, auction management service, advertising, etc.).

5. Name your business.

6. Research the cost of advertising in the various local papers.

7. Create a 60-day advertising budget.

8. Write your business plan and create a cash flow plan.

9. Apply for a sales tax number and a DBA in your business name.

10. Open a business (commercial) checking account.

11. Get a phone number for your business.

12. Design and print letterhead and business cards.

13. Create a consignment agreement, fee schedule, and the various forms you will need for your business. (You can use the ones we provide as a starting point and just modify them.)

14. Organize your workspace, photo setup, and shipping and storage.

15. Get registered, set up, and trained on a software package or auction management service such as MarketBlast, Liberty4, eSavz, or Mpire. Launch a few auctions to gain some experience and work out any bugs in your processes and procedures.

16. Create and print flyers and cards.

17. Launch your advertising and put up flyers.

18. Call your friends and neighbors and let them know what you are doing.

19. Write and distribute a press release announcing your business to the local media.

20. Contact local service groups and offer to speak to them.

21. Track your cash flow and costs weekly and monthly.

22. Start contacting local retail merchants and small business owners in your community to find consignment opportunities.

23. Contact estate attorneys and bankruptcy attorneys.

24. Review your business plan quarterly; update and make adjustments if necessary.

By now you should be making some pretty good money so take a long weekend and fly to someplace sunny and warm!

Glossary

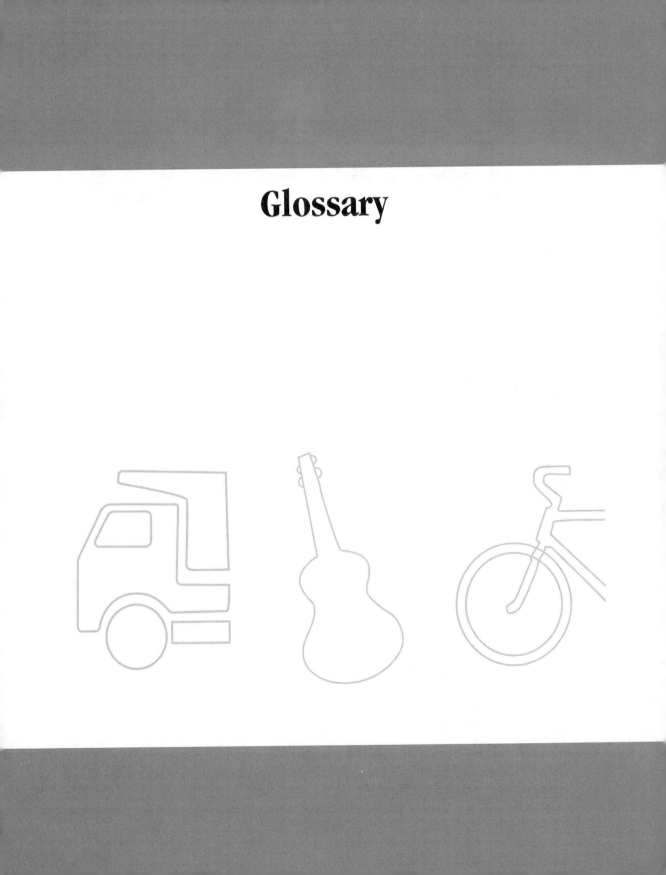

This list includes a glossary of terms used in this book and a larger listing of terms often encountered on eBay and when communicating with eBay members. Over the years eBay has developed its own slang, jargon, and abbreviations. You will often see these terms in auction descriptions and e-mails. I suggest you use care with abbreviations, as they can often cause confusion or misunderstandings with newbies. I have placed them here in case you come across a term you are not familiar with.

Active User   An eBay member who has bought or sold at least once in the prior 12 months.

ADDY   E-mail address.

Adwords   Google's term for pay-per-click advertising.

AG   About good: a term used to describe the condition of an item.

AKA   Also known as.

A/O   All original: an auction term used to describe the condition of an item. The acronym is usually used in the auction title to save space.

AOL   America Online.

AOV   Average order value.

ASAP   As soon as possible.

As Is   Applied to items that are sold at auction without warranties as to the condition of the property. Item may be damaged or have missing parts. See Caveat Emptor.

ASP   Average selling price.

ATM   At the moment.

B&W   Black and white.

BC   Back cover.

Bid Increment   This is the amount by which you must increase your bid over the current high bid. The bid increment is established by the former bid price.

Bid Rigging   The unlawful practice whereby two or more people agree not to bid against one another so as to deflate value.

BIN   Buy It Now.

BIN Rate   The percentage of your items sold with BIN or any fixed-price format.

Blocked Bidders   An eBay feature that allows sellers to create a list of specific eBay members who are not allowed to bid on or buy items they sell. A person on the list will be blocked from participating in all of a seller's auctions.

BRB   Be right back.

BTW   By the way.

Caveat Emptor   A Latin term meaning "let the buyer beware!" A legal maxim stating that the buyer takes all the risk in a transaction.

CC   Originally meant carbon copy. Current usage means to copy someone on a memo or e-mail.

CIB   Cartridge instructions/box (as in computer equipment).

CIF   Cost, insurance, freight. A CIF price includes the shipping cost to you.

COA   Certificate of authenticity: an auction term used to describe an item as genuine (usually certified by an expert).

CONUS   Continental United States, not including Alaska and Hawaii.

CR   Conversion rate.

DBA   Doing business as.

Deadbeat Bidder   One who bids and fails to complete a transaction.

DOA   Dead on arrival (when, for instance, the item you bought doesn't work out of the package).

DSL   High-speed Internet connection through a special phone line.

Dutch Auction   An auction format for selling multiple quantities of identical items in one auction. Bidders choose the number of items they want and how much they want to bid. The final price is determined by the lowest bid among all the winning bidders. The highest bidders win, but all bidders pay the lowest successful bid price.

Emoticon   A specific group of characters used to form a facial expression in e-mails. For example, :-) is a smiley face.

Escrow   A third-party company that holds payment in trust until the seller makes delivery of merchandise to the buyer.

FAQ   A list of frequently asked questions and answers.

FB   Feedback.

Flame   An angry message or feedback sent many times.

Flameout (aka Crash and Burn)   Slang for when you don't follow the advice in this book and your eBay business fails.

FOB   Free on board: you pay the shipping for an item from its FOB location. For example, if I quote you a price for a pallet of goods, FOB Trenton, NJ, that means that you pay the freight from Trenton to your location.

FTP   Method of uploading pages to the Internet.

FV   Final value: the price something sells for on eBay, not including shipping.

FVF: Final Value Fee   The fee eBay charges for selling.

FWIW   For what it's worth.

Gently Used   Used with but little wear.

GMS   Gross merchandise sales.

HP   Home page.

HTML   Hypertext Markup Language.

Hyperlink   A clickable photo or text on a web page that takes you to another page on the Internet.

IE   Internet Explorer (also known by its detractors as Internet Exploder).

IMHO   In my humble opinion.

IMO   In my opinion.

INIT   Initials.

ISP   Internet service provider.

JPG   Preferred file format for pictures on eBay (pronounced J-Peg).

Link   A hyperlink, that is, a clickable photo or text on a web page that takes you to another page on the Internet.

LOL   Laughing out loud.

Lot or Lots   Similar items sold in quantities. Lots are normally sold at discount or wholesale prices.

LTD   Limited edition.

MIB   Mint in box.

MIMB   Mint in mint box.

MIMP   Mint in mint package.

Mint   Never used, in perfect condition.

MIP   Mint in package.

MNB   Mint no box.

MOC   Mint on card.

My eBay   A page that displays your ongoing auctions, status, and auction history.

MYOB   Mind your own business.

NARU   Not a registered user (suspended user).

NBW   Never been worn.

NC   No cover.

Newbie   Someone new to eBay.

NM   Near mint.

No Reserve   See NR.

NPB   Non-paying bidder. See deadbeat bidder.

NR   No reserve price on auction.

NRFB   Never removed from box.

NWT   New with tag.

OEM   Original equipment manufacturer.

OOP   Out of print.

OTOH   On the other hand.

PayPal Verified Buyer   A buyer that has confirmed his or her address and account information through PayPal. This qualifies that user for the PayPal fraud protection plan.

Phishing   A spoofed web site is typically made to look like a well-known, branded site (such as eBay, PayPal, or Amazon) with a subtly different URL. A spoofed e-mail looks as if it came from eBay, PayPal, or your bank. However, the link leads you to the fake web site. Phishing schemes such as these are used to deceive online shoppers into disclosing their credit card numbers, bank account information, Social Security numbers, passwords, and other personal information.

PPC   Pay per click. An advertising program where users pay for each time a viewer clicks through to their web site or eBay store. Companies such as Google and Yahoo show these as "sponsored results."

Primail (PM)   Priority Mail.

Private Auction   An auction in which neither the buyers' nor the sellers' identities are disclosed.

Proxy Bidding   A bidder enters the maximum amount they are willing to spend on an item. eBay will then automatically continue incremental bidding until either that bidder is the high bidder or the bidder's maximum is reached.

Relisting   The process of listing an item that did not sell again on auction.

Reserve Auction   An auction in which the seller reserves a minimum acceptable price. Sellers sometimes disclose the reserve price to perspective bidders.

Reserve Not Met   An auction term that means no bid is high enough to match the minimum price the seller will accept.

Reserve Price   The minimum price a seller is willing to accept for an item to be sold at auction.

Retaliatory Feedback   Negative feedback, posted by an eBay member in response to another eBay member's negative feedback, or when a non-paying bidder posts feedback because you complained about him or her to eBay.

RMA   Return merchandise authorization.

ROFL   Rolling on the floor laughing. See also LOL.

RSVP   Répondez, s'il vous plaît: please reply. In practice, respond as soon as possible.

SCO   Second chance offer.

Shilling   Fraudulent bidding by an associate of the seller in order to inflate the price of an item. Also known as bid rigging or collusion.

SIG   Signature.

Siphoning   Other sellers' contacting bidders and offering to sell them the same item they are currently bidding on, thus drawing bidders away from the legitimate seller's auction.

SKU   Stock-keeping unit.

Snail Mail   Ordinary mail.

Sniping   Bidding at the last possible moment.

$1NR   ***One Dollar*** no reserve: a listing that starts at $1.00 with no reserve. Other variations include $1-NR or $1.00-NR.

Spam   Unwanted e-mail; eBay will discipline you for sending e-mail to bidders in auctions you are not involved in.

Spoofs   See Phishing.

TM   Trademark.

Trading Assistant (TA)   An experienced eBay seller who meets eBay requirements and will sell another person's items on eBay for a fee or commission. Also known as an eBay consignment seller.

Unwanted Bid   A bid that does not meet the seller's terms stated in the auction. Example: A seller states in an auction that the item is shipped only to U.S. locations and the bidder is located overseas. The eBay seller can cancel the bid.

UPS   United Parcel Service.

URL   A Universal Resource Locator: the address that identifies a web site.

USPS   United States Postal Service.

VERO   eBay's Verified Rights Owners program for copyright and trademark enforcement. If you sell counterfeit goods on eBay, the rights owner can file a VERO complaint against you and eBay will shut down your auctions.

VHTF   Very hard to find.

Western Union Auction Payments (formerly called BidPay)   An online auction payment service owned by Western Union.

Winning Bidder Notification (WBN)   The notification sent at the end of an auction to the winning bidder. May be sent by eBay, PayPal, the seller, or the seller's auction management system.

WTMI   Way too much information.

WYSIWYG   What you see is what you get.

Yahoo Shops (aka Yahoo Stores)   A shopping portal operated by Yahoo (separate from Yahoo auctions).

Index

About the Author

Skip McGrath has been an eBay Power Seller since 1999. He and his wife, Karen, started selling antiques and collectibles from their antique shop in the early days of eBay. After gaining experience from hundreds of successful auctions, Skip wrote his first book in 2000, *The eBay Power Seller's Manual*. The manual is still one of the best-selling books on and about eBay.

In early 2000, Skip also launched The Auction Seller's Resource and began publishing *The eBay Seller's News*, a monthly newsletter for professional auction sellers. He also wrote the Auction Tips column for the PayPal periodical.

Prior to working on eBay, Skip had a 25-year career in international marketing where he lived in five different countries and traveled to over sixty countries in pursuit of business.

Skip, his wife, and their Labrador retriever, Tahoe, live on an island in the Pacific Northwest near the Canadian border. They have two sons, one in the U.S. Navy and the other an Able Bodied Seaman on a seagoing tugboat in Alaska.